The Woodhaerst Women

Book 3 of The Woodhaerst family drama trilogy

Patricia M Osborne

White Wings

Books

Published 2025 in Great Britain

by White Wings Books

ISBN 978-0-9957107-6-4

All rights reserved.

No part of this publication may be reproduced, stored in a retrieval system, or transmitted in any form or by any means, electronic, mechanical, photocopy, recording or otherwise, without prior written permission of the copyright owners. Nor can it be circulated in any form of binding or cover other than that in which it is published and without similar condition including this condition being imposed on a subsequent purchaser.

British Cataloguing Publication data: A catalogue record of this book is available from the British Library

This book is also available as an ebook

In Memory of

My dearest mum,

Lila (1932-2014)

and

Sister,

Heather (1956-2009)

Two courageous and inspiring women

A light went out in my heart when you both left this world

Chapter One

Rachel

8th April, 1978

Joe smoothed down the final piece of wallpaper. I stood back admiring the grey shadowed tree design now enhancing the alcoves either side of the fireplace. Duck-white emulsion decorated the remaining walls. 'I reckon we've made a good job of that,' I said. 'There's a lager in the fridge with your name on it if you fancy?'

'Cool. Cheers, babe.' Joe wiped his sticky fingers down the white bib and brace overalls he was wearing. 'What time did you say Mam's arriving?'

'Around one. Lunch is prepared so we can relax for an hour.'

'Awesome.' He wrapped his hands around my waist and kissed me on the neck.

'No time for that though.' Playfully, I pushed him away. 'I hope you're not getting that paste on my best painting clothes?'

'Have you seen the state you've got yourself in? A small bit of paste from me isn't going to make that much difference.' He chuckled.

'Hmm. Suppose so.' I kissed him on the lips. 'You're looking so much better.'

'I'm feeling it.'

'But do you think you're ready to go back to work on Monday?'

'Aye. Jim'll break me in easy. He's retiring at the end of the year and I don't want to miss out on the chance of grabbing his job as foreman.'

'At least she's locked up.'

'Yes. Still can't get a divorce though, can I? I can't believe her father's lawyers found a loophole so she wouldn't have to go to trial.'

'But hopefully she'll be in Forest Vale for a long time. I've heard it can be worse than prison in some of those mental institutions. I feel kind of sorry for her.'

'Sorry for Miranda? How can you feel sorry for the woman who almost killed me?'

'She deserves everything she got but I can't help feeling for her. I mean, a young woman stuck in there with all those insane patients. If she wasn't mad already – although she must've been at the time to stab you like that – it won't be long before she is.'

'Let's not talk about her anymore.' Joe kissed me. 'Are you sure there isn't time?'

I stared into his big, chocolate eyes. 'Go on then.' Giggling, I grabbed his hand and pulled him towards the bedroom.

⁓

Ben crawled through our knees on the grey-shaded carpet while Peggy and Adam inspected the lounge decor. 'I love how springy this is.' Peggy sank her stockinged feet into the deep pile. 'It's so luxurious.'

'Yes, we like it. Came from Courts. They fitted it too.' I twiddled the gold band on my finger.

Peggy frowned. 'I see you're wearing a wedding ring.'

I held it up to show. 'It's only a Woolies one. Although once we're married, Joe said he'll get me a real gold one.'

She frowned. 'But you're not married so should you be wearing any wedding ring?'

'I don't see why not. We're married in all but name. Just because we don't have that piece of paper.'

'Even so. Don't you think it makes a bit of a mockery of marriage?'

'No, I don't. Anyway, I don't see how you can be so judgemental when you had a baby out of wedlock, and let's face it, if you hadn't given me away, or whoever you gave away, then Joe and I would've been married years ago.'

'Now, ladies,' Adam interrupted, 'there's no need for that.' He smoothed his hand against the wallpaper. 'You've done a good job, son.'

'Thanks, Dad. Rachel helped.'

'Teamwork. Always a good thing.' Adam bent down and scooped up Ben. 'What do you think, little man? Do you approve?'

'Dada.' Ben giggled.

'I'm sorry, Peggy,' I said. 'Adam's right, I shouldn't have said that. Why don't you come and help me with lunch?' I led the way. 'I didn't mean to have a go at you.'

'And I'm sorry too. You're right, I've no right to be judgemental.'

'Shall we forget about it? What do you think of the kitchen?'

Peggy peered around, admiring the pine dresser, table and chairs. 'These are unusual.' She opened a louvre door on the fitted cupboard. 'Very modern. Hmm, what's cooking?' She turned to the cooker. 'Isn't this the same one you had in the flat?'

'Yep. Creda Horizon II. I liked it so much I decided to order a new one for here.' I opened the oven door to take out a large quiche and five jacket potatoes.

'Ooh that quiche looks and smells delicious.'

'Ouch.' I rubbed my wrist having caught it on the hot baking tray.

Peggy led me to the sink, turned on the tap on and held my arm under the cold water. 'Keep it there for a few minutes.'

I winced.

'Have you got any antiseptic ointment?'

I shook my head.

'No worries. I've got some in Ben's bag. Won't be a minute.' She disappeared out of the kitchen and was back in no time at all with a tin of Germolene. 'Here you go.' She turned off the tap, dabbed my arm with a towel and rubbed some of the cream in.

'Ta. I can't believe I did that.'

'It won't be the first, I'm sure. I've lost count of the times I've burned myself.'

'Would you get the salad from the fridge, please?'

'Of course.' Peggy went to the refrigerator and lifted out the bowl of prepared salad along with my homemade coleslaw and put them both on the table. 'You've gone to a lot of trouble for us. Thank you.'

'You're very welcome.'

'Shall I call the others?'

'If you don't mind.' I struck a match and lit the stubby red candle in the table centre. The flame swayed.

'Mmm, something smells nice,' Adam said sitting down. 'I hope you ladies have made friends.'

'We have.' Peggy put Ben in a highchair between her and Adam.

'It's great how that thing folds up to go in the car,' Joe said.

Peggy strapped Ben in. 'One of the reasons we chose it.'

Once we were all seated, Adam turned to Joe. 'Are you sure you're ready to go back to work next week?'

'Rachel asked me the same thing earlier and as I told her, Jim, the foreman, will wean me back in gently. I need to be doing something. You know me, I've never been one for sitting around.'

'Just take care.' Peggy patted his hand. 'On another subject, Adam and I were wondering when you'd like to meet Teresa.'

Joe looked at me.

I shrugged. 'It's up to you.'

'How about a week Sunday?' Joe served a huge portion of lettuce, tomato and cucumber onto his plate. 'Invite her for tea at yours and we'll come over. If that's okay with you, Rach?'

'Yep. Sure, might as well see what she's like.'

'You'll like her.' Peggy scooped potato from its jacket into a dish for Ben and mashed it up with cheese.

'How about you, Rach?' Adam asked. 'Have you thought anymore about getting in touch with your real parents?'

'Not really, what with Joe's accident and then getting this place ready but maybe in a couple of weeks. I'll probably decide to meet them. Just to see what they're like.'

'Do you have their address?' Peggy spooned the mash and cheese to Ben.

'Yep, the agency gave it to me.'

'Will you just turn up?' She chewed on a piece of quiche. 'Mmm, this tastes as delicious as it looks.'

'Thanks. It's Mum's recipe. In answer to your question, no, I'll write first. I don't like the idea of turning up unannounced.'

'That's what Teresa did,' Adam said.

'Well, I'm not Teresa.' I sipped water from my glass.

Joe changed the subject. 'How's our Kate doing?'

'Good.' Peggy put a spoonful of food to Ben's mouth but he had other ideas and slapped the spoon away. The food splattered on the floor. 'I'm so sorry.' She leaned down to mop it up.

'Don't worry,' I said. 'We'll leave it until after lunch. I'm sure he'll probably make a lot more mess than that.'

Peggy brushed strands of hair behind her ear. 'At home he has his own spoon which distracts him while I feed him, but that can get a bit messy.'

'Give him a spoon. I don't mind,' I said.

Adam reached for the baby bag and took out a spoon. 'Have you seen Linda recently?' He passed Ben the plastic spoon.

'Not for a couple of weeks,' I said, 'but she and Stu are coming for tea tomorrow. Linda's starting to show. My mum reckons she's having a girl.'

'It'll be interesting to see if she's right. What do you reckon, Peg, do you believe in that stuff?' Adam winked at Peggy.

'I can't say I do. I seem to remember someone telling me I was expecting a girl before Joe was born.'

'Oh, yes, that's right. It was my old Aunt Jane.' Adam turned to Joe. 'Are you still going to your counselling sessions?'

'Yeah, although I'm not sure they're helping me that much, but I'll finish the course.'

'How about you, Rachel?' Peggy asked.

'For the adoption business or being attacked?' I took a bite of quiche.

'Well for both?'

'I didn't bother with the adoption lark, although Mum took it up, as the whole thing messed with her head. She needed to come to terms with the fact that she and Dad hadn't stolen me, that they'd done nothing wrong, and there was no way they could've known about that lunatic attendant at the home switching babies. I've had a few sessions following the attack and my last one is next week but I just want to put it all behind me.'

'Understandable,' Adam said. 'Peg's been having counselling.'

'Really?' I said. 'How's that going?'

'Okay I suppose.' She swivelled the silver bangle on her wrist. 'Meeting Teresa has helped.'

'What's this Teresa like?' Joe asked. 'Does she look like me?'

'Nothing like you or Kate. Or me for that matter. Hard to believe she's my daughter but Aunty Sheila's got photos of my mam at Teresa's age and there's a great likeness. She's a sweet girl. Very artistic. You'll like her, I'm sure. Ben loves her as do Kate and Sheila.'

'I look forward to meeting her.' Joe stacked the empty plates.

Linda nudged me. 'I love it. And you've even got a spare bedroom, just in case, if you know what I mean?'

'Yep, we have. I think we'll be happy here.' I put my hand on her stomach. 'You're blooming.'

'Did you feel her kick?'

'No. What do you mean, her?'

'I'm having a girl. I can feel it. I've even named her. Keep your hand there.'

'You have?'

'Yep. Did you feel it?'

"Sorry, Lind. Maybe it's still too early as you're not five months yet. Incredible though to think there's a little Linda or Stu growing in there.'

'Definitely a little me. Do you want to know her name?'

'Go on then.'

'Anne-Marie. Double-barrelled so none of that shortening her to Anne. What do you think?'

'Cool, but supposing she's a he?'

'She's not.'

'But do you have a boy's name ready?'

She shook her head. 'Nope. She's a girl so we don't need one. How about you and Joe? Do you reckon you'll try for one or wait?'

'I don't know. Part of me wants to have one grow up with yours but the other part says we should wait, and I love my job. I should check those spuds.'

Linda followed me into the kitchen. 'You don't have to give up your job. Lots of mums still work.'

'I suppose so but I'm not sure I like the idea of leaving my child with a stranger.'

'I could always look after him or her. Or Peggy?'

'Hmm, not sure. Anyway, enough of that.' I opened the oven door and the aromas filled the room.

'Yum, that smells scrumptious.'

I gave a final baste to the golden roast potatoes and took out the chicken. 'Want to start carving this for me while I check the veg?'

'Sure.' Linda sat at the table. 'You've set this out nice. You must get it from your mam.'

'You're probably right.' I placed the cooked chicken on a chopping board in front of my friend and passed her a carving knife while I checked the pans on the stove. After turning off the electric rings I grabbed a colander off the hook, strained the boiled potatoes and tipped them back into the large pan. I added a drop of milk and blob of marg, mashing the potatoes with a masher from the utensil set on the wall which we'd received as a housewarming gift from Joe's Aunty Sheila. Once I'd sorted the mash I strained the cabbage, keeping its vegetable juices in a jug, and chopped it finely with a little butter. The carrots and peas just needed straining.

'How's that chicken doing?'

'Just about done. Are the legs for Joe and Stu?'

'That's what I thought, unless you'd rather have one than breast?'

'Nope that works for me. Shall I dish it up on the plates?'

'That'll be ace. I placed four dinner plates onto the table. Another housewarming present but this time from Peggy and Adam.

I added the mash and veg to the plates. 'Oh, I almost forgot gravy.' Taking the frying pan from the drawer at the bottom of the cooker I put it on a ring and added the vegetable juices I'd saved earlier, added in a bit of flour, following with Bisto and stirred, leaving it on a low heat while I got the roast potatoes from the oven. 'Mmm, they smell gorgeous. I reckon they're nearly as good as my mum's.'

Once the plates were finally ready, I called, 'Joe, Stu, dinner's on the table.'

Joe and Stu swaggered in. 'Wow, a feast,' Stu said taking a seat next to Linda.

'If I didn't already love you,' Joe said, 'I soon would with you cooking like this.' He rubbed his stomach. 'I'm starving.' He sat down the other side of Linda.

I tipped the gravy into a jug and put it on the table before sitting down too. 'Oh no...'

'What?' Linda poured gravy onto her dinner.

'I forgot to do stuffing.'

Joe tilted my chin. 'Don't worry, babe, we don't need it. This looks delicious.'

'Thank you, but you haven't tasted it yet.' I cut into the breast of chicken. 'Dig in.'

Linda licked her lips.

'Just one thing missing.' Joe got up and went to the fridge and returned with two cans of lager. 'Here you are, mate.' He passed one to Stu.

'Cheers, pal.' Stu poured the drink into his glass, stopping at intervals to avoid the froth overflowing. 'So, Rach, what did you decide about meeting your real mam and dad?'

I took a sip of water. 'You know what, I'm really not that fussed. As far as I'm concerned, my real parents are my mum and dad. They've been so good to me these last few years. Really been there for me.'

Stu fiddled with his fork. 'But surely you must want to know where you come from?'

'Not really. Not like I did when I searched for Peggy. Maybe it's better to let things lie.'

Joe pressed my arm. 'But, babe, didn't you promise your old man that you would?'

'I believe I said I'd think about it.'

'Hang on, let me get this straight' – Stu put his cutlery down on the side of his plate – 'your old man's encouraging you to meet them? But didn't your folks put up a fight when you wanted to find Peggy?'

'Yep. But this time Dad said these people have been victims in this as much as me. They took steps to hold on to their child and still lost me. But...'

'This chicken is so moist,' Linda said. 'You'll have to give me cooking lessons.'

'Nothing special. I just shoved it in the oven.'

'We saw Mr and Mrs Coles coming out of their house today.' Linda filled her glass from the jug of water on the table.

'Did you? What did you think?'

'A young-looking couple for their ages but then I told you Mam used to go to school with Denise.'

'No, Lind, you didn't. I suppose that makes sense. Same age and living in the same area. The thing is, I don't want to tread on Teresa's toes. She's been brought up by them so therefore they're her parents not mine.'

'Have you met her yet?' Stu asked.

'No, we're meeting her next week,' Joe said.

Everyone tucked in until they finally set their cutlery down. 'That was delicious, Rach,' Joe said. 'Cheers.'

'You're welcome.' I stacked the plates.

'Yes, thanks, Rachel. It was yum.' Stu swigged the lager from his glass. 'You looking forward to meeting your new sister? Are you both going?'

'We're both going,' I said.

'Rachel's coming with me for support,' Joe said. 'According to Mam, Teresa's really nice but we'll make up our own minds. We're going over to Mam's next Sunday for tea. She's invited Teresa, Aunty Sheila and Uncle Malc. It also means we get to meet their new little fellow.'

'Oh yes.' Linda's eyes twinkled. 'A little boy, isn't it?'

'Yes, but that's all we know.' I peered up at the clock. 'Why don't you boys go and watch the footie. Lind and I will clear up in here.'

'Are you sure, babe?' Joe got up from the table.

'Yep, it will give us a chance to have a bit of girlie time.'

Joe and Stu were out of the kitchen in no time at all.

'Wash or dry?' I said to Linda.

'Wash.' She carried the plates across to the sink and ran the hot and cold taps, adding washing up liquid. 'You know, Rach, if you like, I can meet the Coles with you.'

'No, you're all right. Joe said he'll come with me.' I threw the tea towel down on the worktop and put my arms around Linda's shoulders.

She turned around. 'Hey, what was that for.'

'Just that we've both got our happy ever after. I suppose in a way that's one reason I'm not sure about meeting them, and for not wanting a baby yet. I'm so happy I feel something may happen to spoil it.'

'You can't think like that, Rach.'

'I'm trying not to, but after everything that's happened, it's rather difficult.'

She patted my arm. 'You know what, you're right to wait to have a baby, and I reckon you need to keep up with that counselling. Although, you should meet the Coles especially if that's what your dad wants you to do. Changing the subject, how's your Jen getting on?'

'Good.'

'So, she and Phil are an item now?'

'Er, not quite?'

'What does that mean?'

'Well...'

Linda took a carton of orange juice from the fridge. 'Come on, Rach, out with it.'

'You might want to sit down.' I made my way to the table. 'Jen phoned me earlier today.'

'And?' Linda flopped down on a chair. 'She's okay, isn't she?'

I placed two glasses of orange juice on the table. 'Yeah, she's fine, although you're not going to believe this... there is no longer Jen and Phil but there is a Jen and Jan.'

'What?' Linda squinted.

'That's what I said. It seems Jen and Jan have got it together.'

'Well, well' – Linda beamed – 'I never knew your Jen had it in her. Good for her, that's what I say. Whatever makes her happy.'

'Yep.' I smiled. 'I agree, although I dread to think what Mum and Dad will make of it.'

'Maybe Jen's just experimenting and by the time she gets home it will have fizzled out. After all she was in love with that doctor guy and then Phil so she obviously likes men. When's she due back?'

'September. Around the time of your baby's arrival.'

Chapter Two

Rachel

A gorgeous smell of baby talc reached my nose as Joe and I stepped into the hallway. Peggy must've just bathed Ben.

'Go through.' Adam closed the front door.

'You ready for this?' I asked.

'As I'll ever be. Let's go and meet this half-sister of mine.' Joe clasped my hand and we strode into the lounge.

'Ah, you're here.' Peggy came across and kissed Joe and I on the cheek in turn.

Joe peered around the room. 'Where is she then?'

'You mean Teresa?' Peggy repositioned a pair of round, tan framed glasses on the bridge of her nose. 'She's on her way.'

'So what's she like then?'

'Never mind that,' I said. 'Peggy, when did you get the specs?'

'Ha ha. Yesterday. I'm still trying to get used to them. I suppose it was inevitable I'd need them sooner or later.'

'Not necessarily. After all, Dad doesn't.' Joe slipped his jacket off and hung it on the back of the armchair.

'Not yet, although he's booked in for an eye test next week.' Peggy turned to Adam. 'Aren't you, darling?'

'Indeed I am. And if I look as sexy as you in a pair of specs then bring them on.' Adam pulled at his ear. 'You kids fancy a beer?'

Joe glanced at me. 'Rach?'

'Go on,' I said, 'I'll drive. Just a lemonade for me, Adam.'

'Cheers, sweetheart. You're the best. Thanks, Dad, I'll have that pint.' Joe turned around. 'Aunty Sheila' – he wandered over to the sofa and kissed her on the cheek – 'I didn't see you and Uncle Malc.'

'Meet your new cousin.' Sheila looked up with pride.

Joe took the tiny hand of the baby on her lap. 'Hello, Jacob, we've heard a lot about you.'

'May I hold him?' I asked.

'Sure, but you need to sit down first.' Sheila rose from the sofa. 'You can sit here.'

'Ta.' I took Sheila's seat and she passed me the baby before perching close to me on the arm of the couch.

'Hello.' I held Jacob's tiny fingers.

Sheila beamed. 'He's a little darling.' She peered up at Joe. 'And how are you doing now?'

'Good thanks. I went back to work this week. What's it like being new parents?'

'We love it, don't we Malc?'

'Certainly do. He's such a good sleeper too.'

Adam re-entered the room with our drinks and passed Joe a pint of bitter. 'I'll leave yours here, Rachel.' He set a glass of lemonade on the occasional table.

'Cheers, Dad.' Joe put his drink next to mine and lifted Ben from the carpet. 'And how's my little bro? Do you like your new cousin?'

Ben wriggled and moaned so Joe let him back on the floor and Ben sprinted across the room. Joe's eyes twinkled. 'Look at that boy go.'

'Want to feel the difference in weight?' I asked.

'Go on then.' Joe went to take Jacob from me.

Sheila frowned. 'Sit down first, Joe. He's only little and I don't want you dropping him.'

'All right but I am used to holding babies you know. Been holding that one since he was born.' He signalled across to Ben slithering around the carpet like a worm.

Once Joe was settled next to me, I passed him Jacob. 'Feel the difference in weight.'

'He's really light, isn't he? Hasn't got much hair either, unlike our Ben. He had a mop of dark stuff when he was born. Almost black it was.'

Sheila rose from the arm of the couch and took Jacob from Joe. 'He's blond so it doesn't show.' She brushed his crown. 'See, he does have some.'

'Of course he does.' I stood up. 'Here you go, Sheila. Have your seat back.'

'Thanks.' Sheila eased herself down with the baby.

'So, what's this Teresa like?' Joe stretched across to the table, picked up his pint and took a swig.

'I like her,' Sheila said.

Malc rubbed his moustache. 'I've not met her yet so I'm in the dark like you two but Sheila's not stopped raving about her. We've brought photos of your gran, if you fancy a peep.'

'Cool. Yeah.' Joe set his beer down on a mat. 'Mam never spoke about her parents and we've never seen any piccies.'

Sheila handed Jacob to Malc. 'Look after him while I get the snaps.' She leaned over the side of the couch to get the photos from her bag as the doorbell rang.

'That'll be Teresa.' Peggy left the room and moments later returned with a bleached-blonde spiky-haired young woman. 'Joe and Rachel,' Peggy said, 'this is Teresa.'

'Hi' – Teresa grinned emphasising her bright plum lipstick – 'you must be Joe? I've heard so much about you.' Teresa smacked the side of his face with a kiss leaving a red-stained pair of lips on his cheek.

I took a tissue from my sleeve and gave it to Joe. 'I think you need this.'

'Ooh, sorry about that.' Teresa stroked the mark with her fingertip. Her long talon-like, black-painted nails forced Joe to back away. 'I tell you what, Joe,' she said, 'it's a good job you're my brother otherwise I'd be fancying you.'

He wrinkled his nose. 'Hate to break it to you, but it wouldn't make any difference as there's only ever been one girl for me and that's Rachel here. Pleased to meet you by the way.'

Teresa shrugged. 'I was only joking. Peggy didn't tell me you were the serious one. Hi there, Rachel.'

'Hi,' I answered. 'Peggy mentioned you're a poet.'

'Well, I dabble in poetry but I'm not sure I'd label myself a poet.'

'If you'd like me to look at some of your stuff, I can maybe get my editor to publish two or three poems in *The Echo*.'

Teresa blushed. 'I don't think they're good enough for that. I heard you were a hotshot journalist though.'

'I'm a journalist but far from a hotshot.'

Ben let out a scream. Peggy gathered him up from the carpet. 'I think this one needs a change. Rachel, would you mind putting the tea on the table? Everything's ready.'

'Sure. No worries.'

'Thanks, love. You're a good girl.'

Teresa held out her hands to take Ben. 'I'll change him if you like?'

'No, you're all right. You get acquainted with the rest of the family. I shan't be long,' Peggy said on leaving the room as I made my way out to the kitchen.

Teresa followed me. 'I'll help.'

'Thanks.' I removed clingfilm from the dishes and placed them on the table. 'Fancy putting the kettle on?'

'Fancy putting the kettle on?' she mimicked.

I glanced up. 'Pardon?'

She rolled her eyes. 'I said, of course I can.'

I shook my head. Not another crazy woman, please. I'd had enough of them to last me a lifetime.

Ben and Jacob slept while the family grouped around the table. Sheila and Malc. Peggy and Adam. Kate and David. Joe and me, which left Teresa as the odd one out.

I scooped a pilchard in tomato sauce on to my plate. 'Peggy mentioned you're engaged.'

'Yep.' Teresa piled lettuce and a piece of quiche on to hers.

I helped myself to a chunk of French bread from the basket. 'Didn't you invite Teresa's fiancé, Peggy?'

'Yes, I did. It's a shame he couldn't make it.'

'What does he do?' Adam gulped a mouthful of beer.

Joe put down his knife and fork. 'Hang on, haven't you and Mam met him, yet?'

'Nope. I think Teresa's hiding him away.' Adam winked at Teresa.

'Don't you think Peggy and Adam should meet this man you're going to marry?' I said.

'Now, Rachel.' Peggy tapped my hand. 'Teresa will bring him to meet us when she's ready.'

'Exactly.' Teresa blinked. 'Right now, I'm enjoying getting to know my new family without any distractions.'

I supposed that was fair enough. 'What did you say he does?'

Teresa glared at me. 'What is this? The Spanish inquisition?'

'Sorry, I was just being friendly.'

She gave a half smile. 'And I'm sorry, I didn't mean to be ratty. It's just that...' She took out a hankie and dabbed her eyes. 'It's just we had a bit of a row a couple of nights ago and I've not seen or heard from him since.'

'Oh, darling.' Peggy was out of her seat and had her arm around Teresa. 'There won't be any more questions, I promise, and I'm quite sure you'll make up with, whatever his name is, soon.'

'Peter. His name's Peter. Peter Bowles. He's a doctor.'

Adam focused on Kate's fiancé. 'David's a doctor. Maybe you know him?'

'I can't say I do. Sorry.' David's green eyes twinkled.

Sheila took a sip of lemonade. 'How are the wedding plans going, Kate?'

'Really good. I've got a fitting for my dress next week. Rachel too. As you know Rachel and Linda are my bridesmaids.' Kate caught Teresa's glance. 'You can be my bridesmaid too if you like? Can you make next Saturday for a fitting?'

Teresa's smile widened. 'I'd like that. Thank you. I'll make sure I'm free.'

※

Joe and I curled up in bed.

'What did you think of her?' I asked.

'She seems okay. You?'

'Not sure. Something about her?'

'Like what?'

'When we were in the kitchen and I asked her if she could put the kettle on, she mimicked me but then tried to blow it over like it never happened. You're not going to like it, Joe, but I think she could be a bit crazy.'

'Are you sure your judgement's not being knocked after Miranda?'

'Maybe but I don't trust her. I was right about Miranda and I think I'm right now. And what about that remark to you about if you weren't her brother?'

Joe tickled me under an arm. 'Are you sure you're not a teeny bit jealous?'

'Don't be daft. And that bloody big lipstick mark she left on your face.'

'You're overreacting, babe. Come here.' Joe slipped off my nightdress.

'But...'

'That's enough talking.'

Chapter Three

Peggy

Adam bounced Ben on his lap. 'Now you be good for Mama while Dada's at work.' He pecked him on the forehead, got up, and popped him back into the highchair. 'What did you say you're doing today, Peg?'

'Meeting Rachel.'

'You've not done that for a while.'

'No, we haven't, but now with Joe back at work and Rachel free at lunchtime for a change, I snapped up the slot while I could. The weather's supposed to be warm today so I'll leave the car at home and take a nice long walk into town and then Rachel and I will venture to the park.'

'Have a good day.' He pecked me on the cheek.

'See you later.' I was lifting Ben out of the highchair when I heard voices in the hallway so I carried him through to see who Adam was talking to. 'Oh, Teresa, we weren't expecting you.'

'Sorry, impulse again. I wanted to see my little brother.'

'I'd best get on, love. See you tonight.' Adam closed the front door behind him.

'No work?' I asked.

'Got the day off.'

'I'm about to get Ben washed and dressed.'

She held out her hands to take him. 'Let me, please.'

'Okay, if you're sure. His clothes are out ready. It'll give me a chance to clean up the kitchen.'

'I thought maybe we could do something together today.'

'Oh, sorry, Teresa, I can give you a couple of hours but I'll need to leave just after eleven as I've made arrangements to meet Rachel.'

Her smile dropped. 'Never mind. It was just a thought.'

'I know,' I said, 'why don't you join us?' I wasn't sure how Rachel would take that and if I was honest I'd been looking forward to spending a bit of time just with her, and Ben of course, a chance for Rachel and I to have a good one-to-one chat. I'd missed those.

'I don't think Rachel will like that.'

'Why do you say that?'

Teresa bit her lip. 'I'm not sure whether I should say. I don't want to cause trouble.'

'No' – I frowned – 'say, please.'

She carried Ben into the kitchen and I followed her in. She sat down with him on a kitchen chair and he tapped his hands on the table like a drum.

'Tell me, Teresa. What happened?'

'Well, you know when we all came to tea last Sunday?'

'You seemed to get on?'

She shook her head. 'I'm just a good actress. Remember you asked Rachel to set out the tea?'

I nodded.

'Well I offered to help, you know, to give us a chance to get to know each other.'

'That was nice of you.'

'She didn't think so.' Teresa passed Ben to me. 'Sorry.' She put her hands to her face.

'Teresa, whatever happened?'

'Rachel said such nasty things.' Teresa sniffled.

'Like what?'

'That I wasn't welcome here. That you were her mother and not mine.' She got up, helped herself to a tissue from the Kleenex box, and patted her eyes.

Rachel pushed the pram through the gates. 'Wow.' She pointed to the carpet of forget-me-nots. 'Aren't they stunning?'

'They are.' A corner of the park was full of purple and blues. 'What are all these other flowers?'

'Those there on the right are hyacinths and you know what they are on the left, don't you?'

'Are they lilac?'

'Yep.'

Straight ahead a bed of nodding golden daffodils interweaved with red and yellow tulips. 'I love this time of the year.' I glanced into the pram at Ben still fast asleep.

'Me too. And isn't it great to abandon our coats?'

'Hmm, although I heard on the radio yesterday that snow's expected next week.'

'Snow, you're joking.' She stopped at the bench by the pond. 'Shall we sit here?'

'Sure. I've brought lunch, although I think Ben will sleep straight through it.'

'I hope he wakes up before I have to go back to work.'

'He may not. I had an awful night with him. Think he's teething. Shame if he misses the ducks as he loves seeing them. He's even learned to say quack quack.' I passed Rachel a couple of slices of stale bread and as if on cue a couple of mallard and a drake waddled up the bank. I broached the subject about Teresa as we broke the bread into small pieces. 'What do you think of Teresa?'

'She's all right. Why?'

'What have you got against her?'

Rachel squinted. 'Nothing, why?'

'Come on, Rachel. I know.'

'Know what?'

'Teresa's told me what you said.'

Rachel tightened her fists. 'What the hell am I supposed to have said?'

'You told her that I was your mother not hers.'

She tossed her head back and roared with fake laughter. 'I don't believe this. I told Joe she's another crazy woman. I can't deal with this.' She went to stand up but I pressed her back down.

'Don't rush off. Let's talk about it.'

'Talk about what? You've already made up your mind.'

'Then tell me your side of the story.'

She shrugged. 'Not much to tell really except when I asked her to do something she mimicked me. When I tackled her about it she was all smiles, rolling her eyes, and blanking over it like it had never happened. But as for me saying you're my mother and not hers, I'm sorry, Peg, but that's ludicrous and I don't want to have to be dealing with this.' She stood up. 'I'm going back to work. I've a meeting this afternoon and I refuse to let this get to me.'

'Rachel,' I called, but she didn't stop and charged off out of my view. Who was I supposed to believe?

Sheila added a spoonful of Nescafé into each of the mugs. 'This is a surprise visit. Nice though.'

'I needed someone to talk to.'

She poured boiling water into the coffee and brought them over. 'I'll put yours here for when you've finished feeding Ben.'

'Want to tell me what's worrying you? Is it the wedding arrangements?'

'I wish.' I sighed.

'What then?' Sheila nibbled on a ginger nut.

'Rachel and Teresa. I don't know who to believe. They both say the other is out to get them.'

'That's a bit dramatic.'

'Maybe I'm exaggerating but according to Teresa, Rachel's been mean to her. Basically, told Teresa she shouldn't be coming around to see me because I'm Rachel's mother.'

'That doesn't sound like Rachel. Here, let me take Ben so you can have your coffee. Your need is greater than mine.'

'Thanks.' I passed Ben and his bottle. 'No, it doesn't but with everything she's gone through who knows. Maybe she's snapped.'

'She seemed like she was coping fine to me last Sunday.'

'And Teresa?'

'Yes, she seemed fine too, although it did appear that she might be trying to wind Rachel up a bit with Joe. I mean a sister doesn't go around leaving lipstick marks on her brother's cheek and basically tell him she fancies him.'

'She did that?'

'Tried to cover it up that she was joking, and who knows, maybe she was. Maybe that's just how she is. After all, we don't know her, do we?'

'It's all too much.' I sipped my drink.

'Talk it over with your Adam. He'll know what to do.'

'I hope so.' I drank the last of the coffee and put the cup down. 'I'll just change Ben and then I'd better be off to get dinner on the table.'

Kate strained the spaghetti in the colander, served it on three plates and poured the bolognese from the saucepan while I sorted the salad. After putting the dinner plates on the table she asked, 'Shall I call Dad?'

'If you don't mind, love.'

I tossed the lettuce, tomatoes and cucumber into vinaigrette dressing before tipping it into the wooden bowl.

'Yum. This looks nice,' Adam said sitting down.

I glanced at my youngest daughter. 'Our Kate made it.'

Adam picked up his spoon and fork. 'Looks like she's made an ace job of it.'

Kate sprinkled parmesan cheese over the sauce. 'I thought I'd better get into practice. Only three months now until I'm married. Although David said he doesn't expect me to do all the cooking. He said we'll do everything fifty-fifty. I'm so lucky to have such a modern man.'

I rested my fingers on her wrist. 'You are lucky, darling, but so is he. Are you looking forward to your dress fitting tomorrow?'

'I certainly am. Is Aunty Sheila looking after Ben for you?'

'Yes, it's all arranged. She'll come here with Jacob.'

'And you still need to sort out your outfit, Mam. Remember, you're the mother of the bride. That means you have to shine.'

'I'll sort it, love. I promise. There's just so much going on. How about tomorrow afternoon after your fitting? We could hit the shops.'

'That'll work as I'm not seeing David until the evening.'

I coughed to clear my throat. 'While I've got you both here I wanted to ask something?'

'Go on.' Adam shoved a forkful of food into his mouth.

'What do you think of Teresa?'

Kate wrapped spaghetti around her spoon. 'I like her. She's really nice.'

'Adam?'

He shrugged. 'Like Kate says, she's nice. Why? What's brought this on?'

'As you know she turned up this morning...'

'Yes' – Adam took a swig from his glass of beer – 'she does make a habit of turning up uninvited.'

'I don't mind that. It's what she said that's bothering me. She said Rachel was horrid to her last Sunday. Told her that I was her mother not Teresa's and Teresa should stay away.'

'That doesn't sound like Rachel, Mam.'

'I'm with Kate, although...' Adam blinked.

'What?'

'Who knows what's going through that girl's head after the Miranda business. Sounds like the counselling isn't helping. Have you tackled Rachel?'

'Yes, today. She denies it. And she said that Teresa was weird with her.' I shook my head. 'I don't know who to believe.'

Adam reached for my hand. 'Let's go with the flow for now as we've got our Kate's wedding to concentrate on.'

'Okay.' So that was Adam's way of saying I shouldn't bring it up. He wasn't going to be of any help but then at least I still had Sheila to talk to. Right now, I had to put it out of my head and concentrate on Kate and her dress fitting tomorrow. She was going to make a beautiful bride.

Chapter Four

Rachel

Linda pressed the bell. 'Are you sure this is the right place?'

'Yes. 17 Abbotts Way. She works from home apparently. Comes highly recommended from someone Kate works with.'

The door opened. 'Good morning.' A woman with short greyish hair looked from side to side. 'Just the two of you? I thought there'd be more. Which one of you is Kate?'

'Neither,' I said, 'but we are here for Kate's bridal fitting. I take it she hasn't arrived yet?'

'You're the first.' Gold-framed spectacles on a beaded chain fell against her chest. 'Not a problem though. Come through, take a seat and I'll leave the door ajar for the others. Can I get you a drink?'

'No thanks,' I said, 'I'll wait until the others arrive.'

'Me too.' Linda unbuttoned her lightweight jacket.

'So, you two are the bridesmaids?'

'Yes, I'm Rachel and this is…'

'Linda. I'm Linda. Although perhaps Kate should reconsider having me as a bridesmaid because we didn't know I'd be expecting when she asked me. At this rate I'll be the size of a house.'

'Don't worry. We can always take that into account with the style of dress. Perhaps a loose empire line will work. It all depends what kind of look Kate's after.'

There was a tap on the door and Kate, Peggy and Teresa stepped through. 'Sorry we're late,' Kate said, 'we were waiting for Teresa to arrive.'

I might have known she'd be dragging her heels. 'Don't worry, Kate,' I said, 'we've not been here long. Hi, Peg. Teresa.'

'Well now that you're all here,' the fitter said, 'I'll take you through to the bridal area. This way.'

We followed her along the sixties style carpeted hallway and into a large bright room at the back of the house.

'Take a seat. Would you like some sparkling wine?'

'Oh, yes, please,' Kate said, 'although do you have orange juice for Linda?'

'Yes, I have a carton in the fridge. I'm Edna by the way. Kate, we spoke on the phone.'

'Good to meet you,' Kate answered. 'You come highly recommended by Samantha at the hospital.'

'That was kind of Sam. I made her wedding gown along with the dresses for her four bridesmaids.' Edna took a large binder from the bookshelf and passed it to Kate. 'Why not flick through my portfolio while you wait, and see if anything jumps out at you?'

'Thank you.' Kate turned over the first page as the dressmaker left the room.

'Good about free refreshments.' Linda took off her jacket. 'I hadn't realised it was going to be so hot today.'

'I'm sure she bills Kate for it,' I said.

'Well, we can hardly expect her not to.' Peggy glanced at the page. 'That's nice, Kate.'

'It's a bit too low-cut for me and the train looks like it has wings about to take off.' Kate flicked through the contents. 'This one. What do you think?'

'It's rather lovely.' Peggy ran her finger over the picture. 'I like the floral lace and it's very sophisticated. Will you wear a veil?'

'Maybe. This gown's still too low-cut for what I want though.'

'I'm sure Edna can change that,' I said.

'What's that, dear?' Edna entered the room with a tray of sparkling drinks. 'I've added a bit of lemonade to yours, Linda, to give it a fizz effect.'

'Awesome. Cheers.'

'Kate's seen something she likes,' I said, 'but the neckline's a little too low for her. Are you able to adapt it?'

'Everything can be changed. That way the bride gets her own bespoke wedding gown.' Edna checked her notebook. 'How many bridesmaids did you say you're having, Kate?'

'I said two, but sorry, I've changed it to three now. Mam's here for support, that is, unless you can make a mother of the bride outfit.'

'That can be arranged.'

'Ooh, Mam. Seems we don't have to wander around the shops later after all. Perfect.' Kate took a champagne flute from the tray and we all did the same.

'Cheers.' I clinked glasses with the others.

'Edna' – Kate sipped the sparkling wine – 'this is the one I like.'

'That's simple enough to adapt. How are you wearing your hair?'

'I thought up. What do you think, Mam?'

'I think that will be adorable, darling.'

'Then a sweetheart neckline will be perfect. Are you looking at strapless?'

Kate looked at me.

'Go for it,' I said. 'It will be cool in the summer sun as well as showing off your gorgeous slim shoulders.'

'A choker or necklace would set it off,' Linda said, 'or even a locket? Maybe that could be your something borrowed.'

Kate looked up at Edna. 'Then, yes. Thank you. Strapless will be brill.'

'This is what I suggest. A high waistline' – Edna moulded her hands from under her arms to the waist – 'and then let the fabric flow down to a flared skirt with a two-foot train in matching fabric, and a short, lace veil. How does that sound?'

'Amazing.' Kate's hazel eyes twinkled.

'Right, let's get you measured. Pop your wine somewhere and stand up on here.'

Kate passed me her drink and stepped up on the makeshift platform.

'And once I've measured you, we'll move on to the bridesmaids, not forgetting the mother of the bride.'

Peggy beamed.

Edna took a tape measure from around a tailor's dummy and measured Kate from the nape of the neck to the floor, around the bust, and the waist. 'Remind me of the wedding date?'

'29th July,' Kate said.

Edna glanced at the paper calendar on the wall. 'So, today's 29th April, and you'll want it ready at least one month before, which gives me two months to complete, although we may need a last-minute fitting for your pregnant friend's dress. Plenty of time. I'll book you in for the first fitting a month today.'

'Thank you.' Kate stepped down from the platform. 'Do you have pictures of designs for bridesmaids in here too.' She picked up the binder.

'They're towards the back, but let's decide on the fabric for your gown before moving on?'

'Oh, sorry.' Kate blushed. 'Silly me.'

Edna passed Kate the swatches. 'This is the fabric I suggest we use.'

'That floral lace is exactly what I had in mind. Like in the photo in the binder.'

'Yes. And this tulle for your veil.'

'Cool. Thank you.'

'Now for the bridesmaids. Have you an idea of what you'd like?'

'Square necked, high waistline, and tiered layers. Oh, and I'd like them in a soft rose shade.'

Teresa shot up from her seat. 'Pink? Not pink, Kate, please. I don't do pink.'

'You shouldn't have to change what you want, Kate,' I said. 'If Teresa isn't prepared to go with your choices, then maybe she shouldn't be a bridesmaid.'

Teresa put her hands up to her eyes and pretended to cry. 'See what I mean?'

'For God's sake, Rachel,' Peggy said. 'Whatever's the matter with you? This is supposed to be a special day for Kate.'

'Exactly. And that's why we should go with Kate's preferences and not what Teresa wants.'

Teresa sniffled. 'Maybe I shouldn't be your bridesmaid after all. Especially as it now looks like I'm not going to be a bride.'

Peggy rushed over to Teresa. 'Oh dear, I'm sorry. Have you heard from him?'

She nodded. 'He broke up with me.'

'Talk about a drama queen,' I whispered to Linda. 'I don't believe for one moment there ever was a fiancé.'

Edna coughed. 'Perhaps it would be a good idea to take a little break before starting on the bridesmaids.'

Peggy nodded. 'That sounds like a good idea.'

'I'll make some coffee.' Edna left the room.

'Now girls,' Peggy said. 'Let me remind you that we're here for Kate. And Teresa, I'm sure Kate will understand if you'd like to withdraw.'

She blew her nose. 'No, I don't want to let Kate down, and I'd really like to be her bridesmaid because it makes me feel part of the family, it's just…'

'Then you must realise Kate shouldn't have to change her ideas,' I said.

'Rachel has a point, Teresa.' Peggy stroked her cheek. 'Why not check out the fabrics and see if they suit you or not. I'm sure Kate will have a rethink if it doesn't look right on you.'

'Yes of course I will, but I've always wanted bridesmaids in pink, ever since a little girl, haven't I, Mam?'

'Yes, dear. Now, Teresa, are you prepared to give it a go?'

'Okay.' She sniffed.

Edna came back in with a tray of steaming beverages. 'Everything sorted?'

'All sorted,' Peggy said.

'Good. We'll have refreshments first and then get going.' Edna put a plate down on the side. 'Help yourself to my homemade cookies.'

Linda was first to take one. 'Ooh, yum.'

Linda flicked the kettle. 'I see what you mean about that Teresa. She really is a cow trying to turn Peggy against you.'

'I know. I'm not sure where to go from here.'

'Have you arranged to meet her folks yet?'

'No, because if I do that, I reckon she'll get even more crazy. Anyway, what did you think about the bridesmaid dresses in the end?'

'They'll be awesome. I adored the pink and Edna was great about making it looser for me if required. I wonder what Peggy chose for her outfit.'

'Who knows? I'd liked to have been involved in choosing but with Peggy suggesting it was better I left to avoid any more eruptions, I didn't have a choice. It didn't seem fair though. Okay, she's not my mother, but I thought we were close. This Teresa's around for five minutes and already I'm being pushed out.'

Linda touched my shoulder. 'Don't let it get to you. Peggy's in the middle and trying to do right by all. Sit down and have your tea. And guess what? I've made a Victoria sponge.'

'Cool.' It didn't seem fair I was being pushed out. After all Peggy was my mother-in-law in all but name. 'She should've let me be involved but hey, like you say, I'm not going to let it get to me. Bring on that cake.'

I unlocked the door. 'Only me.'

Mum hurried into the hallway. 'Lovely to see you, darling but did we know you were coming?'

'No, it's a surprise visit. I needed to see my mum and dad. That's okay, isn't it?' I heard voices in the lounge. 'Sorry, I didn't realise you had company.'

'It's fine, love. Our visitor was unexpected too. Go through and I'll get you a cup of tea.'

'Thanks, Mum.' When I entered the lounge, I couldn't believe what I was seeing. What was she doing here?

Dad stood up. 'Rachel, darling. We weren't expecting you.'

'I thought I'd surprise you.'

'It's always lovely to see you, dear.' He kissed me on the cheek. 'You've met Teresa?'

I glared at her. 'Yes, we've met. I hadn't realised you were coming here, Teresa. You didn't say.'

'Spur of the moment. You know me, impulsive.'

No, I didn't know her at all. Why was she even here? Had she heard me mention I was coming or was it a mere coincidence? 'I thought you were with Peggy all afternoon?'

'That was the original plan but once she'd had her fitting I decided to come here and meet your parents as I didn't know anything about them. After all, if there hadn't been a mix-up at our birth they'd have adopted me.'

'I see.'

'Here you are, darling.' Mum put a cup of Earl Grey on the small table. 'Do sit down, Rachel. You don't have to wait to be asked. This is still your home.'

'Thanks, Mum.'

'So, Teresa,' Dad said, 'tell us about yourself.'

***

'Did you have a good day?' Joe dropped down the oven door. 'I've cooked us dinner.'

'What a lovely surprise. Thank you. What brought this on?'

'Remember you mentioned that woman in the newspaper who'd managed to divorce her husband almost instantly because he'd put her in hospital?'

'How's that put you in a good mood?'

'I was talking to one of the guys at work this morning. Turns out his sister's a solicitor. He reckons I could have grounds for getting a divorce sooner than waiting the five years.'

'Now that is worth celebrating.'

'Anyway, he gave me his sister's details and I rang her this afternoon. She's booked me in for a consultation next week. Said something or other about me needing to have been married for at least a year but otherwise she reckoned I had a good case.'

'That's amazing.'

'Yeah, and as it's coming up to the first anniversary, it seems likely you and I could get married this year.' He took out a casserole dish and put it on top of the cooker.

'That smells yummy. What is it?'

'Chicken chasseur. Mam's recipe and I've boiled some rice to go with it. Sit down, madam, and I'll bring it over.'

Joe had covered the table in a blue linen cloth and set it with matching napkins, cutlery and wine glasses. He put a tea towel over his arm like he was a waiter and placed a plate of dinner in front of me. 'I'll just get the wine, madam.' He went to the fridge and took out a bottle of Blue Nun and poured a drop into my glass. 'Would madam care to taste?'

I took a sip. 'Delicious, cheers, darling. This is so lovely. Thank you.'

He filled up both our glasses. 'A toast.' He raised his glass. 'To us.'

I clinked my glass with his. 'To us.'

'This means we can start planning our wedding.' He put a forkful of food into his mouth. 'Mmm. Not bad even if I do say so myself.'

'Maybe we shouldn't get ahead of ourselves, Joe. Let's see what the solicitor says first. What day are you seeing her?'

'Tuesday in my lunchbreak. Her office is around the corner from the garage so it should fit in well.'

'That's awesome. But we don't want to steal Kate's limelight so perhaps we should keep it to ourselves for the moment.'

'Yep, you're right. When do you suggest we get married? August? Christmas?'

'August is too close to Kate's. Christmas will be too cold. Let's aim for end of September. By then Linda will have had the baby and Jen will be back home.' I wanted to be excited but something held me back. It all seemed too good to be true.

Chapter Five

Rachel

'This is it.' I stood outside the house up the road from Linda's.

Joe took my hand. 'You ready?'

'As I'll ever be. Thanks for being with me.' I went to tap the knocker when the door opened revealing a woman with long brunette hair.

'You must be Rachel.' She looked at Joe. 'And you must be Rachel's young man.'

'Yes. I'm Joe. Pleased to meet you.'

'Do come in. We're so excited to meet you. I'm Denise.'

The layout of the house was like Linda's with no hallway so we stepped straight into a brightly coloured lounge with fairy lights over the lampshades and blue floral curtains and wallpaper.

'Gordon,' Denise called. 'They're here.'

He hurried into the room. His brown eyes twinkled. 'What a beautiful young woman. I can't believe you're our daughter. If it hadn't been for Dee's blasted aunt, we'd have seen you grow up. Sit down.'

Still clinging to Joe's hand, I lowered us down to a futon covered in matching fabric to the curtains, and glanced around the room. In the alcove adjacent to the fireplace hung a large *Flower Power* tapestry and an acoustic guitar leaned in the corner. My nose tickled and on spotting bunches of daffodils in the vases on the shelves I realised why. 'Who plays the guitar?' I asked.

'That would be me.' Gordon grinned making his Frank Zappa like moustache twitch. I couldn't believe he was my father. So different to my dad or Mike. He was so sexy. His black silk shirt showed off a hairy chest and the tight black jeans accentuated his small hips.

'We're a folk duet.' Denise's tiered skirt spread across the red-patterned rug as she sat down on another futon next to Gordon. 'I sing. Well, we both sing. We only take bookings in local clubs and pubs but it suits us' – she squeezed Gordon's hand, her ice-blue eyes lighting up – 'doesn't it, darling?'

Before Gordon had the chance to answer, I said, 'Really?' Denise even liked the same clothes as me. 'I'm a journalist. Maybe I can feature one of your gigs?'

'That would be wonderful. You look like us, doesn't she, Gord?'

'She does.' He stared at me with his big brown eyes.

'Yes,' Joe said, 'it's easy to see she's your daughter.'

Butterflies stirred in my stomach. Denise and Gordon were lovely. So how come Teresa was such an airhead?

'This must be difficult for you, Rachel?' Gordon said. 'Bad enough finding out you're adopted but to find out your birth parents weren't yours either. Doubly difficult. Teresa's not taken it well but then...'

'What?'

'Maybe we shouldn't say, Gord.'

'No, please. What were you going to say?'

'She's not been an easy child,' Gordon said as a key went in the lock and Teresa strode in.

'Teresa.' Denise jumped up. 'Hello, darling, we weren't expecting you. I thought you said you were out until this evening?'

'Change of plan.' She slumped herself down on the futon next to Joe.

What the hell was she doing here? I specifically remembered Peggy making a point of saying Teresa would be around hers all Saturday which is why I'd arranged for us to come here in the afternoon.

'You've met Rachel and Joe, haven't you?' Denise said. 'Well, they popped around to meet us.'

Teresa touched Joe's arm. 'Of course, I have. I told you, Joe's my brother.'

'I hope you and Teresa can become good friends.' Denise smiled at me. 'Sisters even. Where are my manners? I should make tea.' She went into the next room and Gordon got up to join her. 'I'll help.'

Teresa prodded her fingers in my side. 'What do you think you're doing here?'

'Meeting my real parents,' I said.

'Well stay away. They're my mum and dad, not yours.'

'Teresa.' Joe frowned.

She giggled. 'I'm only playing. You two are far too serious.'

I rose from the couch. 'We're going now, anyhow.' I glared at Teresa, 'Happy now?'

'You sure?' Joe asked. 'She said she was only joking.'

'I'm sure. Come on.'

'Okay,' he said in a soft voice before standing up.

I headed for the kitchen. 'Look, Denise and Gordon, I'm really sorry but we've got to go.'

'Already?' Gordon put a mug down on the worktop.

'Sorry.'

Denise turned to me. 'You'll come back though?'

'Yes. I'll give you a ring.'

<hr />

Stu and Joe strolled out into the backyard for a smoke. Linda had put her foot down and said no more smoking in the house.

'So' – Linda flopped down on the couch – 'what did you think?'

'They're lovely. They are so me. I even look like them. They sing folksongs in clubs. Gordon plays the guitar. Oh' – I laughed – 'they call each other Gord and Dee and they're so affectionate towards each other. You'd never believe they'd been married for all those years.'

'How come you're back so quickly then?'

I sighed. 'Madam turned up.'

'Madam?' Linda squinted.

'That cow, Teresa. She was supposed to be with Peggy all afternoon.'

'So what's your next step?'

'I've suggested Joe go round for his tea at Peggy's next Sunday and he asks her to invite Teresa too. Make out he wants to get to know her better. Not that he wants to, but you know… That way I can try again without interruptions.'

'Would you like me to come with you if Joe's going to be at Peggy's?'

'No, you're all right. I'll be fine now I've met them. I like them and don't feel nervous at all. They're lovely, really lovely, and I understand myself more after meeting them. There's something not right about that Teresa though. They were about to tell us something when she walked in. I reckon my instincts about her are right.'

'I'm so pleased for you. Not about the problems with her, but you know what I mean? Can I ask a favour? Do you think you can get some time off a week on Monday?'

'Why?'

'I've got an antenatal appointment and Stu can't get out of work. Wondered if you fancied coming.'

'What time?'

'It's not until half past three. Would that work for you?'

'Should be fine. I've got to interview Dark Chaos at one because they're releasing a new album and need a plug. You could come if you like? I'm sure Paul would love to see you.'

She shook her head. 'Nah, I don't think so, but thanks. If you meet me at the clinic say quarter past three?'

I took my diary from my handbag and wrote down *meet Lind for clinic just after 3pm* in the fifteenth of May, 1978 slot, to make sure I didn't forget. 'You know they're probably talking about motorbikes out there, don't you?'

'Yeah, although I've told Stu we need to buy a family car before the baby arrives. The Hillman Imp's too small. He's seen a Ford Escort coming up for auction next Friday. Reckons he'll bid. If he wins he and Joe plan to do it up. Quite exciting really.' She picked up an elastic band from the arm of the couch and gathered her hair into a ponytail.

'Your hair's grown so long.'

'I know. A customer at work reckoned that can happen when you're expecting. I'll get it cut once the baby's born. Stu's booked a day off from work next Thursday and is taking me to Chester. We're going to Mothercare to get one of those Moses baskets, order the cot, buy some Babygros, vests and other things. I've been knitting a matinee coat. Want to see?'

'Sure.'

She leaned over to a box by the side of the settee and pulled out a piece of white knitting on two needles. 'This is what I'm making.' She passed me the pattern.

'Awesome. You're so clever. Will you teach me?'

'If you like. See this bit here' – she touched the bottom of the garment – 'that's called rib, and this bit here is moss stitch. It's really easy. Mam taught me. She's made three of them so far in white, lemon, and blue.'

'But not pink?'

'No, she refuses to do pink, even though I've told her I'm definitely having a girl.'

The back door closed and the boys pottered in. 'We should get going, Rach,' Joe said.

I rose from the settee. 'See you soon, Lind, and Monday the 15th is in my diary.'

Chapter Six

Peggy

Adam patted Joe on the shoulder. 'Fancy coming for a pint with your old man?'

Joe looked from me to Teresa. 'Not today, Dad, if you don't mind.'

'What's going on?' I said. 'I've never known you turn down the chance of your dad buying you a beer.'

'I just don't feel like going to the pub today, that's all, particularly as I came around to get to know my new sister a bit.'

'Fair enough.' Adam picked up a packet of Players and a lighter from the sideboard. 'Spare five minutes to have a smoke with your dad out back then?'

'Sure. I expect Mam wants to get tea sorted so we'll get out of the way.' Joe followed Adam through the patio doors into the garden.

'Would you like to help me make tea, Teresa?' I asked.

'Can do but I was hoping you might let me take Ben for a walk as it's such a lovely day.'

'Sorry, love, our Kate and David have taken him out for the day. They'll be back before you go though so you'll still get the chance of a cuddle.'

'Is Kate all right? I've not seen her for a couple of weeks. In fact, I've not seen her since we had the fitting.'

'Yes, she's fine. Been busy that's all, what with the wedding arrangements and extra duties at work. I'm glad you agreed to the pink for the bridesmaid dress. The colour suits you.'

'Really?'

'Yes. I wouldn't have said so otherwise.'

'I've never worn pink before. Felt it was a bit too girlie and I've always been more of a tomboy.'

'You're going to look stunning on the day but you mustn't outshine your sister.' I tapped her on the hand. 'Now let's get that tea sorted. It's only cold meats, salad and jacket potatoes. Kate's eating with David so if you set the table for four. The mats are in that drawer and the knives and forks on the stand. You'll soon get used to the layout around here. Tell me, how are you getting on with Rachel now?'

Teresa took the mats and coasters from the drawer and put them on the table. 'Er... I'm not sure I should say. I don't want to turn you against her.' She set the cutlery down.

I opened the oven and checked the jackets. 'These are looking good. I'll take them out last thing. If something's happened you must tell me.'

'Well' – she took a seat at the table – 'she seems to be everywhere I go. A couple of weeks back, after I left you and Kate at the dressmaker's, I went to see her parents, as they should've been my adoptive parents. I thought Rachel was going out with Joe but she turned up there. Had a go at me for being with her parents, and then last Saturday she and Joe were around my folks. I tried to be pleasant, really, I did, but she had another go at me before storming off.' Teresa put her hands up to her eyes. 'I'm trying, Peg. Really, I am but she's not the easiest person to get on with and she hates me.'

I put my arms around her shoulder. 'Bear with her, love. She's been through a lot. It would be good if you could get on as she means a lot to me and will soon be my daughter-in-law.'

'You're a good woman, Peggy. Better than most. My folks aren't as easy to talk to as you.'

'No?' I opened the fridge and took out a large cheese and onion quiche and the bowl of salad. 'Fancy putting these on the table while I slice up the corned beef?'

'All right.' She got up, came over and took the quiche and salad.

'You were saying about your parents?' I sliced up the cold meat into thin slices and put it on a plate. 'I've got some chicken left over from lunch. Shall I put that out too?'

'That will be nice. I love chicken. Do you have any pickle?'

'You'll find a jar of Branston's in that cupboard up there.'

'Thanks. Yeah, my folks. It was tough growing up in a commune for my first ten years.'

'You lived in a commune? Were your parents hippies?'

'They still are. It was awful growing up there as the lads wouldn't leave me alone, once I started developing like, and Mum and Dad let them get on with it.'

'Really? That's dreadful.' What kind of people were these Coles letting that happen to their daughter?

'They were really strict with me too.'

'With Bobby too?'

'Nope. He couldn't do a thing wrong. They still have a go at me even now yet they were nicey-nice with Rachel last week. I reckon they always knew I wasn't theirs and punished me for it.'

I shook my head. 'I'm sure that's not the case, love. You're probably still in shock with everything that's happened. Were you offered counselling?'

'Yes, but...'

'What?'

'I told them I didn't need it. After all it wasn't going to change anything was it? Anyway, I'm glad that you're my mam. You're much nicer.' She came up and gave me a hug.

'Bless you. I recommend you go for the counselling though. I did, and it's really helped.'

There was a knock on the door. 'I wonder who that can be?' I glanced at my watch. 'It's too early for Kate. You wouldn't get it would you, love?'

'No problem.' Teresa left the kitchen.

I removed the jacket potatoes from the oven and put them in a basket, setting them on the table with the other food, and added coleslaw, salad cream, butter, and cheese from the fridge. 'Who is it?' I called out.

'Sorry, Peg. We were in your area and didn't want to drive past without popping in to say hi.'

'Sheila. What a lovely surprise? You'll stay for tea? We're just about to sit down and there's plenty to go around. Where's Malc and the baby?'

'Malc's getting Jacob from the car. We wanted to make sure you were in before going through all the rigmarole of getting the carrycot out, if you get my drift?'

'Sure. I'll fetch Adam and Joe from the back. Teresa, will you set the table for Aunty Sheila and Uncle Malc while I get the boys in?'

She headed for the cutlery stand.

I pulled open the patio doors and strode out into the garden. Adam and Joe seemed to be in deep conversation. 'Everything all right?' I asked.

'Sorry, love' – Adam stumped out his ciggie – 'we got a bit waylaid.'

I strode closer to them. 'What's going on?'

Adam put his arm around me. 'Nothing for you to worry about, my sweet.'

'Tell me.'

'If you must know Rachel's feeling a bit insecure. She organised for Joe to come around today to keep Teresa here while she's at the Coles.'

'Hmm, Teresa mentioned Rachel's been making her life difficult.'

'You've got to be joking, Mam. You and Dad are totally blind. The girl's a sly bitch. Rachel was right about Miranda, and you'll see, she's right about Teresa too.'

I shook my head. 'Come and get your tea. We've got unexpected visitors too. Sheila and Malc have turned up.'

Chapter Seven

Rachel

I flopped down on a cushioned chair under the flowery parasol in Gordon and Denise's small garden. It was well set out with a round plastic table and chairs, a metal BBQ, and two loungers on the patio. Bumblebees hovered around a couple of mature red geraniums in terracotta pots placed symmetrically either side of the stone slabs. Surrounding the lawn, pansies waved their purple and golden heads in one flower bed while, lilac and pink lupins adorned another. I sneezed as Denise came out of the back door.

'Oh dear. Is it the flowers? Do you suffer from hay fever?'

'Just a bit.' I laughed.

'Here' – she passed me a glass of lemonade – 'this will refresh you in the heat. I made it myself with my grandma's recipe, bless her soul. Plenty more in the fridge too.'

'Cheers. It's glorious out here. You've got a real suntrap.'

'Yes, we like it. I grew up here and remember sitting against that wall sunbathing when I was a teenager. Once Mam and Dad died, being an only child, I inherited it. By the way, I love your skirt.'

'Cheers. Picked it up from Walkers in town. My friend's the manageress. Have you been in there?'

'Oh, yes, I have. Often.' Her ice blue eyes sparkled. 'I bought this skirt in there.'

'You have the most beautiful eyes,' I said. 'I wish I'd inherited them.'

'Yours are gorgeous too. You have Gord's eyes but you must get your fashion sense from me. Talk of the devil.'

'What's that?' Gordon asked as he took a seat.

'I was just saying Rachel has your eyes.'

'Awesome.'

I chortled. 'Nice.'

Denise scooped up a handful of peanuts. 'Are you sure we can't tempt you to have something to eat?'

I was starving but with butterflies partying inside my stomach I couldn't eat a thing. 'No, ta. I'm not that hungry right now. Talking of clothes, your skirt's so similar to mine, isn't it, with the tiers and floral fabric?'

'It is. We obviously like the same kind of gear. What size are you?'

'A ten.'

'Me too. We could swap clothes. I've always wanted a daughter who'd share my outfits.'

'Doesn't Teresa?'

'God, no. She's always going on about her hippie parents and awful dress sense.'

'She has spikey hair so what's the difference?'

'In her mind we're far too old to dress as we do. She'd prefer me in something staid like an old lady would wear.'

'I can't see her problem. You're still a young woman so it's up to you what you wear. Have you lived in this house all your life then?'

'No.' Gordon sipped his drink from the long glass. 'Once Dee had the baby we moved into a commune and although fun at first, it became difficult as Teresa got older.'

'How so?' I asked.

'She was getting unwanted attention from some of the teenage lads there' – Denise sat down – 'and as I had this house standing empty it seemed like the perfect solution.'

'I see. So, when you were at the commune did you take drugs and all that?'

'We smoked a bit of weed but nowt else,' Gordon said.

'What's it like? I've never tried the stuff.'

'It's okay,' Denise said, 'makes you feel a little dreamy but we don't do it now. In fact, we haven't participated in that sort of thing since we moved back in here.'

I laughed. 'That's good to hear. So how long ago was that?'

'Just over twelve years.' Denise picked up her drink. 'Why not tell us something about you? Do you have any siblings?'

'I have one sister. Jen. She's in Paris at the moment but will be coming back in September.'

'What's she doing there?' Gordon helped himself to a fistful of peanuts from the small bowl.

'She went to stay with a couple of my artist friends after giving up her job as a nurse and being dumped by her doctor boyfriend. My friends have an art studio out there as part of their jobs so Jen's mucking in with whatever.'

'Something that's been confusing me' – Denise scratched her head – 'is when you were here last week, Teresa mentioned Joe was her brother. How did that work you and he being together if you thought he was your brother?'

I blinked. 'It was all such a mess. Joe and I were engaged years ago and it was only when I introduced him to Peggy it came to light that we were siblings. Prior to that we had no idea. It was a heart wrenching break-up.'

Denise bit her lip. 'I imagine it must've been. So, what happened then?'

'I got a new boyfriend, Phil. He's one of the artists that Jen's staying with, but once I discovered Joe and I weren't related I knew we had to be together. Wasn't all that easy though as he was married by that time to a girl who lied about being pregnant just to get him to marry her.'

'Married.' Gordon rubbed his bushy moustache. 'What happened?'

'Look, do you mind if we don't talk about that right now? I'll confide in you one day but it's all still a bit raw. The main thing is that Joe and I are now together. Tell me about you two and my family. I understand I have a brother.'

'A brother?' Denise squinted.

'Yes, Bobby. Around the same age as Kate, Joe's sister.'

'This will be coming from our Teresa?' Gordon said.

'Yes.'

'We don't have a son.' Denise sighed. 'Bobby's her imaginary brother.'

Gordon took a deep breath. 'We thought she'd grown out of it. She's always been a troubled child. Didn't stop us loving her, of course, but boy, have we been tested?'

'Gord, are you sure we should be telling Rachel those things?'

'She has a right to know. Especially when it involves her, and she's been expecting to meet a brother.'

'What about her fiancé?' I asked. 'Was that true?'

Gordon shook his head and laughed. 'A fiancé. First I've heard about it.'

'She's a dance teacher though?'

Denise rolled her eyes. 'I'm afraid not. The trouble with Teresa is she's a pathological liar.'

'She writes poetry?'

'Now there is some truth in that statement.' Gordon gulped his lemonade. 'Not that she's any good but it keeps her out of trouble for a bit.'

'And how about painting? The art kind,' I asked.

'Ha.' Gordon snorted. 'I don't think we've ever seen that girl pick up a paintbrush in her life. She used to scream and stamp her feet when we were at the commune if it was suggested she paint a picture. To be honest, I think they were pleased when we moved out.'

'So, let me get this straight. She has no brother, no fiancé, she's not a dance teacher and hates painting.'

'That's her in a nutshell,' Denise said. 'We could never make out why she was like that when we're both so creative and have never told lies.'

'But she has a cousin with a baby?'

Denise squinted. 'No. Is that what she said?'

'Well, that's what she told Peggy. Where did she learn to take care of babies then? She seems to know what she's doing. Changing nappies, bathing, etcetera.'

Gordon stood up to stretch his legs. 'She had a job as a trainee in a nursery but that didn't last long. After nine months they sacked her.'

'Why?'

'She became too attached to one of the babies' – Gordon sat back down – 'and one day she left the nursery with him in a pram, and didn't come back for over three hours. They were worried sick.'

'Was the baby okay?'

'Oh, yes,' Denise said, 'Teresa wouldn't have hurt him.'

'Perhaps I should warn Peggy. I don't know whether you know she has a baby, Ben, he's almost one. Mind you according to Peg, Teresa loves him and Ben adores her.'

'I've no doubt,' Gordon said, 'and she wouldn't harm him, especially when he's her baby brother. We took her to counselling when she was younger because we thought it might have been our fault how she is but it didn't seem to help much.' He shrugged. 'Not sure where we went wrong though. We gave her a good childhood, and like I said, as soon as she was getting bother at the commune, we got her out of there. Maybe it's all to do with genes.'

'She sounds very troubled. She's been awful to me. If she knew I was here now she'd... well I don't know what she'd do, but...' I broke down and cried.

Denise shot up from the chair and put an arm around me. 'Hey, what is it?'

'I've had enough of crazy women to last me a lifetime.' I told them briefly about Miranda without going into too much depth.

'You poor thing.' Denise rocked me in her arms. 'Are you having counselling?'

'Yes, although it's not helped much yet. I don't think dealing with Teresa's nonsense has helped.'

'We'll talk to her,' Gordon said, 'this isn't right.'

'No, please don't. It'll most likely make her worse. She's obviously feeling very insecure. The best thing you two can do is support her and let her know you still love her as your daughter and maybe then she'll slowly recognise I'm not a threat. I'm not trying to take her mum and dad away from her. I would never do that.'

'You're a good girl, Rachel.' Denise squeezed my hand.

I didn't want to be thinking about the past and Miranda so switched to a lighter mood. 'Let me know when your next gig is so Joe and I can come along. We love folk music.'

'Do you?' Denise's eyes twinkled. 'We belong to a folk club. Every second Tuesday in the month at Woodhaerst Village Hall. Why don't you and Joe come along?'

'Does Teresa go?'

'God, no,' Gordon said, 'you'd never catch her in one of those places. Her words not mine.'

'All right then. I'll speak to Joe.' I rose from the chair and picked up my handbag. 'I need to go but thanks for the lemonade.'

'Are you sure we can't get you something to eat?' Denise said.

'No thanks. I'll get a sandwich when I get in. I must rush as I've got an early start tomorrow. Can I leave from the back gate?'

'Yes. Sure. Gord will heat the BBQ next time you come. It's been wonderful to meet you properly.' Denise hugged me.

I wandered down the road to Linda's house and knocked on the door but there was no answer. Their car wasn't there either. Maybe they'd gone to Sandra's or to Stu's folks. That was a shame because I really needed to talk to someone after hearing the revelations about Teresa. I turned around and headed back to my car outside of the Coles house and drove home.

When I got in there was no sign of Joe but then I remembered he'd still be having tea at Peggy's. I needed to eat something. I sloped into the kitchen, flicked the kettle for coffee, and buttered a couple of slices of brown bread. From the fridge I took some grated cheese, stuck it on one of the pieces of bread and added a blob of coleslaw before closing up the sandwich and cutting it into four triangles. Hmm, that didn't seem much to eat so I rooted through the cupboards to see what else I could find. A bag of Golden Wonder cheese and onion. They'd do. With my cheese sandwich, crisps and coffee on a tray I made my way into the lounge, stuck the tray down on the coffee table, put *Rumours* LP on the music centre and flopped down on the settee.

What was I going to do about Teresa? Should I warn Peggy about Ben? No doubt she'd have none of it and think I was causing trouble. I glanced up at the clock. Almost seven. Surely Joe would be in soon. I took a bite of my sandwich but my eyelids flickered. I put the butty down on the plate and let my eyes close.

'Rach.' Someone was shaking my arm.

I jumped. 'What? Who?'

'Hey, it's okay. It's me, Joe. I'm just back. You're going to get a stiff neck sleeping like that. Come on, let's get you to bed.'

'All right.' I yawned. 'I'm done in. It's been one hell of a day.'

'How did it go with the Coles?'

'Brilliant. I really like them but...'

'What?'

'They told me lots of things about Teresa but I'm too tired to go through it now.'

'That's all right, babe. Let's get you to bed.'

I pulled up outside the industrial unit. At least this was an improvement from the last time I'd interviewed the band. I banged my fist on the door knowing I'd need to be loud for them to hear me.

Paul answered. 'Hello, Rach. You're looking well.'

'Hi, Paul. How you doing?'

'Good. Good. Come in.'

'This is quite an upgrade on the other place. And at least it doesn't look like it's about to collapse.'

'It's great. This way.'

I followed him through to a large room. 'It's enormous in here.'

'The acoustics are brilliant too. That room there' – he pointed – 'is our recording studio so it saves us a fortune.'

'Hiya there, flower.' Steve brushed his lips across mine before I could stop him.

'Oi.' I held up my left hand. 'You can't go kissing a married woman.'

'When did that happen? And how come you didn't ask us to play at your reception?'

'Quite recently and we just nipped off quietly. We're having a celebration later in the year or beginning of next. We'll definitely be hiring you then.'

'You know you don't need to pay us a bean. We'll happily play for you for nothing. As a kind of payment for all the promo you give us. Anyway, take a pew.' Paul positioned a wooden chair by me.

'Cheers. So, you have an album coming out then?'

Steve held up an LP cover with a picture of a golden chalice falling to the underworld. It read THE MAGIC CHALICE on the top in large black font and close to the bottom Dark Chaos in white.

That sounds interesting. 'Can I hear it?'

'Sure.' Steve popped the 33rpm record on the turntable.

'Do you mind if I take that armchair over there?' I asked.

'No probs,' Paul said.

'Cheers.' I flopped onto the deep cushion. 'Now I can close my eyes and get a better feel of the sound. Can you start it from the beginning again?'

Steve restarted the LP and I closed my eyes to lose myself in the mythical narratives. Some of it was dark. Some bright. And some were ballads. When it was finished, I opened my eyes. 'I love it. Can I buy one?'

'No,' Paul said, 'you can have one as a gift. Lads come and sign the cover for Rachel.'

One by one they scribbled their names in turn.

'Thank you.' I held the cover close to my chest. 'I shall treasure it and promise to do you a wonderful write-up. Where shall I send my readers to buy one?'

Paul passed me a card. 'Get them to phone this number or they can pick up a copy in the village record shop.'

'Cool. Right, I think that's about it. I'd better rush as I need to meet Linda.'

Paul put his hands in his pockets. 'How is she?'

'Good. She's having a baby.'

'A baby?'

'Yep. Due beginning of September. I'm off to meet her at the antenatal clinic now.'

'Wow. Linda as a mam. Give her my best.'

'I will.'

'I'll see you out.'

'Bye boys,' I called.

'Rachel,' Steve shouted, 'if you ever get fed-up of that man of yours you know where I am.'

I laughed. Not in a million years.

The car park was busy but I eventually managed to find a space as a Morris Marina pulled out. I got out of the car, locked up, popped the keys in my handbag and hurried through into the hospital following the signs to the antenatal clinic. Linda was on the back row of chairs with a shopping bag reserving the seat next to her. She waved on spotting me.

'I'm not late, am I?'

'No. I was a little early. Thanks for coming. How was the band?'

'Great. Their new LP is fab. I'll let you listen later as they gave me a copy for free.'

'I'd like that.'

A young nurse came out from behind a screen. 'Linda Pearson.'

'Good luck,' I said.

'See you in a minute.'

While I was waiting, I jotted a few notes down about my meeting with the boys. This band was going to go far. They needed to record a single, and a ballad track would be perfect for their debut. I must mention that to them.

'That was quick,' I said as Linda eased herself back into the seat.

'They weighed me and tested the sample I brought in so now I just have to wait for the doctor. You can come in with me if you like.'

'Will they allow that?'

'I don't see why not. I'd like you there. I'll tell them that. So how was Paul?'

'Good. He asked after you and I told him you're expecting a baby.'

She smiled. 'What did he say?'

'Not a lot other than wow. Oh, and he sent his best wishes.'

'What about Steve?'

'Still as cocky as hell. Bloody sod kissed me on the lips. Never even got the chance to stop him it happened so fast. Told him I was married.'

'Did you?'

'Waved my ring at him. I'd rather everyone thought we were married than just living together. Some good news though?'

'Yeah?'

'Joe's seen a solicitor and they reckon he can start divorce proceedings once the first wedding anniversary has passed. Could be done and dusted in less than three months which means we'll be able to get married.'

She took my hand. 'That's wonderful news, Rach. I'm so...'

A nurse came into the waiting room, 'Linda Pearson.'

'Ooh that's me. Come on.'

I got up with Linda and strode over towards the nurse.

'I'd like my friend to come in with me.'

'Sorry, dear, I'm afraid that's not possible. If you can go in this cubicle, get undressed and put a gown on. When the doctor's ready we'll open another door the other side to take you through.'

'Good luck,' I said for the second time.

Chapter Eight

Rachel

Betty was on reception browsing the diary when I got into work.

'Betty, you're back,' I said. 'Are you okay? We didn't know why you were off. Have you been poorly? Or on holiday? Mr Strange was very discrete about it all.'

'My mam died, pet. I told him not to say anything. He's been really good. Told me to take as much time as I needed but now with the funeral over, I need to get back to work to keep myself busy.'

I hugged her. 'I'm so sorry.'

'It is what it is. To be honest, we lost her months ago with the dementia, which kept getting worse. Poor Mam. At least she's at peace now.'

'Let me make you a cuppa.' I hurried into the back office, filled the kettle and flicked the switch.

Betty followed me in. 'Thanks, pet. How about you? What's been happening in your world?'

I popped a teabag into each of the two mugs. 'You really don't want to know.'

She rested her hand on my arm. 'Yes, I do. Tell me. I could do with something to take my mind away from my own worries.'

I peered up at the clock. It wasn't quarter to nine yet so there was time. 'Let me get the teas done and then I'll tell you. Although I feel bad loading you up with my problems when you've been going through so much.'

'I'm asking you to.'

I poured water over the teabags and added a dash of milk. 'Do you fancy a biccie to go with that, Betty?'

'No, ta. I must concentrate on my weight. Mam's left me a bit of money so hubby said we'll go abroad this summer so I'd best get rid of some of this.' She tugged at her middle.

'Let's sit down and I'll tell you my woes. I could do with your advice actually.'

'That's what Aunty Betty's here for. Out with it.' She took a sip of tea. 'You make a good cup of cha, girl. I'll give you that.'

'Ta. You remember Teresa, Peggy's daughter, who turned up and has been giving me bother?'

'Yep. You told me that.'

'Well, I met my real mother and father, her parents, a couple of weeks ago, and they told me some things about her.'

'Like what?'

'That she's a pathological liar for starters but then I already knew that. But what does worry me is that she had a job at a nursery and disappeared for hours one day with one of the babies. I ought to tell Peggy and Adam but if I do, I'll just be accused of causing trouble, and I'm not.'

'She sounds like a time bomb waiting to go off. You should tell them.'

'But Teresa always manages to twist things. She's already turned Peggy and Adam against me. They can't see a thing wrong with her.'

'Let me ask you this, pet. If you don't say anything and something happens, how are you going to feel that you didn't speak up to prevent it?'

'I know. I am worried. Joe reckons she'd never hurt Ben and I should leave well alone.'

'Tell Peggy, pet. If she doesn't believe you then that's down to her but at least you'll have given her the chance to watch out for signs.'

'Thanks, Betty,' I said as Mel strode into the back office.

'Morning. Betty. Welcome back. We've missed you.'

'Thanks, Mel. Right, I must get back to reception as Lizzie's late in this morning. Thanks for the tea, Rachel.' She patted my hand. 'Oh, and it's okay to tell the others on my behalf. Too painful for me to go through it with everyone.'

'Okay. Will do.'

'What was all that about?' Mel asked once Betty had left.

I moved over to the kettle. 'Want a cuppa?'

'Thanks.'

'Tea or coffee?'

'Tea thanks.'

I flicked the kettle to re-boil the water and popped a teabag in the mug. 'Betty's mam died. That's why she's been off.'

Mel put a hand to her mouth. 'Oh no, poor Betty.'

'I thought it would be nice if we did a collection to buy her some flowers. What do you think?'

'That's a lovely idea. Would you like me to organise it?'

'If you don't mind as you'll see the others more than I will.' I went to my bag and opened my purse. 'Here' – I passed her two one-pound notes – 'this will start it off.'

Mel took a large manilla envelope from the desk drawer and popped the money into it. 'How's your Jen getting on? Is she still with Phil?'

'I've been meaning to mention Phil to you. They're not together as a couple anymore and I know you've always fancied him so...'

'What? Are you going to matchmake again?'

'Yes.' I chuckled. 'I was thinking, you should write to him, a bit like a pen pal, and get to know each other properly. You'd make a lovely couple.'

'Doesn't he get a say in it?'

'Of course. I'll speak to Jen and get her to mention it to him. If he says *yes,* are you up for it?'

'If he agrees then, yes.'

⊰⊱

John placed the open newspaper down in front of me. 'Have you seen the finished result?'

'No.' I read the headline. DEBUT ALBUM RELEASE FOR DARK CHAOS. 'It looks good.'

'Good?'

'No?'

'No. It's magnificent, Rachel. At this rate the competition will be trying to poach you. Because of this article we've had three other band managers approach us for advertising. 'Keep this up, girl, and you're going to need at least one day a week covering the pop scene.'

'Cool. Talking about that, there's a folk club I'd like to do a write-up on. What do you think of that idea?'

'Folk? Sure, we can run with that. Do you have a date in mind?'

'Not yet. I wanted to run it past you first.'

'I'm all in. We're lucky to have you on board.'

'Thanks. I feel privileged to be working here and Mr Strange has always been so good to me. Poached or not poached, I shan't be going anywhere.' I was sure if I looked in a mirror my face would look like a ripe tomato. When would I grow out of this blushing lark?

'The gaffer will be pleased to hear that.' John drummed his fingers on the desk. 'I've been thinking...'

'Yes?'

'Yes. We should make you entertainment reporter and I'll speak to the boss about having Verity upstairs one day a week to cover the menial tasks. I know she's keen to learn. What do you think?'

'I like the sound of that. Cheers.'

John checked his watch. 'Why not get off home?'

'But it's only half past four.'

'I know.' He grinned. 'Go and surprise that old man of yours.'

The house was quiet when I got in as Joe wouldn't be home for around another hour. He'd be surprised to see me here before him. I unpacked the groceries from the Waitrose carrier bag. Minced beef, tomato puree, spaghetti, one onion, three carrots and two cans of Heineken.

Chopping onions wasn't my thing and it wasn't long before I was booing my eyes out. When Joe was around that was his job, but this evening I wanted the meal ready for when he came in. I stirred the carrot and onion in with the mince. While it was browning, I made myself a cup of coffee, and mulled over Betty's words. *How would I feel if something happened?*

At almost six o'clock, the Bolognese was cooked and smelt yummy. I stirred the spaghetti into a large pan of boiling water so it would be ready for when Joe came through the door in ten minutes. I'd speak to him again over dinner about broaching the subject of Teresa with Peggy. We were meeting for Kate's bridal fitting this Saturday and although it was agreed to meet at Edna's, instead I'd go over to Peggy's earlier and speak to her before Teresa arrived.

The phone rang breaking my thoughts. I hoped it wasn't Joe saying he'd been called out on a breakdown. I strolled into the hallway and picked up the receiver.

'Woodhaerst 56821.'

It was Jen. 'Jen, good to hear from you. Can I call you back later though as Joe's due in any minute and I don't want my dinner to ruin.'

She replied, 'That's fine, Rach. It was just a quick catch up as I'm going out shortly. I'll call you tomorrow if that works?'

I nodded. 'Yep. Tomorrow's good. Look forward to it. Love you.' I put the receiver back in its cradle. I'd ask Jen tomorrow about Mel writing to Phil. It would be wonderful if those two could get together. I wandered back into the kitchen and checked the spaghetti as the front door closed.

Joe came into the kitchen and kissed me on the lips. 'You're home early. Mmm, what's that smell?' He leaned over the cooker sniffing the Bolognese. 'This is a lovely surprise.'

I smiled. 'John was so pleased with my article that he let me off early. Get a quick shower and I'll put it out on the table.'

He wrapped his arms around my waist. 'Are you sure I can't tempt you to join me?'

Chuckling, I slapped his hand. 'I've put my heart and soul into this meal and don't want to ruin it. Besides, there's something I need to talk to you about. Get changed while I put dinner out.'

Joe's lip dropped. 'Okay. I'm going. I can't wait until later though.' He grinned before hurrying out of the kitchen.

Chapter Nine

Rachel

Adam slammed his newspaper down onto the coffee table. 'Do you never give up, Rachel? I know it's all been a shock finding out Peg's not your mother but do you have to try and sabotage her new relationship with Teresa at every opportunity?'

'That's not what I'm doing.' I rubbed my eyes. 'It's just that if I don't tell you and something happened then I'd never forgive myself.' I shot up from the chair. 'Do you think I like having to pass these details on to you?'

'Let's not turn it into a shouting match,' Peggy said. 'You'll wake Ben.'

'She's not who she says she is, and you should know. She's not a dancer. She's not engaged, or ever has been, and she doesn't have a brother. It's all in her imagination. She's a pathological liar.'

'I'd say that's what you're turning into, Rachel.' Adam lit up a cigarette. 'I'd say you're a bit jealous. Isn't it enough that you've got Joe?'

I snatched my handbag from the floor. 'I'm not staying here to be insulted. Peg, I'll see you and Kate later at Edna's.'

Peggy grabbed my arm. 'Don't go off like that. Adam, you're being a little harsh. Rachel's been through a lot and at least she's having counselling to help.'

I shook my head. 'It doesn't matter what I say, you and he are totally blind to Teresa, but I've done my job warning you about her taking that baby, so you can watch out for Ben, and whether you believe me or not, well that's down to you two. I can't do any more.' I took a deep breath. 'I didn't want to tell you but my conscience wouldn't allow me to keep quiet.' I stormed out of the house slamming the front door.

As I was about to get into my car Teresa came along.

'You.' She sneered. 'What are you doing here? I thought you were meeting us at Edna's.'

'I am but I had something to share with Peggy and Adam that couldn't wait.'

'You have to be in control of everything, don't you? You're not happy that you stole my life.'

'What?'

Her face creased like a witch. 'Look at you.' She jabbed me with her long nails. 'That should have been me as the journalist if you hadn't stolen my life. Well Peggy's mine now, not yours and I'll be seeing Rosalind and Charles again too, and before long, none of them will want anything to do with you.'

'You're mad,' I said as Peggy came out of the door.

'What's all the shouting about? Rachel?'

I shook my head. 'Who knows? Ask her? She's a mad woman.'

'Teresa?'

She took a hankie from her pocket and wiped it across her eyes, sniffling. 'I'm not sure what I'm supposed to have done, Peggy, but she just let rip into me.'

'That's a lie and you know it.'

'Rachel, I thought we'd agreed you were going to stop interfering. I think you'd better go and I'm telling you now, I don't want anything spoiling Kate's day when we have the fitting later.'

'Don't worry, I'm going but remember I warned you.'

'What's she talking about, Peggy? What's Rachel said?'

Peggy patted Teresa's hand. 'Nothing for you to worry about, dear. You go on through and put the kettle on. I'll be back in a moment.'

'Rachel,' Peggy said once Teresa had gone in the house, 'please, love, this has got to stop.'

I clenched my fists and took a deep breath. 'I'll see you later.' I got into the car and started it up.

⚜

'Calm down,' Linda said. 'Come and have a cuppa before we leave.'

'They're totally blind, Lind, and think I'm trying to cause trouble but wouldn't you want to know if it were you, and Ben was yours?'

'There's not a lot you can do about it, Rach. They'll need to wake up to her themselves. She's clearly deranged having a go at you like that but she'll never be able to turn your folks against you. Your mam and dad would never let that happen.'

'I know that but I don't want everyone thinking I'm the loopy one.'

'She'll make a mistake soon.' Linda sighed. 'You and me haven't had the easiest of lives, have we? Or Joe for that matter.'

I laughed under my breath. 'You can say that again.'

'Here, get that down you.' She passed me a cup of tea.

'Cheers, and then we'd better go. Let's hope Madam behaves herself while we're at Edna's. I refuse to rise to her jibes so I don't get the blame for spoiling Kate's day.'

Stu and Joe came through the front door. 'You girls still here?' Stu said. 'Thought you'd be gone by now. Me and Joe are about to watch the footie on the telly.'

'We're just going.' I got up, hugged Joe and kissed him on the cheek.

He pulled me at arm's length. 'Hey, what's going on, babe? Are you all right?'

'Not really,' I said. 'Your mam and dad had a right go at me. Didn't believe me at all about Teresa.'

He licked his lips. 'I can't say I'm surprised. They'll have to work it out for themselves.'

'I know but I had to tell them.'

'I understand.' He hugged me tightly.

Kate looked stunning in the wedding gown. The strapless feature showed off her slender shoulders while the high waistline accentuated her lovely figure.

'You look gorgeous,' I said.

Edna stood back and nodded. 'I'm really pleased with it. Fits you perfectly. I'll finish running it up and it'll be ready for you to collect by the end of June. We'll do one last fitting then just in case you've gained or lost any weight.'

Peggy glared at the mention of lost weight. 'She's not likely to lose any, are you Kate?'

'No, Mam.' Kate twirled in the mirror. 'I feel like a princess.'

'You look like one,' Peggy said. 'Wait until your dad sees you, never mind David.'

Edna held up a decorated headdress with pink and white silk roses. 'I've made these for the bridesmaids. Do you like them?'

'I love them,' Kate said. 'Can they try them on with their dresses?'

'Of course.' Edna put the coronet back into the box and brought out a white one. 'And this is for you.' She placed it on Kate's head. 'Obviously you'll have a veil too, but what do you think?'

Kate beamed. 'It's gorgeous. Thank you, Edna. How much extra are they?'

'No extra charge as I've used excess material from your gown and the girls' dresses.'

'But what about your time?' Peggy asked.

'I enjoyed doing it. Something to keep me busy while I was watching the telly. Now' – she went to the rail at the back of the room – 'Linda this is yours.' She turned it part inside out. 'Look here, I've added an elasticated ribbon that can be pulled tighter or looser. The dress has plenty of spare fabric so you have space for your baby to grow. Try it on.'

Linda slipped behind the curtain and came out looking dazzling. Edna placed one of the headdresses on Linda's head. 'Are you girls wearing your hair up or down?'

'They're wearing it loose in waves,' Kate said. 'We've got a hairdresser coming around the house in the morning and she'll do all our hair. Teresa's been growing hers so she can wear it curled like the others.'

Edna passed a frock to me and one to Teresa. 'You girls check yours out too.'

'Thanks.' I popped in the changing room before Teresa. 'It's all yours,' I said when I came back out with my dress on.

Edna adjusted the dress. 'It fits like a glove. Perfect. And while the other bridesmaid is trying hers, it's time to reveal the mother of the bride's outfit. Is that okay, Peggy, or are you keeping it secret for the day?'

'No, that's fine. Thank you.'

Edna went to the wardrobe at the back of the room and came back with a powder blue patterned silk dress and a linen bolero in a matching shade. 'Want to try it on?'

Peggy held it up. 'Yes, please. It looks divine.' She headed for the changing room as Teresa came out.

'You look lovely,' I said to Teresa. 'Here let me.' I placed the headdress on her head. 'You're growing the blonde out too, I see.'

'Yes, I'll look more like Peggy then.'

Peggy came out from behind the curtain. 'I need some assistance in zipping up.'

Edna hurried to her side and zipped up the garment and helped Peggy with the jacket.

'Wow,' I said. The ruched silk hugged her figure yet there wasn't a bump in sight. Peggy had done well getting her figure back in less than a year since Ben was born. 'You look...' I shook my head. 'Words fail me, you just look... A million dollars.'

Peggy blushed. And there was me worrying about still blushing at almost twenty-five. 'The flowery pattern is lovely. Not too loud but enough to hide any unwanted creases.'

'And here's your hat.' Edna positioned the large brimmed hat on Peggy's head. Its shade matched the outfit, and white feathers with a hint of pink on the crown heightened the crimson flowers in the dress.

'Now what about your shoes? I presume you'll wear high heels.'

'Yes, although I haven't got any yet.'

'Hang on.' She brought out a catalogue. 'Check out these crimson stilettos and they offer a matching clutch bag. What do you think?'

'They'd be perfect. Thank you.'

'What size are you and I'll order them on Monday and have them delivered here or direct to your home?'

'Here will be fine thank you. How about Kate and the girls?'

Edna flipped to the front of the catalogue to a white satin pair of bridal shoes. 'These for Kate' – she flicked to the middle and stopped – 'and here these open sandals in rose almost match the bridesmaid dresses. What do you think?'

Kate nodded. 'I love them.'

'I just need the sizes and I'll order them too.'

'Do we need to pay you now?' Peggy asked.

'No, dear. I'll invoice them along with the rest of the order. I'll get these at trade prices so it will save you a few pennies.'

Peggy took Edna's hand. 'Thank you.'

Kate checked her watch. 'We should go. We've taken up far too much of your time.'

'Before you do,' Edna said, 'have you sorted out your flowers?'

'Not yet. Do you know someone?'

'Yes. I have a friend who specialises in weddings. She works from home so doesn't have the same overheads as the high street florists which means you'll get a cheaper price. She only lives a couple of blocks away from here. I'll get you her card.' She headed over to the window and rummaged through the desk drawer. 'Here it is. Ada. Ada Matthews. Let her know Edna sent you. We try and help each other out a little.'

'Thanks, Edna.' Kate put the business card in her purse. 'You've been great. I shall definitely be recommending you.' She winked at me.

Chapter Ten

Peggy

The key turned in the lock. I padded into the hallway as Joe came through the door. 'Hello, love.' I kissed him on the cheek. 'What brings you here at this time? There's nothing wrong is there?'

'Nothing wrong, I just wanted to run something past you without Rachel around.'

'She's not still gunning for Teresa, is she?'

'For God's sake, Mam. Wake up. No, she's not gunning for Teresa as you put it. It's Rachel's twenty-fifth birthday next week and I'm organising a small party round at ours. I wondered if you and the family, including David of course, fancied joining us.'

'Well, you know it's Teresa's birthday that day too? I'm assuming the invitation includes her. Maybe we could make it a joint occasion?'

'Absolutely not, and no, she's not invited.'

'That seems rather harsh.'

'Whatever. So do you fancy it or not?'

'I'll need to speak to your dad as Rachel's not his favourite person right now.'

Joe shook his head. 'Right. I'd best get off then. Oh, before I go, where's my baby brother. I wouldn't mind a quick cuddle.'

'He's not here I'm afraid. Teresa's taken him out.'

'Teresa? You let her take him out even after Rachel warned you.'

'Why not? She's Ben's sister after all. They've gone for a picnic in the park to give me a break. Very considerate of Teresa, I thought. I've managed to clean the house top to bottom, have a bath, prepare dinner, and even curled up on the sofa for a read. That's the first time I've been able to pick up a book since Ben was born.'

Joe rubbed the back of his neck. 'Mam, how long's she been gone?'

'I'm not sure. She left just before noon. What's the time now?'

'Gone five. Don't you think you should be worried?'

The door slammed and Adam was at the lounge doorway. 'Who should be worried and why?'

'You and Mam, that's who. Teresa's had Ben out for hours. I'd certainly be worried if he was my kid. What am I saying? I am worried.'

Adam put his keys down on the hall table. 'Is this right, Peg?'

I looked up at the clock. 'I must admit I hadn't realised the time. Should we be worried?'

'Well I certainly am.' Joe headed to the hallway and picked up the phone handpiece. 'We need to call the police.'

I hurried after him. 'Don't do that. I'm sure she'll be back soon.'

'Stop overacting, son.' Adam patted Joe on the shoulder. 'Your mam's right, she'll be back soon. If she's not back in half an hour, then we'll make the call.'

A key slotted in the lock.

'See, here she is now,' I said.

Joe held the receiver. 'She has a key now?'

I cleared my throat. 'No. No, she doesn't.'

Kate came through the door. 'Joe, how lovely to see you. Is everything all right? You all look kind of... worried?'

'Mam's let Teresa take Ben out and they've been gone since before twelve.'

Kate frowned. 'That doesn't sound too good. Did you tell Teresa she could stay out this late?'

'No' – I trudged back into the lounge and flopped on the armchair – 'I told her not to be too long. Oh my God. I hope they're all right. Maybe they've had an accident?'

'More like she's run off with him,' Joe said. 'I'm phoning the police.'

'No, don't do that. Teresa's my daughter.'

'And Ben's my brother.'

'Half an hour more, Joe,' Adam said, 'and if she's not back then, I'll make the call myself.'

My heart beat faster. 'Teresa wouldn't hurt Ben.'

'No, I'm sure she wouldn't.' Adam put his arms around me. 'Do you have her mam and dad's phone number?'

I shook my head. 'No.'

'Rachel does, I'll give her a ring.' Joe dialled the number.

'Good idea.' Adam led me into the lounge, leaving the door open. 'I'm sure there's a reasonable explanation. Unless...'

'What?'

'There was some truth in what Rachel was saying. You know, Peg, it was a bit irresponsible letting her take Ben out for so long.'

I put my hands to my face. 'You're right. I'm sorry. She offered, and I didn't see any harm but I did tell her not to be too long. You've seen how good she is with him. There's no way she'd hurt him. Ben's not in any danger unless something's happened to Teresa.'

Joe hovered at the door entrance. 'I've got the number. I'll give them a call.'

'No, son. I'll do it.' Adam darted back into the hall and shut the lounge door behind him.

Adam marched up and down the hallway muttering under his breath. Someone knocked on the door and he opened it. 'Where the hell have you been?' he shouted. 'Get out of the doorway while I get my son inside.' He stepped outside to pull the pram up the step. Ben was sitting up giggling. 'Dada.'

'He's had a lovely time.' Teresa grinned. 'And you'll never guess what, but he said my name. Well, he said Tessa but I rather like that. Don't you?'

'We're not bloody interested in that right now.' Adam lowered the pram hood. 'What we'd like to know is where the hell you've been? It's gone six o'clock, past his teatime.'

'Sorry, we were having such good fun that I lost track of time. I'll get his tea sorted now.' She went to lift Ben from the pram.

'No, you won't.' Adam unstrapped Ben and passed him to Kate. 'Can you sort him out, please, sweetheart?'

'Of course. Come on little man, let's get you some tea then a bath.' Kate carried Ben into the kitchen.

'And you, lady...' Adam clenched his fists.

Teresa stepped back.

'What, you think I'm going to hit you? For heaven's sake.'

'Yes, I thought you were going to hit me and I don't even know what I'm supposed to have done.'

'Don't know? Are you stupid as well as a liar?'

'Peggy, what's Adam talking about? It's not like I just took Ben. You said I could.'

'I know, love, but you have been gone rather a long time and we were worried something had happened to you both.'

'Sorry. I should've thought.'

'Yes, you damn well should've done.' Adam opened the lounge door. 'Get in there and answer Peggy's questions' – he took a deep breath – 'and for once in your life tell the bloody truth.'

Teresa put her hands to her face. 'I don't know why you're so upset with me.'

'Don't you? How about you've had our son out for over six hours. We've been worried sick. Why didn't you phone and let Peggy know you were going to be late?' Adam sighed. 'Put her straight, Peg.'

'I'll leave you lot to sort this out.' Joe kissed me on the cheek.

'Bye, Joe. I'll get back to you shortly about that other matter.' I closed the lounge door, signalled for Teresa to sit down, and took a seat next to her.

'Peggy, I'm sorry, really, I am. I didn't notice the time.' She sobbed into her handkerchief.

'I know. I know.' I put my arm around her. 'It's going to be okay.'

'But… you won't stop me seeing him, will you?'

'No, of course not.'

'But, Adam might.' She blew her nose.

'I won't let him, but we do need to talk, and you must be honest.'

'I will. I promise.'

'Why did you lie to me?'

'Lie?'

'Come on, love. We agreed you'd be truthful. Why did you tell me about this girl who doesn't exist?'

She ran her fingers through her hair. 'I don't know what you mean.'

'Adam's spoken to your parents.'

'And?'

'We know everything.'

Teresa squinted. 'Yes, I know. I told you everything.'

'But you told us a bunch of lies. What I don't know is why?'

Sighing, she dropped her arms. 'I suppose I wanted to sound interesting.'

'Was there any truth in what you told us?'

She shrugged.

'Tell me about the baby at the nursery.'

She stared open-eyed.

I took her hand. 'Yes, we know.'

'I didn't do anything wrong. I loved him, unlike his mother who neglected him. She'd drop him off at nursery every morning and never even kiss him goodbye before she left.'

'That didn't make him neglected, Teresa. It could be she was in a rush or maybe she thought it was better for the baby if she made a hasty departure.'

'I hadn't thought of it like that. I just wanted to show him someone cared. I would never have hurt him. The nursery fired me on the spot, they overreacted. Just like Adam. What's his problem?'

'Can't you see what you've done is wrong?'

'What do you mean?'

'Although you had permission to take Ben, you stayed out far too long.'

'Why? You didn't mind when Kate and David had him out all day.'

'But that was arranged.'

'Well, I'm sorry. Next time I won't do that. There will be a next time, won't there?'

'I'm not sure, love. I don't think Adam will allow that.'

Teresa sobbed into a hankie. 'But I love him. He's my brother. I'm sorry.'

'And are you a dance teacher?'

She shook her head. 'I'd like to be though. I love dancing but never had lessons.'

'It's never too late, you know. What about Peter? Was he real?'

'Yes.' She dabbed her eyes. 'He was my boyfriend but chucked me after six weeks because I was too boring.'

'Maybe Mr Right just hasn't come along yet. I'm sorry, love, but I need to ask. Do you have a brother or is Bobby fictitious too?'

Teresa winced. 'He's real to me. He's been with me all my life.'

'But you knew he wasn't real when you told me and the rest of my family. We trusted you and you've thrown that trust back in our faces.'

'Sorry. It wasn't intentional.' She snuggled up to me. 'Please give me another chance.'

'You don't have to impress me. I love you for who you are. There's one more question. Those things you said about Rachel, were they true?'

She stared into space.

'Teresa?'

'Yes, they were true, although...'

'Although?'

'I might've been a bit mean back to her.'

'You know you're going to have to apologise to everyone including Rachel, don't you?'

She nodded. 'I will.'

Adam knocked on the door before entering. 'And if you're going to continue to visit us then you need to agree to getting some professional help.'

I glanced up. 'Have you been listening?'

'Yes, and I heard every word. Now I'm prepared to let bygones be bygones but only if she agrees to counselling. We've been through too much, Peg, and our lives needs to quieten down. We've Kate's wedding coming up, and Ben to consider.'

Teresa rose from the couch, went over to Adam and hugged him. 'I'm sorry, really, I am, and I promise to get help.'

He patted her on the back. 'We'll make sure of it but if I find one more lie crosses your lips then you're out. No more second chances.' Adam pulled her at arm's length. 'Do I make myself clear?'

'Yes.' Teresa sobbed.

He passed her a tissue. 'I think it's time you went home. Your mam and dad are worried.'

'That'll be a first.'

Adam frowned. 'No more lies, remember.'

'No more lies.' She came over and hugged me. 'I'm sorry. Can I come around tomorrow?'

'I think it would be best' – Adam brushed his greying fringe from his brow – 'if you left it for now.'

'When then?' Teresa sniffled.

'Definitely not before the counselling starts?'

'But?'

'You can see Peg away from the house.'

'Adam,' I said, 'that doesn't sound fair.'

'I don't care if it doesn't sound fair, Peg. That's what's happening.'

'But...'

'No, buts Peg, do I make myself clear?'

'But what about Ben?' Teresa asked.

I touched Teresa's hand. 'It's okay, love. I'll bring him with me.'

'No, you won't, Peg. She stays away from my son until I'm happy that she's not going to harm him.'

Teresa looked up at me. 'I'd never harm him, Peggy. You know that.'

'She wouldn't.'

'I've said my piece and that's the end of it.'

'Can I still come to Kate's wedding?'

'Of course you can. Can't she, Adam? She's bridesmaid after all.'

Adam sighed. 'Let's just see how we go, okay?' He rubbed his forehead. 'All this has been just a little too much.'

'He's right, love. Nobody's thinking straight right now. We'll work something out.' I kissed her on the cheek.

'All right. Oh, by the way, Ben took three steps today.'

How could I have missed Ben's first steps? Neither Adam or I responded to Teresa's comment. Instead, he went into the hallway and opened the front door for her to leave.

'Bye, love.' I gave her a hug. 'Give me a ring tomorrow.'

'Okay. Bye then.' She stepped outside.

Adam closed the door behind her. 'You know she needs proper help, don't you?'

'Yes.'

'I mean proper help. Proper professional help. I'll phone her parents later and discuss it with them, and once she's on the road to recovery, I think it would be a good idea for her to go and stay with Mike in the States for a while. Give us all time to breathe.'

'I don't want to turn my back on her. She's still my daughter.'

'I know that, Peg, but it's all a bit too much for us right now.' He shivered. 'When I think of what could've happened to Ben.'

'But she'd never have hurt him.'

'Not intentionally, maybe, but in her state of mind who knows what could've happened? She can come and say goodbye to Ben, but after that I don't want her around him until she's mentally well.'

Adam was making sense but by the same rule Teresa was my daughter and I couldn't abandon her. 'Ben adores her and he'll miss her. Are you banning me from seeing her too?'

'You know I'm not. I'd never ban you from anything. You know that, and I've stood by you through everything. If you want to see her then make it happen away from this house.'

Nothing was ever easy. The last thing I wanted was for Teresa to come between Adam and me.

Chapter Eleven

Rachel

Joe had ushered me and Linda out of the house earlier in the day, saying we should have some girlie time, either shopping or a walk in the park. I anticipated returning home to a nice meal, not a houseful of guests with balloons and streamers hanging from every corner of the room.

'Surprise.' Joe kissed me on the lips. 'Happy birthday, babe.'

It was a surprise all right. Linda and I had to make a hasty retreat upstairs to get washed and changed.

I opened my wardrobe. 'What shall I wear then?'

'This' – Linda pulled out my black flowery maxi skirt with three full tiers – 'and this.' She selected a white gypsy blouse with an embroidered mauve trim.

'Cool.' Linda knew me so well as this was my latest favourite outfit. 'Do you need to borrow something?' I asked.

'You're joking, aren't you?' She took a loose turquoise tunic from a Mothercare carrier along with a brown pair of maternity leggings. 'I'm wearing a sack. Well at least that's what it feels like.'

'You were in on the surprise then?'

'Of course.' She grinned. 'I had strict instructions to keep you away from the house.'

'Some warning would've been nice.'

'And spoil your surprise? Come on, let's get ready.'

I did a twirl. 'Will I do?'

'You look awesome as always.' Linda picked up the heated tongs. 'Sit down and I'll curl your hair.'

'Ta.' I touched her hand. 'You're such a good friend.'

'Soul sisters. Now sit still.' She pulled a comb through my hair. 'So, what's happening about Teresa then? I hear everything blew up.'

'She's getting psychotherapy or something. Got everyone worried sick and running around after her as usual. Attention seeking.'

'You don't think you're being too hard on her?'

'No, why? Do you?'

Linda wrapped a few strands of my hair around the hot irons. 'Well yes, look at it from her perspective. She's had no boundaries.'

'Another one of her lies.'

'What makes you say that?'

'Because Denise and Gordon are nothing like she says. They're good people. Good parents.'

'Well someone's lying, that's for sure.'

'But you trust my judgement, don't you?'

'Hmm' – she bit her lip – 'normally, yes, but don't you think you're being a bit blinded?'

'No.'

She flicked my hair from the sides. 'Maybe you're just seeing what Denise and Gordon want you to see.'

'What do you mean?'

'Well they're not going to admit to you that they've abused her, are they? Let's face it, living in a commune as hippies was rather unconventional and I'd say they act very much like teenagers. All this freedom may have made Teresa feel insecure. Unloved even.'

'You've got to be joking?'

'No, I'm not. I remember when I was younger and used to yell at Mam because she wouldn't let me do something, she said it was because she cared. And you know what? I reckon she made a good point.'

'Denise and Gordon cared.'

Linda put the tongs down and unplugged them from the mains. 'There. All done. You look gorgeous.'

I lifted my hair. 'I love it.'

'You don't think you're being a bit bias? I mean you've met this couple, your real parents, who on the face of it seem like nice people' – she shrugged – 'and you don't want anything to spoil that.'

'Change the subject, Lind. It's obvious we're never going to agree.'

'Sure. What's happening about the next dress fitting? Will Teresa be there?'

'I'm not sure. If Adam had his way, she'd no longer be bridesmaid but Peggy and Kate insisted. After the wedding Adam wants Teresa to go to the States to get to know Mike. They should get on because they're both as screwy as each other.' I looked properly at Linda in her new outfit. She was blooming. I placed my hands on her round stomach. 'You're really starting to show now.'

'I know. Hence the maternity wear.' She put her hand over mine. 'Did you feel that?'

'Ooh, I think I did. Oh, there it goes again. Is it kicking?'

'Not it. She.'

The dining room table, piled high with presents and cards from guests, was pushed to the corner of the room to make space for dancing. Mel and Betty bopped to 'Stayin' Alive', the Bee Gees single. 'That's my favourite,' I said. 'Can you dance, Lind, or is it too much for you?'

She nudged my arm. 'Oi. I can still dance.'

I hovered close to Mel and Betty while we swayed in time to the music. 'Thanks for coming.'

Mel beamed. 'A surprise, eh?'

'Just a bit. Did you do anything for your twenty-fifth?'

'Not as lucky as you having someone to organise a surprise party but the family did take me to a Greek restaurant.'

'That sounds nice. Greek food's yummy. And you, Bett, how are you doing? Is your hubby here?'

'I'm doing well, pet. No, he's not into parties so I came with Mel.'

When the record stopped, I squeezed Betty's arm. 'I should go and say hi to the others. Back soon.'

I circulated around the room and found Mum and Dad. 'You could've warned me.'

'Then it wouldn't have been a surprise.' Dad winked. 'There may be another surprise shortly.'

'What's that?'

Mum grinned. 'You'll have to wait.'

Peggy and Adam strolled over with Ben toddling between them, each holding one of his hands.

'He's walking?' I clapped my hands. 'Clever boy.'

'Yes. I missed his first steps as he took them that day with Teresa in the park' – Peggy chortled – 'but there's no stopping him now.'

I picked him up and gave him a cuddle. 'Who's a clever little man then?'

'Tessa.'

I glared at Peggy.

'He means Teresa. He won't stop asking for her.' Peggy looked at Adam. 'He's missing her.'

'Don't start now, Peg.'

'Am I missing something?' I asked.

'No, don't worry, love. Look' – Adam rested his hand on mine – 'we owe you an apology.'

'An apology?'

'For not believing you, and accusing you of jealousy.' Adam touched my shoulder. 'We should've known better.'

'Yes, you should have.'

'Forgive us.' Adam squeezed my fingers.

'Although, Rachel, you're not entirely faultless.' Peggy scowled at me. 'Be honest now. You've been mean to Teresa too.'

'No, I haven't.'

'I heard you on more than one occasion.'

'I've only ever retaliated. That's all.'

'Leave it for now, Peg,' Adam said. 'This is Rachel's birthday party remember.'

'Okay. Sorry, Rach.'

'I'm sorry too. Seems Teresa had you all fooled. Linda reckons I should feel sorry for her. That it was her upbringing that made her like she is.'

'Who knows what made the girl like it?' Adam released my hand.

I squeezed Peggy's arm. 'Let's put it behind us. I've had enough crazy stuff happening and just want to move on.'

'I'm pleased to hear that. He's not so forgiving.' She looked at Adam.

'Don't start, Peg.'

'I don't blame him. I didn't say I forgave her.' I shook my head. 'Denise and Gordon did their best. She wasn't an easy child and it looks like nothing has changed.'

'Anyway, forget about all of that now.' Adam glared at Peggy. 'Don't let it spoil the party.'

'And we've got Kate's wedding, and Linda's baby to look forward to.'

'And your own wedding.' Peggy grinned. 'Joe said he can start divorce proceedings in a few weeks.'

'Yes, that's right. Was that the doorbell?' I wondered who else could be coming.

Joe came up behind me. 'I'll get it.'

I grabbed Mel up to dance. 'Baby Come Back' was blaring from the music centre when someone put their hands across my eyes. 'Stop mucking about, Joe.'

'It's not me,' he said. 'I'm here in front of you.'

'Then who?'

'Me.' Someone removed their hands and spun me around. 'Surprise.'

'Jen.' I hugged her tightly. 'How? When?'

'You didn't think I'd let your birthday go without being here, did you?'

'Well, yes. Er, I hadn't really thought about it. How long are you over for?'

'Never mind that now. There's someone else to see you too.'

'Happy Birthday, Rach.' He bumped his cheeks on either side of my face.

'Phil. Awesome. Is Jan here too?'

'No, somebody had to stay and look after things.'

'Are you two back together?'

Phil shook his head. 'No, why?'

'Because you're both here.'

'Here for you,' Jen said.

'Does that mean you're a free agent, Phil?'

'It does, but I thought you weren't.'

I nudged him. 'Not me, silly. See Mel there, I think she wouldn't mind getting to know you better. Why don't you ask her for a dance? She loves 'Three Times a Lady', it's her favourite record, and it's a smoochy one.'

'Why not?' Phil headed over to Mel, and Jen dragged me into the kitchen.

'Did you tell Mum and Dad about me and Jan?'

'No, of course not. Are you going to tell them? Be careful though as I think Dad's been having some trouble with his heart again.'

'Phew. There is no Jan and me.'

'Oh, what happened?'

'We decided it wasn't working. Anyway, Jan's got a new woman.'

'Are you all right?'

'Yeah. It wasn't really me but it was fun experimenting. Anyway, I've decided I'm off love for now and going to concentrate on my career.'

'Oh aye? What's that then?'

'To be a cook.'

'A cook? You mean like a chef?'

'Yep.'

'In Paris?'

'Nope, here. I'm going to open a vegetarian restaurant. It should be popular as they're so few and far between in this vicinity.'

'What made you think of that?'

'Jan. She's vegetarian now. I'm also thinking of having a space where local artists can display their paintings and customers can buy them. I'd take a small commission of the sale. What do you think?'

'So, you're home for good? You're not returning with Phil?'

'Home for good, yes. What do you think of my idea?'

'Cool, and maybe you could even have some live music.'

'Oh yes, I like that idea. Depends on the size of the premises I can get though. All I need now is to convince Dad to loan me the money to set it up.'

I chuckled. 'Good luck with that.'

'I've got some money of my own too.'

'Well, I'd invest in you if I had the money, and what's more if you manage to get the project off the ground, I'll do a feature in the newspaper. Have you a name for the restaurant?'

'Not yet. Was hoping you might help me out.'

'I'll put my thinking cap on.'

Chapter Twelve

Rachel

After we'd picked up our gowns, Peggy, Kate and Teresa had gone on to Elmo's but I'd made my excuses. I pulled up outside the Coles and stepped from the car. Gordon was weeding the shrubbery.

'Hi, Rachel, glad you could make it. Dee's at the back. Go through.' He pushed the side gate open. 'I'll just be a min.'

'Cheers.' I strolled down the path and into the garden where Denise was sunbathing in a yellow bikini.

She rolled off the lounger. 'I thought I heard voices. I'll get us a lemonade.' She slipped a blue satin kimono over her swimwear and slid her small feet into a pair of flip-flops. 'How are you?'

'Good thanks. Just been for the final fitting of the bridesmaid dresses.'

'You saw our Teresa then?'

'Yes. She's gone for tea with Peggy and Kate.' I followed Denise into the kitchen. 'Gordon said he's coming in.'

'Thought he might. It's too hot for gardening. Ice and lemon?'

'Ta.'

Using the tongs, she popped a couple of ice cubes and a slice of lemon into each of the three glasses before pouring out the homemade lemonade. 'You said on the phone you wanted to discuss something specific?'

'Yes.' I followed her through to the sitting room.

'What's that then?'

'I wanted to talk about Teresa.' I sipped the drink. 'This is so refreshing.'

'I'll let you have the recipe if you like but you have to promise not to give it to anyone outside of the family.'

I laughed. 'Sure.'

She flopped down on one of the futons. 'Shoot?'

'Sorry?' I took the futon opposite.

'Your questions. Shoot.'

'Ha. Shall we wait until Gordon comes in?'

'If you like. Tell me about Kate's gown. Is it nice?'

'It's strapless with a long train. She looks stunning in it.' I shook my head. 'Never have I ever seen a bride look so beautiful. Her groom's in for a shock.'

'I bet you'll look gorgeous too. You mentioned you were getting married?'

'I did, yes.'

'Although there's no real need. Gord and I never bothered.'

'No?'

'No. Caused a right riot with our families but it was harder in those days. They kept on and on at us to get wed after Teresa was born so in the end we disappeared for a couple of days, came back and announced we'd married at Gretna Green. We told them what made them happy.' She glanced across the room. 'Here's Gord now.'

'Did I hear my name?'

'Yes. Rachel wants to talk about Teresa.'

'What's the girl done now?' He picked up his drink and gulped it back. 'I needed that.'

'Nothing,' I said, 'well at least I don't think she has. I'm curious about her childhood. You know, how she was with her grandparents, holidays, that sort of thing.'

'Why do you need to know that?' Gordon lit up a cigarette which didn't look like any normal ciggie despite what they'd told me about no longer smoking weed.

'I'm just interested.'

'There's no harm in Rachel showing an interest, Gord.' Denise turned back to me. 'We've got lots of photos.'

'I'd love to see them.'

She rose from the futon, went over to the sideboard, took a white shoebox from the cupboard and came to sit next to me. 'We've got that cinefilm upstairs, Gord. Perhaps you could get that down when you've finished your smoke. It'll be fun to see that again.'

'Sure.'

Denise took one batch of the snaps from the box. 'She's five here.'

I stared at the puny, dark-haired child, dressed in a flowery outfit. 'She looks sad.'

Gordon stubbed out his cigarette. 'That's because she never bloody smiled.' He sighed. 'I'll see if I can find that film.'

Denise held another print in front of me. 'Here she is with my mam.'

The girl had a faint smile as she looked up to an older woman. 'You don't look like your mam. How old was she here?'

'Close to fifty. Had me late. She adored our Teresa, her namesake, and Teresa adored her. Broken hearted she was when my mam died of cancer at fifty-two.'

'Gosh. How awful for you all.' Could that be the thing that made Teresa the way she was?

'This one here's at the zoo.'

'Is that Chester Zoo?' Seeing the giraffes took me back to when I was there with Peggy and Mike six or seven years ago. One good thing that had come out of this adoption mix-up was finding out Mike wasn't my father. He was such a jerk.

'Yes, she was seven there. Any other child would be laughing but not our Teresa. Kept moaning the animals were too smelly and she wanted to go home. Gord got so cross with her. I blame myself. I think maybe we should've got her some counselling after my mam died.'

Gordon came back in the room carrying a huge box with rolls of films peeping out. 'It'll take me a while to set this up.'

I browsed through the black and white photos one by one. 'Shame she's not smiling on this one as it's a good one of you two.'

'We loved taking pictures of her but she played merry hell. Had some idea that the camera would steal her soul. God knows where she got that idea from. Gord lost his patience with her on more than one occasion.'

There were many more pictures of Gordon and Denise together looking all loved up. Apart from Teresa never smiling in the photos, they looked like a normal happy family. What would it have been like growing up with these two? Growing up in a commune with them smoking weed? I'd heard communes were all about love, so surely she can't have felt unloved. She must've been devastated when her gran died though. Perhaps that was the root of her problem. Maybe Denise was right and they should've got her some counselling.

'Here we go.' Gordon set the reel going. 'This was her sixth birthday.'

There were lots of girls in party dresses running around with each other but who was that in the corner? Was that Teresa?'

'That's her on the floor.' Gordon rubbed his lip. 'Sulking again. She always was a moody cow.' He chuckled. 'Such a shame because she really was a pretty thing, as you can see from the photos.'

I studied the picture in my hand. 'Yes, she was.' Big eyes with Shirley Temple like hair. If only she'd have smiled.

'We tried our best,' Gord went on. 'Goodness knows where we went wrong. We gave her parties like other kids, trips to the seaside, and zoo, I mean what more did she want?'

'He was right. What more could any child have wanted? Hopefully the counselling would help her now.

Denise gathered the photos back up into the box. 'More lemonade?'

'No thanks. I should be going.'

'So soon. I was going to get Gord to light the barbeque.'

'I promised Joe I'd be back early,' I lied. I had a feeling that Teresa would be back shortly and I really didn't fancy another run in with her. 'How's Teresa's counselling going?'

'All right we think but she doesn't tell us much, does she, Gord?'

'Nope.' He slumped on to the futon. 'She's been worse since discovering Dee didn't give birth to her. We told her it didn't make any difference to us. That we love her and as far as we're concerned she'll always be our little girl, but, hey' – he sighed – 'it's like talking to a brick wall.'

I was right. They were good people. Good parents. 'Right, I must go but will see you both soon. My boss has given me the go ahead to do a feature on the folk club so Joe and I will come along at the next meeting.'

'That's awesome. We've a Ceilidh coming up. You'll love that.' Denise headed to the door. 'I'll see you out the back way if you like. I'm going to steal an extra hour of the gorgeous sunshine.'

'Cheers.' I followed her out.

'See you soon then, Rachel.' Denise slipped off the kimono and lay face down on the lounger.

Before I had the chance to put the key into the lock, Dad opened the door.

I flung my arms around him. 'I love you, Dad.'

'Hey, what's brought this on?'

'Where's Mum?'

'In the kitchen.'

I slipped off my sandals and hurried to find her. 'Mum.'

She put a pan on the stove. 'Rachel? What's wrong?'

'Nothing's wrong.' I cuddled her. 'I just wanted to tell you both how much I love you.'

Dad was standing at the doorway and repeated, 'What's brought this on?'

'I'm so glad you two are my parents.'

Dad scratched his head. 'Has something happened?'

'No, not really. I've just realised how lucky I am to have my life. In fact, I love my life.'

'We love you too.' Dad took me into a bear hug. 'You're our precious gem. You and Jennifer. Your mother and I are blessed.'

Mum wiped her hands down her apron. 'I thought you liked the Coles.'

'I do. They're lovely, but I'm still glad you two are my mum and dad, and Jen's my sister.'

Mum took a casserole dish out of the oven and gave it a stir. 'Are you staying for dinner?'

'No, thanks. I just wanted to see you both.' The aromas from the meal made my tummy rumble. Chilli con carne. Yum. 'Actually, I've changed my mind. I'd love to stay to dinner.' Joe was likely going to be late this evening as he and Stu had gone to look at cars.

Mum set the chilli and boiled rice down on the table. 'Almost like old times,' she said, 'with both our girls here.'

'Let's hope we don't have the arguments.' Dad served himself a good helping of rice and a ladle of chilli.

'No arguments from me.' I served scoops of rice and chilli too although in smaller portions than Dad's.

Jen tasted some food on her fork. 'Have you ever thought of making this as a vegetarian option, Mum?'

'Definitely not.' She placed a bowl of salad and basket of bread on the table before sitting down.

'That's a strange question,' Dad said.

'Not really,' Jen said. 'Jan's a vegetarian and I liked some of the stuff she cooked. Much healthier.'

Dad took a chunk of bread. 'Each to his own I suppose. You'd never get me giving up meat. As a matter of interest how would you make this without the mince?'

'By using soya bean. It gives it the same sort of texture, and apart from that you can add the normal ingredients. I'm thinking of training to be a cook.'

'Right?' Mum took a sip from her glass of white wine.

'Well, you know I've been in Paris these past months and I've been thinking about my future?'

'Yes.' Dad held his cutlery upright.

'I now know what I want to do.'

'Yes, you just said. Train to be a cook.' Dad scooped another helping of chilli onto his plate. 'This is delicious, Rosalind.'

'Thank you, Charles.'

'Yes,' Jen said, 'but more than that, I want to open up a vegetarian restaurant. I imagine it would be a success as there's definitely a call for it.'

Dad put his cutlery down on the side of his plate. 'You might have something in that, Jennifer. What you need is a business plan.'

'I kind of hoped you'd help me with that, Dad, and maybe fund wise too. Not as a gift but a loan like. I plan to go back to college and pass the right exams for cooking, hygiene and so on.'

'Hmm.' Dad rubbed his nose. 'What do you think, Rosalind. Should we take a gamble on our daughter.'

Mum looked at Jen. 'I think perhaps we should.'

Chapter Thirteen

Rachel

Joe locked up the car. 'Will I do?'

'Not half.' My heart skipped a beat at the sight of him in his red tartan shirt and tight black jeans. 'And me?'

'Gorgeous as always, babe.' Joe's new moustache accentuated his smile. He took my hand and we wandered into the village hall where the band was on stage. Gordon was playing the guitar while Denise stood behind a microphone giving out instructions to the dancers. I assumed she was the caller.

Groups dispersed as that specific dance ended and Denise introduced the next one, telling everyone to make a set of eight. Joe and I formed a cluster with six others and moved in routine following the directions with no real idea what we were doing but it was fun and made us laugh. We clapped opposite each other while one couple made a bridge with their hands together held high, and one by one we all went under, extending the bridge until everyone had a turn. I was pleased that Teresa wasn't there. I couldn't quite understand why not though as she'd informed Peggy that she loved dancing. Why was she making up these stories about her parents?

At half time the band stopped for refreshments and headed to the trestle table at the back of the room which was laden with sandwiches, peanuts, and crisps. A smaller table at the side held soft drinks and plastic cups for members to help themselves.

'Are you enjoying it?' Denise asked me.

'Loving it.'

She touched my skirt. 'Looks like we've been shopping at the same place again. I love this crimson, don't you?'

'Yes. My friend, I think I mentioned she's the manageress at Walker's, bought mine for my birthday.'

'Oh yes, your birthday. Did you have a nice time? Sorry we didn't send a card or present but we don't bother with that nonsense. Gord and I feel that if we want to give a pressie then we don't have to wait until it's someone's birthday.'

'With the exception of Teresa?'

'Oh yes, of course. We've always spoiled her. She's our little girl.'

Another lie from Teresa then.

The accordionist approached us. I reckoned he was around my age. He tossed his dark curly hair away from his face and extended his hand. 'Aren't you going to introduce us, Dee?'

'Sure. This is Rachel, she's a journalist for *The Echo* and is going to write an article on us. Hopefully we'll get a few more members from it, and this is her husband, Joe. Rachel and Joe, this is Don, the founder of the folk group. 'Remember we told you about the baby mix-up?'

'Yeah?'

'Well Rachel' – Denise smiled at me – 'is my other daughter.'

'Other daughter?' Don lit up a cigarette.

'Yes, I see it as I've gained another one because obviously I still see Teresa as mine. So now I have two daughters.' She beamed.

'And what a beauty this one is.' Don winked at me. 'Just like her mam.'

I felt heat rising in my face and prayed I hadn't turned pink. 'Pleased to meet you.' I took out my notebook and pen. 'So, what do you call these types of dances?'

'Ceilidhs. Is this your first time?'

'Yes. It's a giggle. How often do you host them?'

'Once a quarter but the folk group is on every fortnight. Members don't have to be able to sing or play, they can just come and listen.' He passed me a leaflet. 'Everything's on there. Use what you like in the write-up.'

'Thanks.' I folded up the poster and put it in my bag along with the notebook.

'I'm just off to the little boys' room' – Don stubbed out his ciggie – 'and then we'll resume the dance.'

'Cheers. Nice to meet you,' I said.

'Don's an okay guy, don't you think?' Denise swigged back an orange juice.

'Sure,' I said. 'I'm surprised Teresa doesn't come here as she loves dancing.'

Gordon took a drag of his cigarette and blew out a smoke circle. 'We've tried, love. How we tried.'

'Don't get upset, love.' Dee rested her hand on his shoulder. 'We'd best be getting back up on stage.' She turned to me. 'We'll catch you at the end.'

'Actually' – I hooked my arm in Joe's – 'we're going to slip off now as Joe's got an early start in the morning. Cheers though. It's been fun.'

'Oh, right. Well, ta-ra then. See you soon.' She slipped her hand into Gordon's and they stepped up on stage.

Giggling, Ben tottered by the ducks. 'Quack quack.'

'He's so clever.' I took a bite of my cheese sandwich and bent lower to pass the crusts to my baby brother. 'Feed the quack quacks.' I turned to Peggy. 'How's Kate doing?'

'Taking it all in her stride. I think she's been far too busy at work, especially running this new support group for teenagers, to worry about getting nervous.'

'What about Teresa?'

'Still going for counselling. Seems to be helping. Adam's agreed she can come to Ben's birthday party tomorrow. You and Joe are still coming, aren't you?'

'Of course, we wouldn't miss it. Three o'clock, isn't it?'

'Yes.'

'That'll give Joe time to get showered and changed after getting in from work. He's grown a moustache, you know?'

Peggy's eyes twinkled. 'Does it suit him?'

'He looks even dishier. If we weren't already together, I'd be chasing after him.' I chortled.

'Teresa's flying out to meet Mike after the wedding.'

'Oh really? Adam heard back from him then?'

'Yes. Return flight tickets arrived yesterday. She's to go out there for a month and "give Adam and I some breathing space" as he puts it. I'll miss her though. I've grown fond of her.' Peggy squeezed my fingers. 'I know you two have had your problems...' Ben fell to the ground and screamed interrupting Peggy. She shot off the bench, scooped him up and tried to console him.

'He was having such a good time too,' I said. 'Is he all right?'

'He will be.' She lowered Ben into the pushchair and strapped him in. 'Shall we take a stroll back to see if I can calm him? I should've watched him more closely.'

'You were watching him, Peg. You couldn't have known. He's doing ever so well for his age walking like that. Are you going to get him one of those horseshoes to give to Kate at the wedding? That will make an adorable photograph.'

'Yes. I picked one up in town the other day. I'll show it to you tomorrow.'

I peeped into the pushchair. Ben's eyelids flickered. 'He'll be asleep before you get back to the car. Will you be able to get him in it without waking him up?'

'I'll probably stay out for a while and give him a chance to have a snooze.'

'Can I push?'

'If you like. How did the barn dance go with the Coles?'

'It was good fun.'

'Shame they've never included Teresa in these dances.'

'They tried, Peg. They really tried. Poor Gordon got really upset when he spoke about it.'

'So he says. Teresa has a different story.'

'Well I know who I believe.' I checked the time on my watch. 'Do you mind if I run on, Peg? I've got a meeting at two.'

'No, you go. I'll have a bit of a wander around the shops as Ben's asleep.' She pecked the side of my face. 'See you tomorrow.'

It was lovely to see Peggy's house buzzing with guests and Ben was soaking up all the attention.

'Happy Birthday, Ben.' I placed a huge parcel in front of him.

'Ooh, look at this, Ben' – Adam placed his son on the carpet and got down next to him – 'it's for you. Pull the paper off.'

Ben leaned on Adam's legs to stand up and toddled across the room. Adam chased after him and brought him back. 'Look.' Adam finished ripping the packaging. 'A Fisher Price garage.

Wow' – Adam glanced up at Joe and me – 'your brother and Rachel are spoiling you. This must've cost you a bit, guys.'

Joe rubbed his moustache. 'Only the best for my baby bro.'

'What's with that?' Adam pointed.

'You mean my tache?' Joe shrugged. 'Felt like a change. Rach loves it.'

'It suits you.' Sheila focused on the toy garage. 'An expensive pressie like that makes this one from his aunty and uncle look a bit stingy.' She passed a small parcel.

'Not at all' – Peggy rocked Jacob in her arms – 'you need your cash to buy this one stuff.'

With Ben's help, Adam unwrapped the gift. 'A Fisher Price chatter telephone.' He turned the dial making the phone ring. 'Hello,' he said in a squeaky voice and put the handpiece next to Ben's ear.

'We could open up a toyshop at this rate,' Peggy peered around at all the presents. The garage, phone, wooden jigsaws, xylophone, Jack-in-the-box, and a fire engine.

'Get him to open mine.' Teresa held out a long, gift-wrapped box.

Adam tore off the birthday wrapping. 'Look at this, Ben.' The cylinder toy on a stick jingled as it spun around. 'You'll enjoy pushing this around, son.'

Ben rustled the paper, more interested in the packaging than the toys.

'It's a good job we bought him a new toybox.' Peggy rose from the settee, still holding Jacob. 'Anyone hungry yet?'

Malc rubbed his stomach. 'Yeah. I'm starving. We missed lunch.'

'You won't go hungry here' – Peggy held Jacob against her shoulder – 'Kate and I have made a feast. I'll just finish setting the table and make tea before you all come through to the kitchen.'

'Where is our Kate?' Joe asked.

'She'll be down in a minute.'

'Is David here?' I asked.

'Not yet but should be here soon.'

Teresa stood up. 'I'll sort the tea if you like?'

'Would you love? That would be a big help.' Peggy said.

'Sure. That way you can spend more time with Jacob and Ben.'

I rose from the armchair. 'I'll help.'

Adam glared at me.

'It's okay,' I mouthed, before following Teresa into the kitchen.

She switched the kettle on at the mains. 'I'll help,' she mimicked.

'Don't be like that. I just wanted to speak to you.'

'Maybe I don't want to speak to you.'

Peggy strolled in. 'Everything all right in here?'

Teresa smiled. 'Yes, we're fine. I was just about to say to Rachel that I know I shouldn't have said those things about her but now I'd like us to be friends. Sisters even.'

I touched the sleeve of her cream crepe blouse. 'This is nice. Let's sit down for a minute.'

She took a seat at the pine table which was packed with plates of food covered in cling film and I sat down next to her.

'You know you said about me stealing your life and stuff.'

She peered up at and nodded.

'Maybe I did steal your life, but if that's the case then you stole mine too. Why don't you give Denise and Gordon a break?'

Peggy stared at me. 'Rachel.'

'It's okay, I'm just saying.'

'They've certainly done a number on you,' Teresa said. 'Brainwashed you.'

Ben screamed from the lounge. Peggy looked to the door. 'I wish you two would sort yourselves out.' She huffed. 'I need to see to Ben.'

'We will,' I said as she left the room. I turned my attention back to Teresa. 'I understand you were lonely growing up. Especially after your gran died, but...'

'What the hell have they said?'

'Nothing. Only that you were cut up after your gran died. And who knows, maybe if I'd grown up without a sister then I too may have invented a brother, but' – I took a deep breath – 'what I still don't understand is why you said all those nasty things about me?'

'Because I hate you, that's why.'

'What? You just said you wanted to be friends.'

'So I did. But I didn't mean it. Go on, run to Peggy and tell her. Let's see who she believes.'

'You really are a piece of work.'

'Rachel.' I glanced up at Adam glaring at me in the doorway. 'What is it with you?'

'It wasn't me. You didn't hear what she said first.'

He shook his head. 'You've got to stop this.'

Teresa smirked at me before turning to Adam. 'I don't know why she's being like this. I've tried to be her friend.' She took a hanky from her sleeve and dabbed her eyes.

He put his arms around her. 'It's all right, love. Don't cry. You go and join the others. Rachel can sort the tea.'

The kettle boiled as she was leaving. I rose to make the tea and gently touched her arm. 'I'm not your enemy, in fact, I'd like to be your friend, or sister even.'

She pulled away. 'That's what she does when anyone else is around. Two-faced they call that.'

Chapter Fourteen

Rachel

'Rach,' Joe called.

Wrapping a bath towel around me, I hurried into the hallway. 'Who was on the phone?'

He put his arm around me.

'What is it? Who was it?'

'Babe, it was Jen. Your dad's been taken to hospital.'

My stomach stirred. 'Oh my God. Is he all right?'

'Jen said they're waiting for the doctor but your dad's a fighter so I'm sure he's going to be fine.'

I put my hand to my face. 'I need to get down there.'

Joe held me close. 'Get dressed and I'll drive you. Afterwards I'll let the newspaper know you won't be in today.'

Joe pulled up outside Accident and Emergency. 'Ring me soon as you know something.'

'Will do.' I got out, slammed the door shut, and hurried to the entrance. I was about to go to reception when Jen charged through a door and wrapped her arms around me.

'Thank God you're here.'

'What's happened? He's not?'

'He's still with us. Let's hurry. I'll let Mum fill you in.'

I followed Jen down the corridor and we stopped outside a ward where Mum was waiting. She held out her arms as we approached. 'Come here, both of you.'

'What happened?' I asked her.

'Not really sure, darling. He was due to leave for work as normal when he suddenly turned a ghastly colour and slumped into a chair clutching his chest.'

'Couldn't Jen have done something?'

'No, I was completely useless. Just froze. Mum managed to call *999*.'

'And thank God they were quick.' Mum sobbed. 'The paramedics had to resuscitate him.'

'Oh my God. Can we see him?'

'Soon, I hope. I'm waiting for the doctor. Ah, here he is now.'

A young doctor came out of the intensive care ward. 'Mrs Webster?'

'Yes, and these are my daughters. How is he, doctor?'

'Let's talk in here.' He signalled to the relatives' room.

'Is he okay?' Mum asked.

He opened the door. 'Please, come and sit down.'

Mum gripped our fingers.

'He'll be okay, Mum.' I guided her to a seat. Jen and I sat either side of her, each holding a hand.

'Please, tell me, doctor...' Mum trembled. 'He's not...'

Oh my God. No, he couldn't be. 'He's not is he?' I echoed.

'No, Mrs Webster, he's still with us, although your husband's condition is critical, and you should prepare yourselves for the worst. If he makes it through the night his chances of survival will increase.' He rested his hand on Mum's shoulder. 'I'm sorry, I wish I had better news.' He turned to me. 'Why don't you take your mother home for a good night's rest? There's nothing any of you can do here.'

'No,' Mum said. 'No, I'm not going anywhere.'

'The hospital will ring if there's any change.' He removed his hand. 'Go home. You need to rest.'

'If I agree, can I see him before we go?'

'I'm afraid not. The medical staff are looking after him. I'm sorry but I must get on.'

Mum got up as the doctor left the room. She headed over to the window and peered out.

I whispered to Jen. 'Do you think he'll make it?'

She shrugged. 'All we can do is hope.'

'I can't believe you weren't able to do something to stop him getting so bad.'

Jen put her hands across her eyes. 'Don't, Rach. I feel bad enough as it is. There was nothing else I could do.'

'But surely as a nurse you should've recognised the signs?'

'If there were any then I didn't see them.' She sniffled. 'Maybe if you weren't always winding him up?'

Mum spun around. 'Stop it, girls.' She raised her voice. 'It's bad enough your father's fighting for his life. I don't need you girls squabbling and blaming each other.'

'You're right, Mum.' I got up and hugged her. 'I'm sorry.'

'I'm sorry too.' Jen joined in the hug.

Mum returned the phone handpiece to its cradle on the hall table. 'Well he's still with us. Thanks for staying the night, Rachel. Is Jennifer up and dressed?'

'Yes, she said she'll be down in a minute. What did the hospital say?'

'Not a lot. Just that he's stable for now but that could change.' She looked at her watch. 'Can you hurry your sister along? I want to get going.'

'I'm coming.' Jen hurried down the stairs.

I unhooked the car keys from the peg. 'I'll drive.'

Mum took the keys from me. 'I'm quite capable of driving, Rachel.'

'But…'

'But nothing. I'd rather drive than sit as a passenger worrying myself silly. Now come on both of you if you're coming. I need to be at my husband's side.'

We headed to the corridor marked *Intensive Care*. The same doctor we'd seen yesterday evening greeted us. 'How are you doing this morning, Mrs Webster?'

'I'm doing okay. How's my husband?'

The doctor coughed to clear his throat. 'He's stable for now but that could change anytime.'

I steadied myself against the wall.

Mum guided me to a chair. 'Sit down.' She turned back to the doctor 'Can we see him?'

'In a moment. I see from your husband's notes he's had heart problems for a few years now.'

Mum clenched her fists. 'Yes. Angina they said. He has a spray.'

'Well, I'm afraid this incident was a heart attack rather than angina. If your husband comes through this, he's going to need to make some major life changes.'

'I'll make sure he does whatever's asked of him, doctor. May we see him now?'

'Yes but' – he glanced at Jen and me – 'only one of your daughters can go in with you at a time, I'm afraid.'

'Thank you, doctor,' Mum said.

He patted her shoulder. 'Prepare yourselves. He's not a pretty sight.'

I wanted to run in to see Dad but I was scared of how he'd look so I turned to Jen. 'You go first.'

'Are you sure?'

'Yes.' I bit my lip.

Jen took Mum's arm. Shaking, I watched them go through. *Please God let him be okay*. Why had this happened when there hadn't been any stress in the house? Well not a lot, anyway. The odd bicker here and there. I buried my head in my hands.

'Rach.'

I jumped. When I looked up it was Jen. 'How is he?'

'He looks dreadful. You can go in for a minute.' She hugged me briefly.

'Thanks.' I pushed open the door and slowly made my way to his bed dreading what I'd see. Mum was sitting beside him holding his hand. 'Rachel.' She beckoned me closer.

Dad's eyes were closed and he had an oxygen mask over his face. A monitor at the side of him blinked green. My stomach turned. 'Dad.'

'We'll keep praying.' Mum gripped my fingers. 'Take your sister to the canteen and get some breakfast. I'll be along shortly.'

'Okay.' I left the ward and hurried along the corridor to the *Ladies* where I spewed up. Every time I was happy something always spoilt it. I flushed the cistern and came out of the cubicle to find Jen waiting.

'You, okay?' She wrapped her arms around me.

'I will be. Just shock. Mum said for us to go to the canteen and get something to eat.'

'Good idea.' Jen took my arm.

The following evening Joe turned up at Mum's. 'It's Joe.' I called through to the lounge. 'Are you sure you don't need me to stay?'

Mum came into the hallway. 'No, love. You get off home and rest. Your father's doing better and hopefully he'll be transferred to a regular ward by the morning.'

'But if he's still in intensive care, Mum, does that mean he may relapse?'

'The doctors said they need to keep him there for another twenty-four hours so they can monitor his progress but they're confident he's going to be fine. You get off home.'

'Okay.' I hugged her. 'Love you.'

'I love you too. Joe, take care of my girl.'

'I will, Mrs Webster. I hope Mr Webster recovers quickly.'

'Thank you. Now you two get off. Jen's serving our dinner and then we'll be off to bed.' Mum closed the door as we headed down the footpath.

Once in the car, Joe asked, 'You all right, babe?' He turned the ignition key.

I nodded. 'Think so.' I broke down and sobbed.

'Hey.' Joe put his arms around me. 'He's going to be all right.'

'I know.' I sniffled. 'It's just...'

'What, babe?'

'Every time I'm happy something bad happens.'

'Your dad will be fine. He's a fighter. You know that.' Joe put his hands back on the steering wheel. 'Shall I call in at the chippie on the way home so we don't need to cook?'

'I don't think I could eat a thing but sure, you must be hungry after a day's work, so, yes, it's a good idea.'

'You need to try and eat something too.' Joe flicked the indicator and turned right. The road was quiet so we managed to get to the chip shop in no time at all. 'I'll get two cod and chips.'

I pulled him back. 'Nothing for me.'

'Okay, I'll get one portion and you can have some of mine.' He glared at me. 'And I won't take no for an answer because I promised your mam I'd look after you. You want to have the energy to visit your dad tomorrow, don't you?'

I nodded.

'Good.' He patted my hand. 'I'll be back in a mo.'

The following day Dad had been moved to Pine Ward so I headed down the corridor and followed the signs. I pushed open the double doors and found him in the first bay on the right. At least his face had a little pink in it and he didn't have the oxygen mask covering his mouth and nose.

'How are you?' I kissed him on the cheek.

'Feeling a little battered to be honest, love.'

I held up a bag of grapes. 'I've brought you these.'

'My favourite.'

'When do you think they'll let you out?'

'They said I could be home before the weekend.'

'That's good.'

The sound of bleeps went from a bed further down the ward. A rush of doctors and nurses hurried in. The next thing they were pushing the patient out of the double doors.

I looked at Dad. 'What's happening?'

He squeezed my fingers. 'It's all right, Rachel, that's not going to happen to me.'

'Are you sure?'

'Yes.'

'You gave us all a scare.'

'I know and I'm sorry. I've been trying to do too much. I tend to forget I'm not a youngster anymore. Your mother and I have agreed I should retire and we're planning a little holiday down the coast to help me get my strength back.'

'That sounds like a good idea.' I remembered when I'd taken Joe down to the sea to convalesce it had done him the world of good. 'Well make sure you do what the doctors tell you.'

'Your mother will see to that. She's already got a dietary plan from the nurse. It seems I need to lose a few pounds and exercise more. Too many hours sitting at a desk.'

Chapter Fifteen

Peggy

A ribboned sash with *Bride* fell across Kate's chest, and pinned to the crown of her shoulder length hair hung a short veil. Her hazel eyes twinkled. She'd come such a long way since the teenager diagnosed with anorexia nervosa. Now she was a confident young woman supporting others suffering as she had.

Debs, the landlady of The Black Horse, stood behind me with an arm around my shoulders. 'A wonderful family you have, Peg.' She slipped down into the chair next to me. 'You've had your share of drama, mind. Haven't you? I wouldn't wish that on anyone.'

'We have, but I'm blessed. I have three daughters although only gave birth to two.'

'Nice that Joe and Rachel get their happy ending after all.'

'Yes. It'll be their wedding next.'

'I bet Rachel's hen will be rowdier than this one. I presume she'll want to hold it in here.'

'I imagine so. You put on such a good spread for us.'

'Has Joe started divorce proceedings yet?'

'In a couple of weeks. I can't believe I didn't see through that psycho Miranda.'

'You and me, chuck. You and me. I thought Rachel was being bitchy but she recognised something in the girl that none of the rest of us did.' Debs organised the triangular sandwiches onto the plates. 'Your Kate looks immensely happy.'

'She is.'

'What about the groom? Where've they gone for the stag?'

'Not sure. Some posh place in Chester that David's doctor friends organised.'

'Will they be at the wedding tomorrow?'

I shook my head. 'In the evening. It's just family and close friends in the day as Kate didn't want anything big. She doesn't like being in the limelight and it's going to be tough for her walking down that aisle tomorrow as it is. Thank goodness she'll have her dad on her arm.'

Debs patted my hand. 'He's a good man, your Adam. One in a million.'

'You're all right though with your Harry?'

'Oh sure. He's the best. We weren't blessed with kids but my Harry's been more than enough for me. Married fifty years this September. Not many around can say that.'

'That's wonderful. Will you have a party?'

'Oh yes. Watch this space. It'll only be in here but I've an inkling Harry's cooking up something special for us to celebrate afterwards. A cruise maybe. He knows that's something I've always wanted to do.'

'You must've got married young.'

'We did. I was sixteen and he was seventeen. Ran off to Gretna Green because we couldn't get our folks to agree. Said we were too young. Everyone reckoned we'd never last.'

'Well, you showed them.'

'We did.' Debs chuckled. 'How you getting on with that one then?' She signalled to Teresa. 'Is she fitting in?'

'We're getting there. Poor love has had an awful life.'

'And she and Rachel managed to iron out their problems?'

'Unfortunately not. There still at loggerheads. Honestly, Debs, I'll have no hair left at this rate. All I want is a quiet life.' I took a breath. 'Teresa desperately wants to be friends with Rachel, but Rachel won't have any of it. She won't have anything said about Teresa's mam and dad either. According to Rachel they're good people and good parents but' – I shook my head – 'what do I do? There's only so much I can do to try to keep the peace.

'Sounds like a tricky situation.'

'It is. And it's not helped because Adam's still a bit wary about Teresa and I don't want him starting to think that Rachel's right.'

'Hmm. You don't think that she could be?'

'Not at all. It's just Rachel being Rachel. I love the girl dearly but she doesn't like to be wrong.'

'I see. What are Teresa's parents like then? I heard they were heavy in the folk circle.'

'From what I understand yes, plus they're geriatric hippies.'

Debs tossed her head back in laughter. 'Geriatric hippies' – she nudged my shoulder – 'what are you like, Peggy Davies?'

'I'm being serious.'

'Has Teresa been telling you porkies?'

'No. Not at all. In fact, Rachel agreed. But like I said though, they can do no wrong in her eyes.'

Debs picked up a couple of the plates. 'Fancy bringing some of the food across for me, chuck?'

'Sure.' I picked up two trays of sausage rolls, sausages, and cheese and pineapple on sticks.

'Here you go, you lot.' Debs placed the plates down on the table. 'Heard about your dad, Rachel. How's he doing now?'

'His recovery is slow. He and Mum are off to Southport next week to help him recuperate. My boss has let them use his place on the beach.'

'The sea air will help. Come on you lot, get this down you? If there's one thing I've learned as a landlady is that if someone's going to drink then they need to eat. Especially when you've got a wedding the next morning.'

'Why she didn't have the hen on a Thursday evening like I did,' Linda said, 'I'll never know.'

Kate grinned. 'Probably because I'm not drinking.'

'Well, I hope your groom can say the same.' Linda bit into an egg and cress sandwich.

'He can. David's like me and barely drinks.'

'Well at least, you, David and me, will be okay. Can't say the same for the rest of them, especially Stu and your brother.'

'As long as they don't try and do something stupid to my groom.'

'They won't,' I said. 'Your dad's there to keep everything under control. Nothing's going to go wrong tomorrow. Your mam and dad will be the proudest parents alive.'

Teresa glared at me.

'Don't worry, love, when it's your turn we'll be saying exactly the same to you. And to Joe and Rachel on their day too.'

Teresa took a sip of vodka and lime from the glass. 'I doubt I'll ever find anyone.'

'You don't know that,' Rachel said. Then added under her breath, 'With a bit of luck you'll meet a nice yank out in the States and do us all a favour and stay there.'

I tapped Rachel's hand. 'Be nice, Rachel.'

Chapter Sixteen

Peggy

The hairdresser packed up her tools into the bag. 'That's all of you done. Don't forget to send me some piccies, Kate, once you're all poshed up, to use for my portfolio.'

'I won't.' Kate smiled. 'Thanks Mandy.'

'You're going to be a gorgeous bride.' She squeezed Kate's hand.

'I'll see you out.' I led the way into the hallway and opened the front door. 'Once again, thank you. You've done a great job on us all.'

'You should wear your hair like that more often. You certainly give Farrah Fawcett a run for her money with it styled like that.'

'That's very kind of you. Will we see you at the evening reception?'

'I'm hoping so, although my mam's not been that good so can't look after the little ones, but we're hoping our neighbour will step in.'

'Fingers crossed,' I said. 'Hope your mam feels better soon.'

'Thanks.'

After closing the door behind her, I re-entered the sitting room and admired the girls. The three bridesmaids' hair bounced in loose waves while Kate's was piled high with ringlets at the side. 'Gorgeous the lot of you,' I said.

'You can talk,' Linda said. 'Look at you with a fringe and your sides flicked back. I reckon it's knocked ten years off you.'

'Thank you.' I ran my fingers through my hair. 'It does feel lovely and soft. Where did you find Mandy, Kate?'

'Through one of the girls in the support group. Mandy's her aunty.'

'She's done well, not only with your hair but make-up too. You all look so glamorous.'

Kate hugged me. 'You do too, Mam.'

I peered up at the clock. Time's getting on girls. I think we should be getting dressed. We should hurry as I know your dad wants to take a couple of piccies before we leave for the church.'

There was a knock on the lounge door. 'Safe to come in, yet?'

'Yes,' I said, 'we're just going up to get changed.'

Adam entered the room. He looked so dishy in the dark suit with its grey waistcoat and tie that my heart skipped a beat. All these years we'd been married yet he could still do that to me. On the left side of his lapel a red carnation contrasted with the white shirt.

Butterflies flapped in my stomach. 'You look so handsome.'

'You don't look so bad yourself, Mrs D, and that's before you get your glad rags on.'

Adam and I waited at the bottom of the stairs as Kate headed down with Rachel holding her train. Linda and Teresa followed behind.

My eyes misted up. 'You look stunning, Kate.' The silk bolero added at the last-minute set off the strapless lace gown. A small coronet of white silk roses held her short tulle veil in place. I passed her shoes and she stepped into the satin stilettos adding four inches to her height.

'What a picture.' Adam kissed Kate on the cheek. 'I'm going to be the proudest father alive today having my baby girl on my arm down the aisle.'

Her face turned a gorgeous raspberry red. 'Don't, Dad.'

I laughed. 'Wait until your groom sees you. He's going to be bowled over.'

'Oh, Mam.' She hugged me. 'You look beautiful too. You could easily be our sister.'

Now it was my turn to blush. I stared at Linda. 'And you're positively blooming. Edna's done an amazing job with your dress. It drapes perfectly.'

'Cheers.' She touched her bump. 'I can't wait for this one to come out.'

'Not long now. September, isn't it?'

'Yep. Just over four weeks. Oops. She's kicking. She's due on the first but I reckon she'll come early.'

'How do you know it's a she?' I asked.

Linda beamed. 'I just do.'

'Right, ladies' – Adam lifted Ben out of the playpen – 'enough chit-chat. Your car's waiting.'

In the hallway I stepped into crimson high-heels, and Adam passed Ben to me.

'We'll see you at the church.' Adam moved close to my ear. 'Our Kate's right. You look amazing.'

I was waiting with the bridesmaids in the vestibule when Joe came out.

'What are you doing out here. You should be in the church. And who's looking after Ben?'

'Aunty Sheila. Look, Mam...'

'What is it?'

'I don't know how to say this but...'

Rachel moved forward. 'Joe, what is it?'

'It's the groom. He's not here yet.'

'What? Where the hell is he? Kate's going to be here any minute.' I looked out. 'Here she comes now. What should we do?'

'Joe,' Rachel said, 'run out and get them to go around the block a couple of times. She can't be here before David.'

'Yes,' I said. 'That's a good idea. Thanks, Rachel. Hurry, Joe. Your dad's getting out of the car.'

He hurried down the footpath and spoke to Adam. Adam climbed back into the car and said something to Kate.

'My poor girl.'

'Don't worry.' Rachel hugged me. 'There'll be an explanation. There's no way he'd stand up Kate.'

'That's what you think,' Teresa muttered. 'Looks like Kate's going to be jilted at the altar.'

I couldn't believe what I'd overheard. 'What did you say?'

Teresa smiled. 'I said there's no way he'd jilt Kate at the altar. Why?'

I huffed. 'Right.' Was Rachel right about the girl? Maybe Adam was right about the trip to the States being a good thing.

Joe came running back.

'Is Kate okay?' I asked.

'Yeah, she laughed. Said it was like one of those comedy films. She said there's no way David wouldn't be here. That there must be a reason.'

'I hope so.' I glanced at my watch. 'But where the hell is he?'

'He'll be here,' Joe continued. 'He wouldn't even touch a drink last night because he was scared of oversleeping. The whole night all he talked about was how he couldn't wait to be married to our Kate.' He looked up. 'They're back again.' He waved the car to go around again.

I glanced across at Teresa and Rachel. Looked like they were at loggerheads again. I wasn't sure how much more stress I could take. 'Come on David.'

Linda held her stomach. 'Oh God. You can stop that now, Anne-Marie.'

'What's happening?' Rachel asked. 'You're not going into labour, are you?'

'Bloody hope not. It's probably Braxton Hicks. I've been getting them a lot lately. My midwife said it's my uterus getting ready for the big day.'

A black Ford Corsair with a cream ribbon across its bonnet parked up. 'Looks like that's them now,' Joe said. 'We can breathe again.'

The groom and best man got out of the vehicle and hurried up the footpath.

'You're late.' I said. 'What happened?'

David caught his breath. 'Jonathan's car broke down. Thank goodness he was able to borrow his brother's. Anyway, I'd best get in there.'

'Yes, you had. Our poor Kate's had to go round the block three times. Get yourself in there.'

'I'm going.' David breezed into the church with Jonathan behind him.

Ben gurgled baby talk on my lap with the occasional coherent word of baba, dada and mama. He looked delightful in a pair of navy shorts, white shirt and red tie. Joe, next to me was a younger version of Adam. Finally, the organist played *Here comes the Bride*. David and his best man rose and Joe and I turned to see my daughter on the arm of the man I loved. She held her head high, her small hands cuffing the red and white floral bouquet dressed with pink ribbon and gypsophila. Her hazel eyes sparkled. My tummy fluttered. I couldn't have been any prouder.

David and his best man, in matching attire to Joe and Adam, turned their heads as the bride moved closer.

Joe leaned towards me. 'Is that really my kid sister? Boy, she scrubs up well.'

Rachel, Linda and Teresa kept their distance behind Kate, so as not to tread on her long train.

Joe put his hand to his mouth. 'And check out my girl. Isn't she's stunning?'

He was right. Rachel was. The rose-coloured dress emphasised her dark hair and brown eyes. She had the perfect figure for the empire line bodice. Even though she wasn't my daughter, it didn't stop me feeling pride. Then there was Teresa. I hoped I wasn't wrong about her. She looked lovely too. I liked how she'd grown out the bleached blonde and let the true brown colour come through. She caught me looking and smiled. Her flight to the States had been booked for two weeks today and Mike was looking forward to meeting her. Hopefully he'd behave more like a father to her than he had when we thought Rachel was our daughter. Not that it sounded like he had to work that hard to be an improvement on Gordon Cole if Teresa was to believed. Having heard that snidey comment earlier I was now doubting myself.

David smiled as he reached Kate at the front.

The vicar stepped down from the altar. He began the service with thanking us all for coming and introduced some preliminaries before saying, 'Who gives this woman Katherine Joyce to marry this man David Andrew today?'

Adam stepped forward. 'I do.'

Kate twisted round to Rachel and passed her bouquet before turning back. The bridesmaids and Adam joined us on the front pew.

Chapter Seventeen

Rachel

Kate grinned before answering, 'I Katherine Joyce take David Andrew to be my wedded husband, to have and to hold from this day forward' – she took a breath – 'for better for worse, for richer for poorer, in sickness and in health, to love and to cherish, till death us do part' – she stared into David's eyes –'according to God's holy law. In the presence of God I make this vow.' She let out a deep breath.

Joe squeezed my hand and I squeezed his back. Kate had her princess wedding which was wonderful but mine would be different. I had no intention of wearing a traditional bridal gown and veil for starters, neither were we getting married in church, but Joe and I hadn't told our parents yet. Peggy would have something to say about it for sure, but the way we saw it, it was our wedding and we'd waited long enough for it.

David slipped the wedding ring on to Kate's fourth finger of her left hand. 'I give you this ring as a symbol of my love…'

Peggy watched the couple while Ben slept peacefully on her lap. The best man passed Kate the groom's ring. Her eyes twinkled as she slipped the ring on to David's finger and repeated the vows.

Afterwards the vicar addressed the congregation. 'In the presence of God, and before this congregation, Katherine and

David have given their consent and made their marriage vows to each other...'

Ben opened his eyes and gave a small cry. Peggy rocked him. 'Shh now. Your big sis is getting married.'

Adam held out his arms. 'Here, give him to me.'

Peggy passed him over and Ben instantly stopped and re-closed his eyes.

The vicar continued, 'I therefore proclaim that they are husband and wife.' He glanced at David. 'Here's where you'd normally kiss the bride.'

Everyone chortled as David took Kate into his arms and gave her a long lingering kiss.

The vicar waited before bringing their hands together. 'Those whom God has joined together let no one put asunder.'

David and Kate kneeled at the altar and the minister said, 'Blessed are you, O Lord our God, for you have created joy and gladness, pleasure and delight, love, peace and fellowship. Pour out the abundance of your blessing upon Kate and David in their new life together. Let their love for each other be a seal upon their hearts and a crown upon their heads...'

Adam passed his handkerchief to Peggy and she dabbed her eyes.

We bridesmaids congregated at the back of the vestry while David and Kate signed the register. Teresa stuck her tongue out at me when she thought no one else was looking. I turned away. It was Kate's big day and I wasn't going to spoil it by retaliating.

Joe stepped forward along with David's best man and witnessed the bride and groom's signatures. Alan, the newspaper photographer, took a photograph of Kate holding the pen over the register.

'Now one with the bridesmaids.' He ushered us around the desk. I made sure I wasn't close to Teresa. 'Say cheese,' Alan instructed. Next it was Kate and Adam. Alan took a few more shots before folding up his tripod. 'I'll see you outside the church.' He went out the side entrance to get set up.

'Are you ready?' the vicar asked.

We followed Kate and David down the aisle. Peggy joined with Ben as we reached her pew. Her outfit fitted like a glove and Mandy had styled her hair to perfection.

We all gathered into the function room at the back of The Black Horse. Trestle tables had been set in a square around the edge of the room. In keeping with tradition, David and Kate were in the middle of the top table flanked by Adam and Peggy. But tradition was broken with Ben in a highchair squeezed in-between Peggy and David's father while his mum was placed the other side of Adam. The best man and I took the end places. My immediate neighbour was David's dad. Joe took the first seat turning the corner on the right of me, so although he wasn't on the top table, we were close enough for him to hold my hand or play footsie. Thank goodness Teresa had been put on the opposite turning corner near the best man. They seemed to be in close conversation.

Brian and Rose, David's mum and dad, were of a similar age to my parents. I hadn't chatted to Rose yet but Brian was very talkative. An early retired banker. They'd bought a cottage in Devon and had driven up for the wedding. David's best man,

Jonathan, had been friends with him since Infants. He appeared nice enough. Certainly, he had a friendly smile.

Harry, the pub landlord, clapped his hands. 'If I can have your attention, please.'

Everyone put their cutlery down and quietened.

'I'm pleased to have the honour of introducing the speeches and to begin with my dear friend, whom I've known for many years, Adam, father of the bride.' Harry took a seat next to his wife, Debs, in the corner of the room and everyone applauded as Adam stood up.

He coughed. 'I always knew this day would come with me having to stand up here making a speech. What can I say? Well for starters, having a daughter like Kate has been a delight, although at times a little choppy.' He chuckled. 'Seriously though' – he turned to Kate and squeezed her hand – 'it's been an honour to be your dad.' His attention went back to the guests. 'Both Kate's mam and me are so proud. She was a gentle child and has grown up to be a tender caring woman, so much so, she gives an enormous amount of her free time to support others. I couldn't be prouder than I am today to have witnessed my beautiful girl become David's wife. Without further ado, I'd like you all to join me in a toast. To Kate.'

Everyone stood up and raised their glasses. 'To Kate.'

'And on that note' – Adam put his glass down – 'I'll hand you over to the groom.' Adam returned to his seat as David rose from his, turning to Kate before facing the guests. He took a sip of his drink.

'No one warned me I'd have to do a speech if I got married.' He chuckled. 'Only kidding. First of all, I believe I need to thank some lovely people. For starters, my stunning wife's mam and dad for not only giving me this gorgeous woman, but for making' – he spread out his hands – 'all of this happen today. And thank you to my own mother and father for all they've done for me, bringing me up and supporting me through medical school.' He turned to each of them in turn and smiled. 'Which brings me to...' He gave a nod to Debs in the corner of the room and she headed over with two baskets of flowers packed with red, yellow and purple blooms. David passed one to his mam and one to Peggy. 'From us both.' He gave out a present to me along with the other bridesmaids. 'And then there's my beautiful bride,' he continued. 'Thank you, Kate, for making me the happiest man in the world.' He lowered his head to kiss her and dropped a wrapped item in front of her on the table.

She opened the box to reveal a string of pearls. 'They're gorgeous, David. Thank you. And I have something for you.' She passed him a small parcel.

'Thank you, darling.' He leaned over and kissed her lips. 'Now, there are a few more people I need to thank.' He went through a list of everyone who'd helped to make their day special. 'And last but not least' – David held his glass high – 'please join me in raising your glass to my wonderful wife, Kate, and our future together.'

Everyone rose and raised their glasses. 'To the wonderful bride. To the bride and groom.'

David took a deep breath. 'Oops, I almost forgot one special person. To Jonathan, my best man. Not only for today but for being my friend since we were kids.' David bent under the table and picked something up. 'A gift for you too, my friend.'

Jonathan strode over and shook David's hand. 'It's been a pleasure, pal.'

'And as Jonathan's already standing up, it seems a good time to hand the reins over to him.'

'Cheers, Dave.' Jonathan headed back towards his seat but remained standing. 'Thank you for those kind words and the gifts for the bridal party. To everyone who doesn't know, I'm Jonathan and work with Dave as a doctor in the local hospital but we've actually known each other, and been best friends, since we were' – he held his hand low in the air – 'this high. Now traditionally I'm supposed to tell you some stories about the groom. Well I'd be lying if I didn't say he'd been the best friend ever.' He followed with some amusing anecdotes about he and David growing up together. Finally he said, 'Seriously though, I couldn't be happier for my pal. He's loyal, the best friend ever, and he'll make the perfect husband. Not only will he love Kate, but he'll take good care of her, so no worries there, Adam.'

'Glad to hear it.' Adam chortled.

'And Kate, Dave's one lucky man. You're even more striking than usual today. A princess, and I promise your prince will never disappoint, or if he does, come and see me.'

This time it was Kate's turn to laugh.

Jonathan finished up with the telegrams. 'And last but not least. This one's from all the guys and gals at the hospital. To Kate and Dave. Congratulations. Some of them will be at the party this evening.' He picked up his glass. 'And now you lot have sat down long enough so please rise and join me in raising your glass to the happy couple. Mr and Mrs Erikson.'

The tables had been culled down to a couple at the side of the room where guests could sit either side. A disc jockey and his equipment had been set up at the back of the room and flashing lights flickered on the ceiling and floor. Debs had allowed Peggy and Sheila to put a couple of travel cots upstairs in one of the bedrooms for Ben and Jacob. Sheila clutched the monitor.

A couple of waiters ran around the room taking orders and bringing the guests drinks from the bar.

Harry took the microphone. 'It's now time for the bride and groom's first dance.'

Everyone clapped and David led Kate to the floor as the vinyl 'How Deep is your Love' spun on the turntable. The groom glided the bride around the room as her train trailed the floor. Kate stared into David's eyes. I turned to Joe. 'It's clear to anyone they're madly in love.'

He kissed my lips. 'Just like you and me. Shall we join the happy couple.'

'Sure.' I turned to Linda. 'Are you and Stu getting up?'

She hugged her bump. 'I think I'll sit this out. To be honest today's been a bit draining.'

I patted her shoulder. 'I understand. You sit back and relax.'

Joe took my hand and we strolled up as 'Can't Smile Without You' started. Peggy whispered something to Sheila before Peggy and Adam headed our way and, in a few seconds, the makeshift dance floor was crowded with couples swaying.

'Look.' I tapped Joe's arm as Jonathan led Teresa to dance.

She scowled at me.

'Did you see that?'

Joe rolled his eyes. 'I thought you two were getting on better now.'

'She's two-faced. Pretends she's being nice but whenever no one else is around she's forever making digs at me. Of course when I retaliate Peggy thinks I'm the bad person. Seriously, Joe, that girl can't be trusted.'

'I don't know, Rach. You don't think you maybe wind her up a bit?'

'No, I don't. Anyway, you're supposed to be on my side.'

'I am, darling. I am.' He brushed his lips against mine. 'Changing the subject. You know you look divine. It's taken me all my time today to keep my hands off you.'

'I feel the same but the waiting will be worth it. We can't leave before the bride and groom. That wouldn't be right.'

Through the evening we were up and down dancing. It was obvious poor Linda was feeling cheated. 'Wait until the baby's born,' I said. 'You can make up for it then.' I turned to Teresa. 'You and Jonathan looked cosy.'

She frowned. 'What's it to you?'

'Nothing. I was just saying.'

'Why?'

'Just being nice.'

'Now say it like you mean it.'

I sighed. 'I give up.'

The music stopped and Harry took the microphone again. 'Can I have your attention?'

The room went silent.

'The bride and groom are now leaving.'

Everyone followed Kate and David out to the car where a colleague from the hospital had been elected to drive the couple to the hotel. A red Ford Escort had been decorated with a flower arrangement on the back window and a placard saying *Just Married* hung from the bumper along with tin cans rattling on string. We took the opportunity to throw more confetti over the bride and groom.

Peggy and Adam kissed Kate in turn. 'We love you darling,' Peggy said.

Adam tapped David on the shoulder. 'Look after my baby girl.'

The bridal couple climbed into the back seat of the vehicle and everyone waved as it drove out of sight before heading back inside.

'I think that's our cue to get off home too,' Peggy said.

I glanced around the room. 'The DJ's packing up now so I imagine it's time for everyone to go. It's been a long day.'

Chapter Eighteen

Rachel

'Got time for a drink and a catch-up?' Mel pulled the door shut to the newspaper office and turned the key in the lock.

'Yep, go on. Can't stay long though otherwise Joe will wonder where I am. We definitely need a catch-up though.'

We headed across the road to The Black Horse and up to the bar.

'Hello there, girls,' Harry said, 'we don't normally see you in here at this time.'

'Nope, but it's been bedlam at work of late' – I climbed on the high stool – 'so we've not had a chance to chat for days. It's quiet in here.'

'Give it another half hour and they'll all start pouring in. What can I get you both?'

'Just two diet cokes' – I got my purse out – 'as we're both driving.'

'Okey-dokes.' He popped a slice of lemon into two glasses and poured in the coke.

'Help yourselves to ice.'

Using the tongs Mel grabbed a few cubes of ice and dropped them into both our drinks while I paid. 'Cheers, Harry. Let's sit over there,' I said to Mel and we made for a table by the window.

Once we were seated, I asked, 'So, what's happening with you and Phil.'

She took a sip of coke. 'Well, we're still corresponding by letter, and he wants to meet up once he's back here.'

'Are they still planning to return in September?'

'Phil is but Jan's contemplating staying out there. I think her relationship is serious.'

'Good for her.'

'Anyway, how was the wedding?'

'Aw, Kate looked beautiful. Wait until you see the photos. I popped a couple of films into Boots and they said they should be ready by tomorrow. Shame you couldn't make it.'

'I know. I was gutted. One of those twenty-four-hour stomach bugs.'

'Do you know where you picked it up from?'

She shook her head. 'No idea at all. Anyway, be yours next.'

'Yeah, I can't wait. Joe's started the ball rolling for the divorce. We've got Linda's baby coming first though. She's convinced it's a girl. I don't know what she'll do if she pushes out a boy.'

'I'm sure she'll love it whatever. So, how's it going with Teresa? Is she still being a pain in the arse?'

'Absolutely she is. You'll never guess what?'

Mel flicked her hair behind her ear. 'No, I won't so you'd better tell me.'

'She only got off with the best man at the wedding. Dishy he is too.'

'Yeah?'

'Doctor as well.'

'Shucks. I knew I should've been there.'

I held up my finger. 'You've got Phil, remember.'

She smiled. 'Well, I hope so.'

'Why don't you come to the barn dance at the folk club next time we go? They're great fun.'

She gritted her teeth. 'I don't know about that. I'd have no idea what to do.'

'You don't need to know. That's part of the fun. Say you'll come.'

'Go on then. You've twisted my arm. Let me know when.' She swigged back her drink. 'I suppose I should let you get off home.'

I checked the time on my watch. 'Gawd, yes. Joe will be wondering where I am.'

Chapter Nineteen

Peggy

I flicked the switch on the kettle. 'In answer to your question, Rachel, I've no idea what Adam will say.'

'Then why are you letting her stay?'

'Because she can't go back there. It isn't safe.'

'Still pouring out a pack of lies, I see.' Rachel dragged her hair back into a ponytail.

'Please don't start this again. I know you can't see any wrong in Denise and Gordon, but, love, you're not the one who's living under their roof. Sometimes people hide who they really are.'

'Exactly. Just like Teresa. She's playing you.'

I clenched my fist. 'Don't keep on, love. My nerves are already hitting the roof, and this bickering with you girls isn't helping.'

'I'm sorry you think like that but...' Rachel looked to the door. 'Adam may have come around with her spending time with Ben, but moving her in.' She sighed. 'I'll lay odds he isn't going to like it.'

'It's only for a few days at first because don't forget she's off to the States next week. I'm sure he'll be fine.'

'Keep telling yourself that.'

'She's my daughter. I can't reject her again.'

'That seems a bit over the top. Or did she say that?'

'No. She didn't. But I remember you saying that to me once.'

'I'm sorry about that. I've grown up a lot since then.'

'Then act like it and stop all this tension. Help me convince Adam that it's the right thing to do.'

'You've got to be kidding.'

Before I could answer, Teresa wandered into the kitchen with Ben. 'He needs changing. Would you like me to do it?'

'If you don't mind, love. Thanks.' I spooned coffee into a couple of mugs.

'Course not. I love caring for him.'

'Tessa.' Ben gurgled as Teresa carried him upstairs.

'See. She'll be a big help, and I need that now our Kate's gone. It's not like I don't have room with both Joe and Kate left home.'

'True, although I bet Adam doesn't see it like that.'

The door slammed. 'Shh. That'll be Adam. Not a word now about Teresa.'

'Sure.'

He strolled into the kitchen. 'Rachel, hello, love. This is an unexpected visit.'

'I'm not staying. Just dropped in to give a book to Peg. Joe and I are popping around Stu and Linda's shortly. I'd best be off now though.' Rachel gave me a kiss on the cheek. 'See you soon.'

'Bye, love.'

'Oh, Rachel' – Adam followed her into the hallway – 'can you ask Joe to pop around tomorrow after work? There's something I need to discuss with him.'

'Sure. See you then.'

'Sit down, love,' I said to Adam when he came back in. 'I'll get you a cuppa.'

'Ta, love. I'm gasping.'

I transferred water from the kettle into the teapot. 'How was the breakdown?'

'Not too bad. Didn't take me too long to sort so they could get on their way.' He sighed. 'You know sometimes I'm so bloody sick of this job when I can't even have a Sunday off in peace.'

'Think of the overtime.'

'Money isn't everything. I'm losing family time I can't get back.'

'I know what you mean. We should book a holiday.'

'That's not a bad idea. Anywhere in mind?'

I poured tea from the pot into the mug and added a dash of milk. 'I've heard Bournemouth's supposed to be nice.'

'Hmm, be crowded this time of the year.' He peered up at the ceiling. 'Who's that up there?'

'Teresa.'

'Oh.' He squinted. 'I didn't know she was coming around tonight.'

'It was a surprise visit. How do you fancy going to The Black Horse later?'

'What about Ben?'

'I'm sure Teresa will babysit.' I placed a mug of tea in front of him on the table.

He sighed. 'I'm not sure about that, love. Yes, she seems to be doing a lot better but... I just don't know.'

I shut the kitchen door. 'Er' – I bit my lip – 'don't get cross but...'

'Now why does this sound like I'm not going to like it?'

'I've said she can move in with us for a while.'

He almost choked on his tea. 'Please tell me you're joking.'

'I couldn't say no. She's homeless.'

'Like hell is she homeless. She's got a home with her mam and dad.'

'But she doesn't feel safe there. Gordon's been violent. Remember, it was your idea for Teresa to come into our lives.'

He let out a deep breath. 'That was before she ran off with our son. And now you want her here 24/7.'

'She won't be here that much. She goes to the States next week. And what with work, or out seeing Jonathan, we'll hardly know she's here.'

'Now why don't I believe that?' He picked up his packet of Players and took one out dabbing it on the box.

'Do you know that Gordon used to lock her up in the cupboard under the stairs? No wonder she's like she is.'

'We only have her word for that. Rachel's normally a good judge of character and she said they're nice people.' He struck a Swan Vesta, lit the cigarette, and shook the match until the flame went out.

'Please, Adam. We should support her.'

'Perhaps we should speak to her parents.'

'No, we can't do that. It'll just make things worse for her.'

He drew on the cigarette. 'Okay, she can stay until she goes to the States, but any nonsense and she's out. And you never know she might decide to stay there with Mike.'

'Is that what you're hoping?'

'No, I don't know, maybe, but you have to admit it would be easier for us all.'

'All except Teresa. She needs love and security. We can offer that.'

He tapped ash into the ashtray. 'I've said, yes, you don't need to keep going on.'

'There's more.'

'More?'

'Yes. Her stuff has to be collected.'

'And?'

'Well, she can't go on her own, and I don't want to go without you. I don't trust that Gordon.'

He sighed. 'Okay we'll go with Teresa and get her stuff. Get Sheila to look after Ben though.'

⊰⊱

Adam pulled up outside the Coles.

Teresa slid out from the back seat. 'It doesn't look like they're home as their car's not here.'

'Let's get in there quickly, then.' Adam stepped out of the Cortina 1600E. 'You stay here, Peg.'

They hurried down the path. Teresa put the key in the lock, pushed open the front door and they disappeared into the house. My hand trembled as I turned the radio on to try and relax. That Gordon sounded a nasty piece of work. Hopefully Adam and Teresa would be in and out before the Coles returned. Admiring their well-kept garden occupied my mind while listening to Tony Blackburn. Bees and butterflies hovered over the striking pinkish, red, purple, and golden blooms.

A car pulled up behind. My heart hammered as some guy got out and slammed the door. It must've been Gordon because he fitted the description Rachel had given. Medium build, dark hair, and a bushy moustache. He stared at me before trudging over. 'You know that's my parking spot.'

I wound down the window. 'Oh, is it? Sorry. We're a bit lost so my husband's gone to try and find someone for directions. We're looking for Highland Close. Do you know it?'

He sniffed, wiping his nose on his shirt cuff. 'Never heard of it. He'd better not be bloody long.'

A woman came over fitting Denise's description. 'Sorry,' she said, 'my husband's having a bit of a bad day. He's not normally that rude. Are you darling?'

The man grunted.

I stepped out of the Cortina. 'He shouldn't be long.'

'Whatever. Dee give us a hand getting the shopping in, love.' He paced back to his vehicle and opened the boot. The woman joined him and unloaded a couple of Waitrose carrier bags.

'Did you find out what they're doing here?' she asked in my earshot, before passing the bags to him.

'Nope. She reckons they're lost.' His gaze went to the house as Teresa and Adam came out with the luggage. 'What the hell? That's our Teresa with a suitcase.' Gordon hurried through the rattling gate and sprinted down the path bashing the lavender bush with the shopping bags then dropping them by the doorstep.

I rushed down the path after him.

He held Teresa's arm. 'What's going on, Tess?'

'Peggy and Adam know all about what you're like and they've said I can move in with them for a while. I'll bring this back in a few days.' She signalled to the case.

'What do you mean know all about me?'

Adam prodded Gordon. 'You should be ashamed of yourself.'

Gordon squinted. 'What are you on about, mate? Why should I be ashamed?'

'You've been mentally and physically abusing your daughter. So much so that she's too scared to live under your roof for one day longer.'

'Look, mate, I don't know what she's told you but that's simply not true. Tell him, Tess.'

'It is true.' Teresa backed away. 'Please don't hurt me.'

I put my arm around her. 'It's all right, love. We've got you.'

Gordon held up his hands. 'If that's what you want, love, then go.' He sniffed. 'If you change your mind though, remember, this is always your home.' He turned to Adam. 'I've never laid a finger on my daughter. It's all lies and I' – he shook his head – I simply don't know why she's saying these things.'

※

The cup shook as I passed it to Adam.

'Darling,' he said, 'you're shaking. Sit yourself down.'

I lowered myself into the armchair.

'Here, have this.' He passed me his cup of tea. 'I'll get another.'

'Thanks, love.' The cup and saucer quivered in my hand. 'At least she's safe now.'

'Where is she?'

'Upstairs unpacking.'

'You know, Peg, that Gordon seemed really genuine. You don't think the girl could be lying to us?'

'Why would she? That's what these abusers do. Make out they're the good guys so people don't suspect them. Don't be fooled.'

'Hmm. I'm not so sure. Especially when Rachel gives a different story.'

'Believe what you like, but I trust my daughter.'

Adam patted me on the arm. 'I should go and get Ben.'

'It's all right, I called our Sheila. She said he was asleep and she'd hold on to him overnight. I'll go round in the morning to pick him up. Thank you for today.' I sipped the drink.

Teresa stacked the dinner dishes and headed over to the sink.

'Can you come and sit down for a minute, love?' Adam tapped the chair at the table.

'I don't mind washing up. It's the least I can do.'

'You can do them later.'

'You're not going to make me go back to them, are you?'

'No, if you'd let me get a word in edgeways. Come and sit down.'

Teresa turned off the tap and made her way back to the table. 'What did you want to speak to me about?'

Adam coughed. 'Like I said, we're happy for you to stay but there are a few conditions.'

She looked him directly in the eyes. 'Anything.'

'First of all, the obvious one is, we don't ever want a repeat with Ben like the time you disappeared with him.'

'No, there won't be. I promise.'

'Secondly, once you're back from the States, you need to find somewhere else to stay. So you'll need a proper job.'

'But I have a job.'

'No, I said a proper job. Full time employment. Not a cleaning job for a few hours here and there.'

She leaned on her elbow. 'But I'm no good at anything else.'

'How about a shop assistant?' he asked.

She bit her lip. 'But I've no experience.'

'Woolworths is a good place to start,' I said. 'Rachel worked there for a while, and Linda. They both loved it. I'm sure Rachel would put in a good word for you with the manager if you asked her.'

'Do you really think I could do it?'

'Yes, absolutely,' I said.

'Or' – Adam drummed his fingers on the table – 'I noticed Waitrose down the road are advertising. Why don't you pop down there tomorrow and get an application form?'

Teresa smiled. 'Thanks, Adam. I will.'

'And once you're working,' I said, 'there's nothing stopping you going to night school to get some exams.'

Chapter Twenty

Peggy

Teresa was upstairs packing for her trip tomorrow. Her flight wasn't until nine in the evening but the airline had advised check-in three hours beforehand. Adam had booked us into a hotel close to Heathrow Airport overnight for after we saw Teresa off. 'I'm getting too old to travel there and back in one day,' he'd said.

A key turned in the lock. I wondered which one of my kids it was. I headed out to the hallway. 'Ah, Kate and David. You're the first to arrive.'

Kate gave me a kiss on the cheek. 'Well, you did say, don't be late.'

She slipped her sandals off and put them neatly at the side of the door. 'Is she okay?'

'I think so. Come and sit down.' They followed me through to the lounge and took a seat next to each other on the settee. 'Obviously,' I continued, 'she's nervous.'

'Yeah, but what an adventure.' Kate brushed her fringe out of her eyes. 'Stop worrying, Mam, she'll be fine and it'll do her good. A chance for her to travel, meet new people, including Mike. She's not a kid but a grown woman.'

Light footsteps came downstairs and Teresa peeped into the room. 'Hello, you two. Peggy never mentioned you were coming.'

'Didn't she?' Kate grinned.

Teresa squinted. 'What's going on?'

Kate grinned again. 'Can I tell her?'

'Go on then.' I smiled.

Teresa glanced around the lounge. 'Tell me what?'

Kate's gorgeous hazel eyes twinkled. 'Mam's arranged for a little goodbye party for you.'

Teresa's cheeks flushed. 'For me?'

'Yes' – I patted her arm – 'you didn't think I'd let you go without a proper goodbye to everyone, did you?'

'A party. Awesome, thanks.'

'Not exactly a party. Just a few family members to wish you well before your trip.' I headed over to the sideboard drawer and took out a small parcel. 'Before everyone else arrives.' I passed her the gift.

Teresa blushed again. 'Thank you.' She ripped off the wrapping. 'A journal.'

'I thought you could write what you do each day. You never know you might be able to turn some of it into poetry or even a story.'

'It's lovely. Thank you.' She held me tightly in a hug, so much so, I had to pull us apart. 'That sounds like our Joe,' I said. 'Unfortunately, Rachel can't make it.'

Joe strolled into the room. 'Hi, Mam.' He turned to Teresa. 'Bet you're excited?'

'I think so.'

'I hear you've been seeing a bit of my best friend Jonathan?' David said.

Teresa tittered. 'Yes, we've had a couple of dates. He's asked me to write to him while I'm away.'

'That's a good sign.' Kate popped her handbag down on the armchair. 'He's a nice guy. You could do a lot worse.'

Teresa's eyes lit up. 'He's lovely. I just hope he doesn't get bored of me.'

'He's not that kind of guy,' David said.

There was a knock on the door. 'I'll get it.' Kate headed back into the hallway and came back in carrying Jacob with Sheila and Malc in tow.

After the pecks on the cheek with my sister, her husband and son, I said, 'Tea's out ready if you want to come through to the kitchen. I've done a buffet so we can help ourselves and have it on our laps.'

'This is so wonderful of you to do this for me, Peggy.' Teresa hugged me again, wetting my face with her tears.

'Hey.' I patted her back. 'No need for that, you're only going for a month not a lifetime.'

'It's not that.' She whimpered. 'No one else has ever been so kind to me.'

Poor girl. That Denise and Gordon had really done a number on her. No wonder she was so messed up.

Adam grabbed a trolley from outside the terminal, lugged Teresa's suitcase on, and pushed it through the entrance with us following behind. He glanced around before pointing. 'Looks like check-in's over there.'

I thought about the last time we were here all those years ago with Rachel, must've been at least six years ago now. She had her parents, Linda, Stu, Joe, Sandra, Adam and myself, seeing her off, but poor Teresa only had us two. I'm sure Kate and Joe would've come if it hadn't been so far to travel. Sheila had taken

Ben last night so we didn't have to worry about him. Thank goodness he'd never been a clingy baby like Joe. Ben loved going to Aunty Sheila's and she was marvellous, taking everything in her stride, managing to take care of Ben and Jacob. I wasn't sure I'd be able to cope with such ease but then she was a few years younger than me.

Adam heaved the suitcase onto the scale.

'Passport.' The TWA stewardess smiled.

Teresa handed it over. 'I've never flown before.'

'Don't worry, we'll look after you. What with drinks, snacks and meals, you'll be back on the ground before you know it.'

'Thanks.'

'The gate's not open yet but shouldn't be long.' She passed Teresa her passport and boarding card. 'Keep an eye on the board.'

'Thanks.' Teresa turned to me. 'What do we do now?'

'Find a seat until you're called,' I said.

Adam searched the area. 'It's busy this evening, but look over there, three empty seats.'

Once we sat down, Adam said, 'Now have you got your cash and travellers cheques?'

'In here.' She patted her handbag.

'And have you packed your journal?' I asked.

'That's in here too. I thought I'd make a start on the plane.'

'That's a girl.' Adam tapped her arm. 'Any problems you ring us. Reverse the charges if necessary. Not that I foresee any as Mike will look after you, I'm sure. I know he's looking forward to meeting you.'

'As I am him.'

A voice came over the Airport Tannoy system advising a gate was open but we couldn't hear it clearly.

'I'll check the update.' Adam headed over to the board. After standing in front of the panel for a couple of minutes he beckoned us over.

Teresa grabbed my hand as we got up from the chair and made our way over to Adam.

He signalled to the board. 'Time for you to go through.'

Teresa's face paled.

'It'll be okay.' He reached for his wallet from his jacket pocket. 'Get yourself a vodka and lime or something once you've gone through.' He handed Teresa a fiver. 'Just one mind, to steady your nerves.'

I passed her a Danielle Steel book. 'Find somewhere comfortable to sit and read while you're waiting. The time will pass quickly. I couldn't put it down and you can carry on reading it on the plane.'

'*Now and Forever*. It looks good. Thanks, Peggy.' She hugged me tightly, broke away, and hugged Adam. 'I really appreciate all this, and for letting me move in with you both.'

Adam patted her on the back. 'We know.'

'Write to me,' I said, 'and ring me once a week.'

'Will do.' She popped the book in her bag and headed to the gate, waving just before she went through.

'Do you think she'll be all right?' I asked.

Adam put his arm around my shoulder. 'She'll have a whale of a time. Let's go and find that hotel, have some dinner, and an early night. I don't know about you but I'm knackered.'

Adam was a good man. I was lucky to have him.

Chapter Twenty-One

Rachel

While waiting on one of the antenatal chairs I scribbled an idea in my notebook for a new article about pregnant women. Linda was the last patient to go through despite arriving over an hour early. She came out of the consultant room beaming.

I gathered my stuff together, shoved it in my bag, and stood up. 'It went well then?'

'It sure did. The doctor said everything's going as it should and she'd be surprised if I manage to make it to my due date.'

'But that's only a fortnight away.'

'I know. She reckons this one's going to pop out.'

'Well so long as it doesn't start today.' I chortled. 'We have plans remember?'

She nudged me with her elbow. 'Anne-Marie will come when she's ready, and if that's this afternoon then so be it.' Linda chuckled.

Gawd, I hoped it didn't happen while she was with me. I had no idea what to do. 'Come on then, where first?'

'Coffee and something to eat. I'm famished.'

'Righto. Elmo's?'

'No. Wimpy. My stomach's screaming for a knickerbocker glory.'

'Yummy. My treat.'

We headed out of the clinic and across the road. 'Shall we take the park route?' I asked.

'That'll be nice.' Linda panted. Poor girl was huge. I don't think I'd ever known a pregnant woman to be so big. She'd put on weight all round too. Even her normal slim face was plump.

'Are you sure you're okay walking in this heat? I can easily fetch the car from the car park and drive us closer to the café.'

'Nah. Doctor said keep moving. I'm itching to meet my daughter so anything that helps.' She hooked her arm in mine and we strolled through the park's tall iron gates. The maples had started turning from green to yellow, and some were already a spectacular red. We were greeted by a bed of dahlia blooms in gorgeous colours. Golden, burnt orange, and scarlet spikey heads and some smaller in yellow, peach and lavender. As we passed the pond, I asked, 'Would you like to stop and sit here for a while?'

'Nope.' Linda touched her large bump. 'I need food. A nice big juicy cheeseburger.'

'I thought you wanted a knickerbocker glory.'

'I do. That's for afters.'

I shook my head. She may want all of that but would she find room? As we left by the back entrance of the park, the stunning maple branches waved farewell in the light breeze. We crossed the road at the traffic lights, turned right into a side road, and stopped outside the Wimpy.

I peeped inside. 'It looks a bit crowded. Sure you want to go in?'

'Hmm. Maybe not, although that couple by the door look like they're getting ready to go.'

I headed inside to the man and woman. 'Hope you don't mind me asking but are you leaving?'

The woman stood up. 'We are, and this will be a good place for your friend to sit. There's a lovely breeze from the open door.'

'Thanks.' I beckoned Linda.

'How long have you got to go?' the woman asked Linda.

She hugged her bump. 'Two weeks although the doctor reckons I won't make it that long.'

'Hope it all goes well. We've got a six-month-old. This is our first time out without her. Feels strange.'

'I might see you in the baby clinic one day then. My name's Linda.'

'Gemma.'

The man sighed as he stood outside the café holding two loaded up Mothercare carrier bags.

'I'd best go. I think he's getting a bit fed up.'

Linda giggled. 'Probably all that shopping you're making him do.'

'Yes.' She laughed. 'We're done now though. Going home for half an hour's peace before my mam brings our little one back.'

'Good luck.' Linda eased herself into the chair closest to the door.

'She seemed nice.' I sat opposite Linda.

'Yeah. She did.'

A grey-haired waitress came over. She peered over her large, amber-framed spectacles. 'What can I get you ladies?'

Linda perused the menu. 'Cheeseburger and fries for me.'

The woman scribbled it down in a notebook. 'And your friend?' She glanced at me.

'A portion of fries for me, oh and a black coffee, please.'

She turned back to Linda. 'Can I get you a drink?'

Linda leaned forward. 'Just a glass of water, please. Cheers.' She flopped back in the chair. 'I'm totally knackered and we've not even done the shops yet.'

'Are you sure you're up to it? It's warm out there so I'm not surprised you're exhausted.'

'I must go to Mothercare even if we don't do anything else. Especially now the doctor thinks I won't make the two weeks.'

'You could write a list for me. Why don't I drive you home after this?'

She shook her head. 'Nah, I want to choose the stuff from Mothercare myself.'

I shrugged my shoulders. 'If you insist.'

'I do. I'll be fine after having a rest and something to eat and drink.'

'If you say so.'

A young lad around sixteen shouted. 'Cheeseburger and chips?'

I put up my hand. 'Over here.'

'Cheers,' Linda said.

'And a bowl of chips.'

'That's me.' I smiled. 'Quick service too. Thought we'd have to wait ages. You're busy this afternoon.'

'Yeah, but it's thinning out now. Be quiet by three. I'll get your drinks. Black coffee and a water, wasn't it?'

'That's right.' I sprinkled salt and vinegar on my chips and popped one in my mouth. 'Mmm, I hadn't realised how hungry I was.'

'Me too.' Linda munched on the burger. It oozed with mustard and tomato ketchup.

I laughed.

'What?'

'You've got ketchup around your mouth.'

She wiped the serviette across her lips. 'Has it gone?'

'Yeah.'

After a couple of bites, she put the burger down. 'I've gone off it now. Want it?'

'No, thanks.'

She held her stomach. 'Not much room in here for food.'

Poor Linda. It must be so hard for her carrying all that extra weight. 'Won't be long,' I said. 'You'll soon have your figure back.'

'No one told me how hard this pregnancy thing was. Puffing and panting, not able to sleep at night because you can't get comfy, and I'm one of the lucky ones cos I didn't get morning sickness.'

'You're not making it sound very appealing.' I chuckled.

'It'll be worth it.' She smiled. 'Does that mean you and Joe are thinking...?'

'Not sure.' I grinned. 'Maybe.'

Linda puffed and panted as we trudged.

'Please, let me take those bags,' I said.

'No. You're already loaded up.'

'It doesn't matter.'

'Nah, I'll be okay, let's make for that bench over there and take a rest.'

'Okay.'

Swaying, she headed to the seat on the corner. Tyres screeched. A car screamed around the bend. I looked up as a green Vauxhall Viva zigzagged towards us out of control. 'Linda, look out.'

She stepped forward.

'Linda,' I screamed again.

She turned to me. 'Rach.'

The car boarded the pavement with a screech of tyres. A loud thump. The Mothercare carrier bags split and terry nappies, body vests, babygrows and pink dresses scattered. Two men and a woman ran towards the car. I couldn't see Linda. Where was she? I rushed forward past the car. In the windscreen the driver glared, wide-eyed. The engine restarted. The car reversed. It sped away.

Someone shouted, 'I'll phone for an ambulance.'

'Linda,' I shouted pushing my way through. 'Move move.' I shoved people away. 'It's my friend. Linda. Linda,' I shouted again. People cleared a pathway, patting me on the back, arm or shoulder, as I hurried through. 'Linda.' I screamed.

She was on the ground. A pool of blood seeped around her head. *Oh my God*. I covered my mouth. My heart pounding, I crouched down and took her hand in both of mine. She didn't react, her eyes were closed. God, was she breathing? 'It's going to be all right, Lind,' I whispered. 'The ambulance is on its way.'

⁃

Joe had his arm around me. 'She'll be all right.'

'But what if she isn't?' I sniffled. 'And the baby?'

'Look, here comes Stu now.' His voice tailed off as we both glanced up and took in the look on Stu's face. I'd never seen him cry before.

I jumped up from the seat in the waiting room and headed towards him. 'What's happened? Is it the baby?'

He shook his head. 'No.' He whined. 'They think they can save the baby.'

'What then?'

Stu turned away sobbing.

'What? Tell me.' I tugged at his arm. 'Tell me what's happening, please.'

He was trembling. 'She's... She's... She's gone, Rach.'

'Stu,' I said, 'you're not making any sense. What do you mean, she's gone?'

'She's dead, Rach, for God's sake. How much clearer can I make it?' He charged through the double swing doors towards the exit. I ran after him with Joe in tow.

I tugged at his arm. 'Stu, please, tell me it isn't true.'

He shook me off. 'Leave me be.'

I screamed. 'No. No. She can't be. She can't be dead.'

Joe hugged Stu. 'My God, mate. I'm so sorry. You said they can save the baby?'

'They think so.' Stu sniffled 'They're doing the operation now. Said nothing else could be done for Lind. They fought hard to save her but the head injury was too traumatic. She's brain dead.' He put his hands across his eyes. 'What am I going to do without her?'

What was Stu going to do? How would he cope with a baby and no Linda? How was I going to cope without her? Linda was more than a best friend, more like a sister. We'd done everything together. She was to be my bridesmaid. 'No.' I screamed, over and over and I didn't care how many people stared.

A baby girl. Seven pound and eleven ounces. Doing well, Stu had said. Linda was right. She'd known all along she was carrying a girl. Her Anne-Marie.

Sandra and Keith charged through the double doors and up the corridor towards me and Joe. I met her halfway and hugged her.

'My baby girl can't be dead.' She screamed.

'I'm so sorry.' I hugged her tightly.

Joe put his arm around her. 'You have a granddaughter.'

'Where's Stu?' Sandra asked between sobs.

'He's in with the baby,' I said.

'Have you seen Linda?' Sandra blew her nose.

'Not yet. They've said Stu can see her shortly. I think they're making her look... well you know, after the operation. I sniffled. 'I still can't believe she's gone. We were out shopping. She'd had her antenatal appointment only a few hours earlier and when they said the baby could arrive before two weeks none of us thought this would happen.'

'I'm going to find a nurse. I need to see my daughter.' Sandra headed up to the nurses' station and I followed. 'Can someone help me?' she asked a young nurse. 'I'd like to see my daughter. Linda Pearson.'

'I'll just find out if she's ready. I know her husband is in with the baby. If you can sit back down, I shan't be long.'

The nurse disappeared but was back within a few minutes. 'I'll take you through.'

'You want to come in with me?' Sandra asked, gripping my hand.

I glanced at the nurse. 'Will that be okay?'

She nodded. 'That will be fine. This way.'

We followed her into a side room. 'Take all the time you need,' she said.

Slowly we headed towards the gurney where Linda lay. 'She looks like she's asleep.' I wiped my eyes but the tears wouldn't stop. I'm not sure who had the loudest sobs, me or Sandra. I stroked Linda's face. 'I'm going to make sure you get justice.' I kissed her cheek. If I had my way the bastard who did this to her would be behind bars for the rest of his life.

Sandra turned towards me and fell into my arms crying against my chest. I had to be strong for her. I was cursed. Bad things happened when I was around. There were no happy ever afters, only in fairy tales.

A policeman and policewoman were speaking to Stu and Joe as I approached. 'Here's my fiancé now. She saw what happened.'

'He came up on the pavement,' I said, 'and he didn't stop. Have you caught him?'

'We think we've found him,' the policewoman answered.

'Well, I hope he's going to jail for life. Was he drunk?'

She blinked. 'If it's the same car, the driver's dead too. Can you tell us what you remember about the vehicle?'

'Yes. It was a green Vauxhall Viva. K reg and I think it had 69 somewhere in it but I can't be sure.'

'How can you be so sure of the make?' the policeman asked.

'My fiancé's a mechanic so I can recognise most cars.'

The policeman nodded. 'In that case it was the same car. We don't know yet whether he was under the influence or whether there was a medical reason for the accident. We think he may have been a joy rider. Wrapped the vehicle around a lamppost about two hundred yards up the road from where Mrs Pearson was knocked down. We're trying to trace the owner of the vehicle. The driver was only a young lad. Seventeen, eighteen maybe, so no doubt has parents will be devastated by this news.'

'They may be devastated but their son inflicted it on himself.' I raised my voice. 'My friend was minding her own business and now her baby girl is left without a mother.'

'We understand.' The policewoman patted my arm. 'We're sorry for your loss.'

I rocked the transparent crib. 'She's beautiful. So much like Linda.'

'She is.' Stu lifted her out. 'Would you like to hold her?'

'May I?'

'Sure.'

'Let me sit down first.' I lowered myself into the hospital chair.

'Here.' He passed the infant to me.

My eyes misted as I stared into the newborn's face. 'Your mam would've loved you. She did love you.'

Stu put his hand on my shoulder. 'She would've. What are we going to do, Rach? How will we ever get past this?'

I shrugged. 'I don't know, but I suppose we have to. I think Anne-Marie will help.'

Stu ran his fingers across his forehead. 'How the hell will I cope? I mean, I need to work.'

'Maybe Sandra will help? Or Sheila. I know Lind mentioned going back to work and I believe she'd already spoken to Sheila about it. Perhaps between Sandra and Sheila it'll be doable. What about the garage though? Surely, they'll allow you a few weeks to get sorted.'

'I'm sure they will but that won't pay the bills, will it?'

'You know Joe and I will help you in any way we can.'

'I know. My parents are on their way in. My mam never really liked Linda. Said she was a bad influence on me. She was rabbiting on the phone about naming the baby Grace after my grandmother.'

Anne-Marie gave a high-pitched cry. I rocked her. 'See even she objects. She's your daughter, Stu, yours and Linda's, and you know as well as I do that Linda named her Anne-Marie almost instantly from when she first found out she was expecting. Don't let your mother sway you from that.'

Chapter Twenty-Two

Rachel

Joe perched next to me on the bed. 'You, okay?'

I shook my head. 'Not really.' Each night since it had happened, I'd laid awake going over and over everything in my head. Linda bursting with joy as she came out of the consultant's room, the giggles in Mothercare as we picked up terry nappies, chose body vests, babygrows, and dresses, popping them into the shopping basket. I was concerned about her buying baby dresses but she was insistent. She had no doubt she was carrying a girl and even encouraged me to purchase a pink cuddly rabbit for her Anne-Marie.

'I just can't believe it, Joe. I can't believe my best friend has gone.' I sobbed.

'I know, babe.' He put his arm around me. 'Say *no* if you don't want but...'

'What?'

'Stu's been on the phone.'

'How is he?'

Joe shrugged. 'As you'd expect. Like you really, a bit in denial. He needs to drop off some clothes for Linda at the funeral parlour.' He pulled me closer to him. 'Now remember say *no* if you're not up to it but he's asked if you'll help him choose something for her to wear.'

I dabbed my eyes with a tissue. 'Doesn't he want to do that himself?' I sniffed.

'Well, no, otherwise he wouldn't have asked you.'

'But what about Sandra?'

'Stu's asked you. You and I have to be strong for him as he's going to need us over the next few months.'

I squeezed Joe's hand. 'I'll try.' The tears refused to stop.

※

It was weird being in Linda's bedroom going through her wardrobe. I slipped an apple-green tiered floral maxi skirt off the hanger and paired it with a white broderie-anglaise gypsy top. From her jewellery box I selected a steel pendant set with a cut-glass emerald stone and placed it with the blouse.

Stu came in with Anne-Marie screaming in his arms. 'I don't know what to do, Rach. She wants her mam. I'm no good for her.'

'That's not true.' I laid the clothes out on the bed. 'Linda wouldn't have known what to do either, you'd have learned together. Here. Pass her to me.'

Stu handed over the baby. I rocked her like we'd done with Ben when he was a newborn. 'She might have colic.'

'Colic. Is that serious?'

'I don't think so, but it can be painful for babies, and stressful' – I patted him on the shoulder – 'particularly for Mums or Dads. Might be worth mentioning it when the health visitor comes around. Didn't the hospital say someone would be around this week?'

'Yeah. I think she's coming today, or maybe tomorrow, I can't bloody remember.' He rubbed his brow. 'How the hell am I supposed to take care of a new baby when I can't even look after myself?'

I touched his hand. 'You will, because you have to. Anne-Marie will get you through this.' I stroked her strawberry blonde fuzz. 'She's going to be your mini-Linda. Already at five days she looks like her.'

Stu smiled. Probably the first time I'd seen him smile since Linda's death. 'I know.' He blinked. 'Supposing, I'm not up to the job, Rach, and not only let Linda down but Anne-Marie too. My mam and dad have offered to take her back to Dorset with them.'

'What? Not for good?'

'Yeah. They've offered to bring her up. Said the sea air will be good for her and as they're both retired, she wouldn't be left with strangers all day.'

'You can't do that. Anyway, I think Sandra would have something to say on the subject. As long as you don't allow your mam and dad to take Anne-Marie you won't let Linda down. Now, let's not have any more talk like that.'

'I'll try.' He lifted the corner of Linda's skirt. 'Is this for Lind?'

'Yes. Do you remember the outfit?'

'Sure.'

'But do you remember what's so specific about it?'

'No. I know she liked it though.'

'She called these her lucky clothes.'

'Why?'

'Because she was wearing them the night you proposed.'

He closed his eyes and a smile crossed his lips. 'Oh yes, I remember now.' He re-opened his eyes. 'She looked enchanting that evening. Her gorgeous auburn hair hung in waves across her shoulders, and her stunning green eyes sparkled when I asked her to marry me.' He took a handkerchief from his jean's pocket and blew his nose. 'She was my life, Rach. How am I going to cope without her?'

I put Anne-Marie down in the carrycot and held Stu in my arms. 'We'll help you.'

I pushed open the glass door into the funeral parlour. Stu followed with Anne-Marie. She looked gorgeous in the pink lace dress he'd chosen for her to wear. One of the outfits Linda had bought in Mothercare less than an hour before she was killed.

'Mr Pearson.' The funeral director moved closer to look at Anne-Marie. 'She's beautiful.'

'Thank you.' Stu gave a half smile.

'Take a seat and I'll make sure Linda's ready for you.' The undertaker disappeared through an arch.

'I'm not sure I can do this, Rach.'

'Yes, you can. Linda needs to meet Anne-Marie.'

'Can't you take her?'

I squeezed his hand. 'I'll come in with you, if you like?'

The funeral director returned. 'She's ready for you now. Take your time. Go in whenever you're ready.'

'Thanks.' I turned to Stu. 'Ready?'

His face paled. I took his shaking hand as we inched through the arch and turned right into the small low-lit room, greeted by soft instrumental music and flickering candles. The coffin was on a raised platform in the centre. Stu held back, but I put my arm around him and guided him to the open casket.

'Look, Stu,' I said, 'she just looks like she's asleep.'

He lifted his head to glance inside. 'Oh God, I'm sorry but I can't do this.' He passed Anne-Marie to me. 'You do it. Please, Rach.'

I patted his arm. 'Okay. You sit outside and wait.'

'Look what you made, Lind.' I held Anne-Marie over Linda. 'And you were right, a girl, your little Anne-Marie.' My eyes poured tears and my words were full of sobs. 'We're going to help Stu bring up your gorgeous daughter and we'll make sure she knows everything about her lovely mummy.'

Anne-Marie let out a low-pitched scream. I moved to the door entrance. 'Stu, can you take her?'

He headed over, his eyes glazed from tears. 'Hey, what's up little one?' Stu took Anne-Marie. 'We'll wait in there.' He signalled with his head.

'I shan't be long.' I re-entered the chapel of rest and took a seat next to my friend, not saying a word just holding her ice-cold hand and remembering. Remembering the last ten years since we'd been friends. I smiled at the bad influence she'd been to me at times. I smiled at the good times when we'd first met Stu and Joe. That time I'd got cross with her on the park bench after that woman told us all off for canoodling. I was embarrassed and scared while Linda thought it was a hoot. How she'd supported me when I'd learned Joe was my brother, although thankfully that had been a mistake. Linda may have been a messed-up teen but she'd grown into a stable, loyal wife and would've been an ace mam.

I stood up and leaned over the casket. She looked stunning, her hair and make-up done to perfection and the clothes looked gorgeous. They were the right choice. I dug into my bag, took out a photograph of me and Linda, and put it next to her, along with a letter I'd written. 'I love you, my friend and I'll never forget you.' I kissed her cold forehead.

Chapter Twenty-Three

Rachel

The organist stopped after the congregation finished singing 'Abide with Me'. I closed the hymn book and took the notes from my bag.

The vicar signalled for me to go up to the lectern. 'Rachel, Linda's best friend, will now read a eulogy.'

Joe squeezed my fingers. 'I'm here if you need me.'

'Thanks.' Shaking, I headed to the platform.

The vicar whispered, 'You'll be fine.'

I climbed two steps, looked out to the congregation, took a deep breath, and referred to my notes. I coughed. 'Stuart, or Stu as we've always known him, has asked me to say a few words about his wife, Linda. She was my best friend but more than that, she was like a sister. We first met at Woolies over ten years ago and connected almost instantly. Although we were both sixteen, Linda had left school and was in full time employment whereas I'd continued my education working Saturdays only. Once my 'A' levels had finished, she convinced me to go full time at Woolworths, although I didn't need much persuading. I was tired of studying and loved the idea of earning more cash. My parents blamed Linda for this decision, saying she was a bad influence.' Smiling, I glanced across at Mum and Dad. 'Thankfully, once they got to know her, they came to love her.

Of course, I won't say she was always a good influence because that wasn't the case. If she were here, she'd tell you that herself.'

The congregation gave a little laugh.

'But I loved her and now that she's gone part of me has gone too. I didn't know her as a child, I only know what Linda and her mam told me. She was pretty with freckles on her nose, an animal lover, and she adored jigsaws spending hours putting the pieces together on wet weekends. In her younger years she had a couple of pets. Whiskers, a tortoiseshell cat, and Pepper, a black and white rabbit, although Sandra tells me she was the one who ended up cleaning out the hutch.'

The congregation offered up another small laugh.

'She was a troubled teen,' I continued. 'Although proficient at whatever she put her hand to, she couldn't always see that herself. Her confidence was low despite becoming one of Woolworths' youngest supervisors' – I looked out to the congregation and spotted Mr Peters and Gloria – 'and when I persuaded her to go for the manageress job at Walkers, a new boutique' – I glanced at Mr and Mrs Walker in the fourth pew on the right – 'she took to the job like she'd been doing it forever. She knew exactly which colours suited someone and what type of blouse to wear with a certain skirt to make the perfect outfit, or which piece of jewellery set it off. Mr Walker said he'd never known a young woman with such natural flare in fashion.' I turned over the page and coughed to clear my throat. 'It was love at first sight when she met Stu. They met on a blind date, set up by his best friend Joe, my now fiancé. For the first date we all went to the pictures and afterwards Stu took Linda home on his motorbike. From that day the four of us spent as much time together as possible. Strolls in the park, playing darts at The Black Horse, or coffee at Elmo's. At one point Stu and Linda went through a rough patch but true love always finds a way and it wasn't long before they were back together and Stu was down on one knee proposing.

Linda became the perfect wife. I teased her on more than one occasion about being a Stepford wife. She was a brilliant cook and a skilful baker. Her cakes were the lightest sponge I'd ever tasted. She learned new skills in homecraft including curtain making, blinds, and accessories. All Linda ever wanted was to have her own family, a husband and a horde of kids, so it was no surprise when she became pregnant quickly after she and Stu married.

From the moment her pregnancy was confirmed she insisted she was having a girl, and at only the size of a plum, she named the baby Anne-Marie. Somehow, Linda knew she was having a girl, and she was right. Stu, Sandra, Joe and I will make sure Anne-Marie grows up to know how much her mummy loved her and what a wonderful woman she was.' Sniffling, I dabbed my eyes. Joe came to my side and wrapped his arm around me.

'I shall miss her every day' – I looked towards the coffin – 'but don't worry, Linda, Joe and I will be there for Stu and your gorgeous baby girl.' I let Joe lead me back to the pew and once there let out my tears.

Sandra hugged Anne-Marie to her chest as we stood by Linda's graveside, her coffin in place ready to be lowered. At least the rain had stopped and the sun was out. Joe held my hand as I sobbed. He had his other arm around Stu. Through a mist of tears, I glanced around at the mourners. Phil was here with Mel. I wondered when he'd got back. Harry and Debs from the pub, Elmo, Mr and Mrs Walker, Mr Peters, Gloria, Stu's parents, Sandra and Keith, Peggy and Adam, Kate, my mum and dad with Jenny by their side. Many more people who I didn't recognise. Maybe they were customers from either Woolies or the boutique.

When Linda's coffin was lowered into the ground, I wanted to scream but instead squeezed Joe's hand tighter. Stu buried his head into Joe's shoulder.

The vicar said, 'In sure and certain hope of the resurrection to eternal life through our Lord Jesus Christ, we commend to Almighty God our sister Linda and we commit her body to the ground, earth to earth, ashes to ashes, dust to dust.'

Anne-Marie gave a high-pitched cry. Was she able to sense it was her mam? Or maybe she was hungry? Sandra shielded the baby under her coat to protect her from the cold wind.

Stu, Joe and I moved closer to the grave and each threw a red rose onto the coffin. Joe held me tightly. Other mourners followed. Some tossed a handful of soil while others threw roses. Peggy took Anne-Marie from Sandra while she wept in Keith's arms.

The vicar spoke again, 'O God, by whose mercy the faithful departed find rest, send your holy Angel to watch over this grave. Through Christ our Lord. Amen.'

Stu fell to his knees. 'Linda, Linda,' he screamed.

I pulled back from Joe. I had to be strong. 'Stu needs you,' I said. 'Go to him.'

'Are you sure?'

'Yes. He needs you more.'

Joe helped his best friend from the ground. Stu cried in his arms.

Harry and Debs handed out tea and coffees to the mourners as they entered The Blackhorse.

Stu sat with his parents. Keith, and Sandra holding Anne-Marie, joined them. I was about to sit down with my family when Mel and Phil came over to me.

'Phil' – I gave him a hug – 'when did you get back?'

'Last night. There was no way I wouldn't come. I had to be here for you. How are you holding up?'

My eyes misted up again. I moved out of his hold. 'You know.'

He blinked. 'She'll be missed.'

'She will. How long are you back for?'

'For good. Jan's staying out there though.'

Joe was by my side. 'Phil, Mel. Thanks for coming.'

'There's no way we wouldn't be here,' Mel said.

Phil shook his head. 'Such tragic news. Linda was such a bubbly young woman.'

'She was.' Joe lit up a cigarette and passed the packet to Phil. 'Smoke?'

'Cheers.' Phil took one.

Joe flicked his lighter and Phil bent his head closer and took a puff to light the cigarette.

'We're just heading over to sit with our families,' Joe said. 'Why don't you join us?'

'Thanks, although we don't want to intrude?'

'You won't be,' I said. 'They'll be pleased to see you both, particularly Jen.'

'It will be lovely to see Jen again.' Phil smiled. 'She was great company in Paris.'

We picked up our coffees from the ledge and headed over to the others.

'Mum, Dad, Peggy, Adam' – I set my cup and saucer down on the table and pulled a chair out – 'you remember Phil?'

Dad stood up. 'Yes of course. How are you, son?'

'Good thanks. How about you, Mr Webster? I heard you've been poorly?'

'Dicky heart but doing all right thanks. Retired now. Rosalind and I have moved to the seafront at Lytham St Annes. We've not sold up here yet but that's the plan.'

'That sounds wonderful.' Phil turned to Peggy and Adam. 'And how are you folks?'

Peggy fiddled with the gold cross chain around her neck. 'We're doing okay thanks.'

'Wish we were getting together under happier circumstances.' Phil sipped his coffee. 'How's your little lad? Ben, isn't it?'

'He's doing well, thanks' – Peggy dabbed her eyes with a tissue – 'my sister's looking after him. Yes, so sad about poor Linda. She was like one of the family. Have you met her daughter?'

Phil shook his head. 'No, not yet.'

Mel, still standing said, 'Do you think they'd mind if I went over for a peep?'

'I got up from the table. 'No, Mel, Stu would love that, I'm sure. I'll take you over.'

Chapter Twenty-Four

Rachel

I awoke to rain thrashing on the window and Joe standing over me.

'At last, you're awake. I've been trying to wake you for the last ten minutes.'

I held my head. 'Sorry. I shouldn't have drunk so much last night.'

Joe perched on the bed next to me. 'I've made you a cuppa.'

'Thanks.' I glanced at the alarm clock. 'Aren't you late for work?'

'The governor's given me extra time off which brings me to...'

I pulled myself up into the sitting position. 'What?'

'I've spoken to your boss too. He's happy for you to take more time, and not only that has offered us his place at Southport.'

'Again? That's so kind of him.'

'I know.' He passed me the cup of tea. 'And at no charge.'

'Cheers.' I took a sip. 'But we can't go. We need to be here for Stu.'

'No, we don't because Stu's going back with his mam and dad.'

I put the cup down. 'Not for good, I hope?'

'Nope. He's got a month off work but whether he decides to stay there that long, I don't know.'

'I slipped out of bed past Joe, put on my dressing gown, headed over to the dressing table and sat down at the mirror. 'He will bring Anne-Marie back, won't he?'

'You don't have to get up yet.'

'I do, and you didn't answer me. He is going to bring Anne-Marie back home?'

'As far as I know, yes. I don't think he'd dare not do, after you told him he'd be letting Linda down.'

'He told you that.'

'Yes.' He stood up and stared out of the window. 'That rain's awful.'

'And you want to go away in it?'

'The weekend's looking good.' Joe put his arms around my neck.

I leaned the back of my head into him. 'All right then, let's do it. Maybe getting away from here could help.'

※

This time when we drove into Coastal Lane and stopped outside number seven it was Joe driving. He pulled on the handbrake. 'You all right, babe?'

I rubbed my eyes. 'Not really, but there's nothing you can do to help.'

He patted my leg. 'It'll get easier. Come on, let's get inside and I'll put the kettle on.' Joe stepped out of the car, took the suitcase from the boot, and headed up the path. I got out, locked up the Ford Escort, and reached Joe as he turned the key in the lock. When we pushed open the door the heat hit us just like it had last time and we were greeted by the sweet floral perfume from a vase of chrysanthemums on the sideboard, and the woody smell from the lively flames in the grate.

'I'd forgotten how lovely this place was.' I sniffed the golden and pink-blush blooms. 'These are gorgeous.' I sneezed. 'But not so great for my hay fever.'

Lapping waves with a rhythmic rise and fall entranced me. They danced outwards away from the shore with a soft ripple gliding across the shingle. I picked up a large pebble. 'Look, a wishing stone. See the white line that goes all around it?'

Joe put his arm around me. 'What are you going to wish?'

I shrugged. 'My wish won't come true. I want to wish that Linda hadn't died but we can't undo something like that. Maybe I should wish for a time transporter so we could go back and make sure she was nowhere near that blasted car.'

'You should make a wish, babe. Linda would want you to.'

'Okay.' I moulded the stone in my palm before taking it in my fingers, held my arm back, and threw the nugget into the sea, wishing that, if I couldn't bring my friend back then I'd wish there was definitely a heaven and she was happy there.

Joe rubbed his upper lip. He suited that moustache and beard. 'You know the decree nisi should be through any day.'

'That's awesome. Must've been awful for you still married to that screw-up.'

'Yeah, but I was thinking…'

I kissed him on the lips. 'What?'

'Six weeks afterwards the absolute will come through. Maybe we should be setting a date.'

I pulled away from him. 'Not now, Joe. I can't even contemplate something like that.'

'But it's what Linda would want.'
'Maybe, but not now.'

We lay on the bed with the drapes wide open so we could gaze at the stars.

'That there' – Joe pointed – 'is Orion's belt.'

I curled up closer to him. 'You remembered.'

'I did.' He stroked my hair. 'Rach, you do still love me?'

'Of course. What sort of question is that?'

'And you do want to marry me?'

'Yes.'

'Then why can't we set a date?'

'It's too soon. I don't want to be thinking of a happy ever after when my friend has barely been in the ground.'

'Sorry, babe. That was a bit insensitive of me but…'

I sighed. 'What?'

'If this has taught me anything, it's that we should grab happiness while we can. I want you to be my wife. I want you to have my baby. I want us to be a family. Before…'

'Before what?'

'Before it's too late. Supposing something happened to you? Or something happened to me. Wouldn't you want a child we'd made to help you through it?'

'I suppose so.'

'Then when can we get married?'

'Let's say sometime in spring. How about March? But we keep it to ourselves and when we do get married, we slip off and have a quiet affair.'

'That's fine with me.' He smothered my neck with kisses and slipped off my nightdress.

I succumbed to his seduction, losing myself in our lovemaking, escaping from reality for a short while.

Over the next few days Joe and I walked for miles along the beach. We even had a bit of a paddle although the water was awfully cold. We made love each night and morning and for short periods of time I was able to forget my best friend had died. Eileen kept us provided with her wonderful casseroles so we didn't need to worry about cooking.

On our sixth day when we were strolling along the shoreline, Joe said, 'Hey, I was going through the local rag that Eileen left for us and it seems an Indian restaurant opened in the village last week. Walking distance too. Do you fancy it?'

'I don't know.'

'Come on, Rach. Remember our first Indian meal when we were with Mel and that dickhead what was his name?'

'Sam. Yes, I do. Awkward, but the food was yummy.'

'Let's do it, then. I'll take a hike around there after dinner this evening and book us in for tomorrow, and I'll let Eileen know there's no need to cook us dinner.' He pleaded with those gorgeous chocolate eyes.

'Okay.'

'Thanks, Rach.' He picked me up and swung me around. 'You know, babe' – he stroked my cheek – 'Linda wouldn't want you to stop living.'

'I know but...'

'Let's go for a paddle.'

'What now?'

'Yes. Nothing more romantic than being in the water under the stars.' He pulled off his socks and shoes, rolled up his trousers and ran closer to the waves. 'Come on.'

I smiled. 'Okay.' I pulled off my boots and tights. Threw them next to Joe's socks and shoes and joined him.

He took my hand and we strode into the gushing waves. I jumped out again.

'Chicken.' Joe held out his arm. 'Come on.'

I gritted my teeth and re-took his hand and we strode out knee deep into the groaning sea.

⊱

The owner opened the door for us. 'Welcome. Shall I take your coats?'

'Thank you.' I slipped off my black maxi coat and passed it to him.

'I'll keep mine with me, cheers.' Joe patted the pocket of his leather jacket. 'Got my wallet and stuff in here.'

'Of course.' The waiter folded my coat over his arm and showed us to a table close to a stairway. He pulled back a chair for me. 'Madam.'

'Thank you.' I sat down facing the front.

'This is nice.' Joe took off his jacket and hung it over the back of the chair.

'Yes.' I glanced around the quaint restaurant with its identical small square tables covered in white and plum linen cloths matching the chair cushions.

The waiter passed a menu to each of us. 'Can I get you some drinks?'

'Do you have any lager?' Joe asked.

'Yes, sir. We have Heineken.'

Joe looked at me. I nodded.

'A pint please,' Joe said, 'and a half with lime.'

'Yes, sir. Can I get you some poppadoms?'

'Yes, thank you.' I perused the menu once the waiter left our table. 'Shall we be a little more adventurous than our first time?'

'Sure. Why not?'

'How about we get two mains and have half each?'

'Sounds good. Do you want to choose?'

'I could do, or we could choose one dish each?'

'Nah. You go for it.'

'Okay.' I looked down at the menu. 'Let's go for a chicken dhansak and a chicken biryani.'

'That sounds cool.'

'The dhansak's quite spicy but I'm sure you tried it when we went out with Stu and Linda.' I wiped my eyes. 'Oh, Joe, we'll never be able to do that again.'

Joe squeezed my hand from across the table. 'I know, babe, but hold on to the memories.' He picked up the menu. 'Now, what about side dishes, and you love that garlic naan.'

'All right. Mushroom bhaji, lady's fingers, that's ochre, Bombay potatoes and saag aloo?'

The waiter returned with our drinks, four poppadoms and chutneys. 'Are you ready to order?'

'Yes, thanks.' Joe repeated what I'd suggested and added, 'Oh and a garlic naan and a chapati, please. We plan to share.'

The waiter scribbled on his little notepad. 'Shan't be long.'

Joe raised his glass. 'To us.'

'To us.' I clinked my glass with his.

The door opened. A large group chatting and laughing came through. Another waiter showed them to their tables on the opposite side of the restaurant to us. He pushed four of the small tables together. The noise heightened as they all sat down.

'There goes our quiet evening.' I munched on a poppadom.

'We shan't let it spoil things.'

The laughter got louder. This wasn't right. They were carrying on as normal. Feeling my tears, I said, 'Sorry, Joe. I can't do this.' I hurried outside, perched on the wall by the sea and wept.

Joe was by my side. He tightened his arms around me. 'It's all right, babe.'

'No, it's not. This isn't right. We shouldn't be here enjoying ourselves when my best friend is dead.'

Joe faced me, putting his hands on my shoulders. 'Rach, Linda wouldn't want you to stop living. She'd want you to make the most of your life. You're still here. I'm still here. We can't waste that.' He kissed me softly on the lips before taking my hand.

We trudged along the sand under the starlit sky. Moonlight reflected in the gently humming waves.

'Choose one,' Joe said.

'Sorry?'

'Pick a star.'

Sniffling, I blew my nose. 'Why?'

'Humour me. Just do it.'

'All right. That one there.' I pointed.

'Okay. That's Linda looking down and she doesn't want you to be sad.'

I wiped my eyes. 'I've been thinking...'

'Yeah?'

'We should head back home tomorrow.'

'Really? We don't have to go yet. There's no rush.'

'I know, but I don't want to abuse our employers' goodwill, plus I need to get in touch with the baby shop about the pram.'

'But you can't sort out delivery until Stu's back.'

'No, but I can distract myself from thinking too much if I'm back at work.'

'I know what you mean, and if that's what you want, then we'll pack up and go home tomorrow.'

'Thank you.'

Joe held my hand tightly. 'It will get easier, babe. Early days right now.'

Chapter Twenty-Five

Rachel

Lizzie was on the phone when I passed through reception and gave me a little wave as I entered the back office. Betty hurried over from her desk. 'How are you, pet?'

I shrugged. 'You know.'

She put her arm around my shoulder and guided me to the kitchen area. 'Sit yourself down and I'll make you a coffee.'

'I should really get upstairs. John will be wondering where I am.'

'No, he'll be fine.' She filled the kettle. 'Now sit down like a good girl and let Aunty Betty take care of you.'

My throat closed up. I didn't want this. Why couldn't people just leave me alone? I took a deep breath and forced a smile.

Betty spooned coffee into the mug and poured on boiling water. 'Here you go.' She squeezed my hand. 'I wished I'd been here when you got back from Southport. Did it help going away?'

I thought back to the sea, the stars, and the wishing stone, which seemed so long ago now. I smiled. 'It was nice.'

'And what about you, pet. How are you really doing?'

'Better when allowed to lose myself in work. Look, thanks for the coffee, but I really should be getting upstairs.' I picked up the coffee mug.

Betty patted me on the back. 'Don't bottle things up, pet.'

Joe came into the kitchen. 'That's better,' he said. 'Sometimes I wish I had a job like yours where I didn't have to worry about showering and changing before I can even sit down for a cuppa.'

'I bet.' His hands were the worst. Poor bloke. He'd spent hours cleaning the stubborn grease off them the night before Linda and Stu's wedding. Stu's were the same. The penalty for working on cars, I supposed. I was glad I didn't have that problem. 'At least you're clean now. Sit yourself down as dinner's ready.' I headed to the stove and took out the chicken casserole. It smelt nice but I wasn't hungry. I dished up a huge portion for Joe, and a smaller one for myself, along with boiled rice, and placed the plates on the table.

'Mmm, this smells gorgeous, Rach.' Joe picked up his cutlery and tucked into the food. 'Yum. It tastes good too.' He glared at me. 'You not eating?'

'Yep. Just a little slower than you.' I slid some casserole onto my fork and forced it into my mouth, feeling like I was going to gag. Joe was watching me so I shoved in another couple of forkfuls before setting my knife and fork down into the finished position.

'You need to eat more than that.'

I sighed. 'I'm not hungry.'

'Rach, you've barely eaten anything for weeks. Your clothes are hanging off you.' He squeezed my hand. 'Please, eat. Do it for me.'

'I can't eat another bite.' I held my stomach. 'I'm going to be sick.'

'Are you pregnant?'

I shook my head. 'No. I'm just not hungry.' The doorbell rang. Glad of the opportunity to escape I shot up from the table. 'I wonder who that is. I'll go.' I hurried out of the kitchen into the hallway and answered the door. 'Stu.'

'Hi, Rach. Sorry for turning up unannounced but I've just got back from my mam's and needed to see a friendly face.'

'Where's Anne-Marie? You've not left her in Dorset, have you?'

'No. She's in the car. I wanted to make sure you were home before getting her out. I'll be two ticks.'

I left the door ajar and rushed into the kitchen. 'It's Stu. He's just got back. I'll get him some dinner.'

The front door closed and Stu pushed the carrycot on wheels into the kitchen. 'Hi, Joe.' Stu put the brake on the pram.

Joe rose from the table and hugged Stu. 'How you doing, mate?'

'All I can say is I'm surprised I've got any hair left.' He shook his head. 'My bloody mother drove me mad. I swear if I didn't get out of that house, I'd have killed her.'

'Sit down.' I peeped into the carrycot. Anne-Marie was sleeping. 'She's grown.'

'Yeah, and I think you were right about that colic as she seems to have settled the last day or so.'

I served out dinner for Stu and put the plate in front of him. 'You must be starving driving all the way back from down south.'

'Cheers, Rach. Yeah, I am. Left this morning but had to make a couple of stops to feed and change Anne-Marie.'

'She's beautiful. I can't believe she's almost six weeks.' I turned away to hide my tears. Almost six weeks since Linda had died too. I blew my nose. 'Can I get you a cuppa, Stu, or a beer?'

'A cuppa would be great. Better not have alcohol as I'm driving with precious cargo.'

'You can always stay the night.' Joe turned to me. 'That would be okay, wouldn't it?'

'Sure. It won't take me five minutes to make a bed up, and I presume you have nappies, clean clothes, and milk for Anne-Marie in the car.'

'Yes. Yes, I do. Cool. I'll have that beer then. Cheers.'

I took two cans from the fridge. 'I'll get some glasses.'

Joe pulled on my sleeve. 'It's okay, Rach, we'll drink from the can. You not having one?'

'No, ta.'

Stu had almost cleaned his plate. 'This casserole's lovely.'

'Fancy some seconds?' I asked.

'Sure. If it's going. I'm absolutely starving. Didn't even have brekkie as I had to get out of the house quickly to prevent me from doing time.' He chuckled.

'Oh dear, that doesn't sound good.' I headed over to the stove. 'Would you like some more, Joe? There's plenty.'

'Go on then. I'll keep my mate company.'

'So, what went on between you and your mam?' I dished up a couple of helpings of the stew and placed the plates in front of the boys.

Stu shook his head. 'She drove me bloody mad. Kept going on and on that Anne-Marie's name should be Grace. I told her Linda had chosen her name and I'd no plans to change that.

'And this morning she started on about it again, only this time added, what difference did it make to Linda when she wasn't even here anymore.' Stu swigged the beer. 'For God's sake. I nearly swung for her. I know she never liked her but to say that.' He sighed, shaking his head.

I joined Stu and Joe at the table. 'I'm glad you didn't listen to her.'

'No way would I. Linda's wishes are my wishes. Anyway, like you pointed out earlier, Anne-Marie's almost six weeks which means I have to register her and wondered if you'd come with me, Rach. You too, Joe, if you like. I'd rather not go on my own.'

'Of course,' I said, 'I'll give Betty a ring in a moment and ask her to let Mr Strange and John know I'll be in late tomorrow.'

Stu squeezed my hand. 'Thanks, Rach.'

※

Stu wheeled Anne-Marie into the register office building. He looked up at the sign. 'This way.'

I held the door while he pushed the pram into reception. 'We've come to register a birth,' I said to the woman behind a typewriter.

She glanced up and fixed her glasses in place. 'Do you have an appointment?'

'No.' Stu blinked. 'Sorry, I didn't know I needed one.'

The woman smiled. 'It's all right. We can still fit you in.'

'Phew.' Stu let out a deep breath. 'Thank God. Today's the deadline to do it.'

'You left it a bit tight then. What's your name?'

'Stuart Pearson.'

She turned to me. 'And you must be the baby's mother?' She smiled.

'No.' I moved closer to the desk. 'No, I'm a friend. Her mam died.'

'I'm so sorry.' The receptionist came out from behind the desk and peeped into the carrycot. 'Looks like Dad's doing a grand job though. Let me see if the registrar can fit you in now.' She headed to a door on the right, knocked, and walked in.

I put my arm around, Stu. 'You okay?'

He nodded. 'Think so. Cheers for being with me and for doing the talking.'

The woman returned. 'You can go in now.'

'Thanks.' I picked up Anne-Marie from the carrycot and followed Stu into the room.

Chapter Twenty-Six

Peggy

Joe brushed a hand through his hair. 'Please, Mam, you've got to help me do something. She's wasting away.'

I put a mug of tea in front of him. 'What does she say?'

'She won't talk about anything. "Just wants to lose herself in work," as she puts it.'

'To be honest, love, it's not that I haven't bothered trying to see her, but she's not been answering my calls, and I haven't pushed it because I know she needs time to grieve. Should I come over to yours?'

'Yes, please, come on Sunday. Bring Dad too and I'll take him out for a pint, that's if you can get Kate to babysit Ben.'

The front door slammed shut. Kate hurried into the kitchen. 'Hello, big bro. How are you?' She lowered her voice to almost a whisper. 'I was so sorry to hear about Linda. How's Rachel coping?'

'Not great to be honest but then they had been best friends for years. I don't suppose I'd cope any better if it had been Stu.'

'No.' She bit her lip.

'When does Teresa get back from the States?'

'She doesn't,' Peggy answered. 'At least not for a while anyway. She's met someone out there and decided to stay. Dad's promised to take me out there to visit.'

Joe smiled. 'That's wonderful. Good on Dad. Can't be easy for him with Mike out there.'

'No, you're right. I was quite shocked.'

'I'm pleased things are finally working out for her.' Joe gulped the rest of his tea and placed the mug on the draining board. 'Right, I'd best get off, otherwise Rach will wonder where I've got to.' He kissed me on the cheek. 'See you Sunday.'

Joe opened the door. 'Hi,' he whispered. 'Remember, pretend this was your idea.'

'Sure, love.' I kissed him on the cheek and Adam shook his hand.

'Who's at the door?' Rachel came into the hallway. 'Peggy, Adam. Is everything okay?'

'Yes, all fine,' I said. 'Kate's looking after Ben and Adam happened to mention we'd not seen you for a while, so, I hope you don't mind but we thought we'd pop in to see how you're doing.'

'Oh right. Come in but excuse the mess' – she headed into the lounge and picked up an office file from the sofa and plumped up the cushions– 'only I wasn't expecting visitors.'

We followed her in. Adam peered around. 'Looks tidy enough to me.'

Rachel put the paperwork on the sideboard and took a navy velvet scrunchie from a trinket dish. She dragged her hair back into a ponytail making her face look gaunt. 'Sit down and I'll put the kettle on. Tea? Coffee?'

'Actually, Rach,' Joe said, 'do you mind if I take Dad to the pub? He's not been there since it changed hands.'

'No, course not, but why don't we all go?'

'Well, you'd better stay here, babe, cos if you remember, Stu's turning up later. It would be awful if he arrived and found an empty house.'

Rachel twiddled her chunky gold bangle. 'Oh yes, okay. You go then, but don't stay out too long.'

'We won't. We'll be back before closing.' Joe brushed his lips against hers.

He was right, she looked so thin and had aged at least ten years. 'Tell you what, Rachel' – I slipped off my coat and placed it on the back of the settee – 'why don't I come and help?'

She shrugged her shoulders. 'If you like.'

I followed her into the kitchen and she flicked the kettle on. 'Coffee or tea?'

'Coffee sounds nice.' I took two china mugs from the hooks under the cupboard. 'Tea or coffee for you?'

'Nothing for me, Peg. I don't fancy anything right now.'

'Then don't do one especially for me. Look, come and sit down, only I'd like to talk to you.' I took a seat at the table.

She clenched her fists. 'This is a set-up, isn't it? Out with it then.'

'Not at all.'

'Yes, it is' – She raised her voice – 'Joe's got you here to speak to me and that's why he's gone out with his dad. Okay, say your piece. I'm sure you're dying to.'

'Rachel. Don't be silly.'

'Silly, am I?' She flung her arms in the air. 'Why the hell can't people just bloody leave me alone?'

I stood up and put my arms around her. 'Joe's worried about you, and seeing you now, I can understand why. He said you're not eating. How much weight have you lost? A stone? More? Why aren't you eating?'

She pushed me away. 'It's none of your business.'

'You're not going down the road our Kate did, are you?'

'If you mean, am I anorexic, then no. For God's sake, Peg, my best friend has died.'

'I know that, love, but you have to try and move forward.'

'So, tell me' – she took a deep breath before raising her voice even louder – 'if it had been your Sheila, how would you be feeling?'

I shook my head. 'But that's different. Sheila's my sister.'

'Exactly, you don't bloody understand. Linda may not have been my sister by blood but we were sisters. We helped each other through everything. I was her bridesmaid and she was supposed to be mine. But now that's not going to happen, is it?' Rachel screamed at me, punching my arms, before finally settling down and sobbing into my chest while I stroked her back.

Chapter Twenty-Seven

Rachel

I parked the Escort, locked up, headed to the gallery and knocked on the door.

Phil opened it. 'Hello, you. What a wonderful surprise.'

'Well, you did say to come and check out what you've been doing with the place. You mentioned something about reopening?'

'Yes, that's right.' He opened the door wider. 'Come in, don't stand out in the cold. October's hit us with a vengeance.'

'Cheers. You putting the kettle on?'

'Naturally. I may even have some Jammie Dodgers.'

I followed him into the kitchen. 'I thought I'd do a write-up in the newspaper to help you get a little more footfall.'

'Always thinking of others.' He put the kettle on the stove.

'Don't you think you should get an electric one?'

'Nah. This lets me know when its boiled, particularly helpful if I'm moving around the gallery.'

'Good point.' I took a seat at the table and dug into my bag for a notebook. 'It must be lonely here for you without Jan.'

'A bit, and strange you should mention that as I'm planning on putting in an ad for a young apprentice. You still black no sugar?'

'Yep.'

He spooned Nescafé into two porcelain mugs. 'That way I'll be helping a college leaver while at the same time not floating around in this huge space on my own.'

The kettle whistled. He took it off the stove and poured boiling water into the mugs. After stirring he brought the coffees over to the table. 'Actually, maybe we could kill two birds with one stone. You could do an advert with the write-up.'

'Sure. I can do that.'

'Now where did I put those biscuits?' He rooted in the cupboard. 'Ah, finally.' He pulled out a packet. 'I knew I had them somewhere.' He placed the biscuits in front of me. 'Help yourself.'

'No, I'm all right, thanks. Coffee's fine for me.'

He perched on a seat next to me. 'Am I hearing correctly? Rachel Webster's turning down a Jammie Dodger?'

I hid my face behind the mug.

'You're not doing too well, are you?'

'I'd be doing a damn sight better if people stopped going on at me.'

He took my hand in his. 'People care. It's good to talk about these things.'

'So they say, but to be honest, I'd rather not.'

'Have you told Joe how you're feeling?'

I shrugged. 'Sort of. Not really. I don't know. He doesn't understand. He wants to set a date for the wedding.'

Phil smiled. 'That's good, isn't it?'

'Is it?'

'I'd say so after you've waited this long.'

'I know but now it's different.'

'Don't push him away, Rach.'

'You don't understand. No one does. Now please, I don't want to talk about it anymore.'

'Fine, but just one more thing.'

I bit my lip. 'Phil, I really don't...'

'Listen' – he held my hand tighter – 'if Linda were sitting here now instead of you, what would you be wanting her to do?'

I squinted. 'What do you mean?'

'Let me make it clearer. Would you want her to live her life or stop living?'

'Live her life of course.'

He released my hand. 'I rest my case. Let Joe in. So, about this wedding?'

'I told him March but that was really just to shut him up.'

'A spring wedding would be nice.'

'I suppose so. Anyway, enough about me. How's it going with Mel?'

It was his turn to shrug. 'You know. She's a lovely girl and all that but at the end of the day she's not you.'

'Oh, Phil. Please don't carry a torch for me.'

'Easier said than done but I'll do you a deal.'

I swallowed a mouthful of coffee. 'Go on?'

'I'll stop mooning over you if you promise to try and move on with your life, and get yourself married to that great guy of yours.'

'All right' – I kissed him on the cheek – 'I'll try.'

'Good girl. Wait there, I've got a present for you.'

'For me?'

'Yes.' Phil hurried out of the room and returned in minutes with a large canvas.

'A new painting?' I asked expecting a picture of the Eiffel Tower or River Seine.

He turned the frame around.

'Oh my God, Phil. It's beautiful. How?'

'Jen gave me an old photo of you both for me to work from.'

I studied the picture. 'It's wonderful.' I wiped my eyes with a tissue. 'You've got Linda down to a T. Her auburn hair and gorgeous green eyes. Linda and I had our arms around each other's shoulders. 'We look so happy.'

'Do you remember where you had it taken?'

I licked my lips. 'I'm not sure. Blackpool maybe? We went there with Joe and Stu. The pebbles on the beach, the waves on the sea, the cerulean blue sky, and you've even got the seagulls. 'This is so thoughtful, Phil. Thank you.'

He placed the picture against the wall. 'I'm glad you like it.'

'Are you still taking commissions?'

'Yes, why?'

'I wondered whether you'd do me a portrait of Linda from the photo.'

'I can but there's no need to pay me.'

'No, I must. I'd like to buy it as a Christmas present for Stu. Does that give you enough time?'

'It does. Mate's rates then.'

'No. I don't want any special deals. Charge what you'd normally charge.'

'Very well. I'll start work on it tomorrow.'

'Thank you and thank you for my lovely gift. May I take it home today?'

'Do you mind if I hold on to it for a little longer? Only I'd like to frame it.'

'Like I said, you're so thoughtful.' I gulped back the coffee. 'I suppose we should get to work. Want to show me what you've been up to?'

John was just leaving as I arrived back at the office. 'What you got for us?'

'Phil's organising a reopening of the art gallery. He's also looking for an apprentice so I said I'd run an ad alongside the article.'

'Is he now?'

'Yes. To help him with the workload but I think it's also a little lonely for him there on his own.'

'Hold off the advert for now, Rachel, as I have someone in mind for that post.'

'You do?'

'Yes. My daughter. She left college earlier this year and has a job at Budgens while working out what she wants to do for a career. She studied art, and she's good at it too. It would be perfect for her.'

'I'll give Phil a ring and put the feelers out for you.'

'Thanks, it would make me and her mum happy knowing she was with someone we could trust.' He peered up at the clock. 'I'd better be off but I'll speak to my daughter tonight about it. Why don't you tidy your desk and get off home too? Mel will be locking up in a few minutes.'

'Will do. Have a good evening,' I said as he left the office.

Phil had probably left the gallery for the day so I'd ring him at home this evening. That was if Anne-Marie would let me. I chortled to myself. I wondered whether Mel had to rush home. We hadn't spent any proper time together since Linda's accident. I cleared my desk, locked up the drawer, and headed downstairs.

'Hi, you.' Mel fastened her mac. 'Time for a drink?'

'Great minds. I was thinking the same. Can't stay long though as I promised to babysit Anne-Marie this evening so Stu and Joe can get out for a while.'

'The Black Horse?'

If we went there I knew Harry and Debs would start asking questions that I didn't want to answer. 'Tell you what,' I said, 'let's go somewhere no one knows us. How about The Three Horseshoes.'

'Okay.'

I took my maxi coat from the hook, pushed my arms into the sleeves, and buttoned it up as Mel locked up the building. We crossed the road at the zebra crossing and headed down the alleyway where the pub was set back in a corner.

We pulled open the door and found an almost empty pub with just a couple of old blokes propping up the bar. 'What do you fancy to drink?' I asked Mel.

'Half a cider, thanks. Shall I get us a table?'

'If you like.' I slipped off my coat. 'Can you take this for me?'

'Sure.' She took my coat and headed to the back of the pub.

'A diet coke and a half of cider,' I asked the barman.

'Coming up. Anything else?'

'Um, let's go all out' – I chuckled – 'I'll have two packets of cheese and onion crisps too.'

'Righto.' He drew the cider into a glass from a beer tap, flicked the lid from a bottle of coke and poured it into another glass and popped both onto a tray. 'And two packets of crisps.' He plonked the crisps next to the drinks.

I handed him the cash, picked up the tray and made my way to Mel who was sitting in one of two armchairs by a roaring fire. 'Nice spot.' I put the drinks down on the table and sank into the deep-cushioned chair.

She picked up her glass. 'Cheers. It's been ages since we had a drink out with just the two of us.'

'I know. Got any news?'

'Not really. Do you babysit much for Stu?'

'Only a couple of times so far but happy to do it whenever he likes. I don't like the thought of him in the house on his own every evening. It's good for him to get out with Joe.'

'Did you manage to sort out the problem with the pram?'

'Yes, the shop was really understanding. When I explained what had happened with Linda, and how Stu needed something more portable than a Silver Cross, they recommended a Tansad instead. The soft bodied carriage comes off the chassis wheels and slides easily onto the back seat of the car. Much better for Anne-Marie to sleep in too, for example when she stays over at ours, or when she's at Sheila's in the day while Stu's at work. A lot more practical than that carrycot on wheels.'

'Glad it all worked out.'

'And because the Tansad was cheaper it meant I had an extra hundred pounds to spend on other stuff in the shop too. I picked up some dresses, matinee coats, booties, that sort of thing. Stu was well pleased. You seeing Phil tonight?'

'No. He said he's too busy with the gallery stuff.'

I wondered whether he was fobbing her off. 'Did you know he's looking for an apprentice?'

'He mentioned something in passing.'

'Well John reckons it would be perfect for his daughter.'

'I didn't know he had a daughter.'

'She left college in the summer. He has a son too. Fifteen, I think.'

Mel crunched on a crisp. 'I don't think Phil's really into me. Has he said anything to you?'

'What makes you think that?'

'He doesn't seem that keen. It's like he'd rather be friends than boyfriend and girlfriend.'

'And how do you feel about him?' I sipped the coke.

She shrugged. 'I'm not sure. We don't have any chemistry. In fact, I'm thinking about breaking up with him. What do you think?'

I touched her hand. 'You must do what's right for you, Mel. No one else can answer that.'

Chapter Twenty-Eight

Rachel

I put the phone down. 'I'm going to take an early lunchbreak if you don't mind.'

John stubbed a ciggie into an ashtray. 'No problem. Is everything okay?'

'I think so. Actually, it was Linda's mam. She's got Anne-Marie today and asked if I'd like to meet them at the park café.'

'That's good news, isn't it? Hasn't she refused to see the child since her daughter's funeral?'

'Yes, that's right. Let's hope it's good news. It'll be good to meet up which is why I'm loathe to say *no*.'

'And you mustn't. How old is the baby now?'

'Almost three months. Eleven weeks to be precise. You sure it's okay for me to go early?'

'Absolutely. And don't worry about rushing back. We've nothing in the diary.'

'Cheers, John, really appreciate that.' I hurried downstairs, unhooked my coat, and rushed past reception giving Lizzie a quick wave. As I left the building the cold November wind hit me. I slipped on my knitted hat and wrapped a matching scarf around my neck.

I hadn't seen Sandra since Linda's funeral. In fairness to her, it wasn't all her fault as I hadn't made any effort either. Neither of us had wanted to see anyone but at least I'd seen Stu and Anne-Marie on a regular basis, as well as throwing myself into work, whereas Sandra had refused to see anyone.

Scarlet maples welcomed me with waving branches as I rushed through the open metal gates. The park was quiet except for a few dog walkers. A small golden and white spaniel scampered towards me.

'Amber,' a woman called.

I glanced over. My heart pounded. Linda?

'I'm really sorry.' The woman attached a lead to the dog. Close up I could see the woman was nothing like Linda. It had been her black felt hat and auburn hair flicking at the sides that had thrown me.

'That's okay.' I bent down and stroked the animal's head. 'She's lovely. She is a she?'

'Yes. She is.'

'I thought she must be because she's so pretty.'

The woman picked up the dog. 'She's great company too.'

Amber stared at me with big round eyes. My pulse increased. Was Linda communicating to me through the dog? I was going mad. Linda didn't even have brown eyes. 'Look at her,' I said to the owner, 'she's gorgeous. It must be hard to get cross with her?'

'Yes.' She tousled Amber's floppy ears. 'You're spoilt, girl, aren't you?'

I gave the dog another pat. 'Nice to meet you, Amber, but I have to go now. Bye,' I said to the woman.

'Bye, enjoy your day.' The woman returned Amber to the footpath and they went off in the opposite direction.

I hurried to the café, pushed open the door, and was greeted by the immediate heat. At least the sun was shining and had thawed the early morning frost. I peered around the café and spotted Sandra by a window cradling Anne-Marie. I made my way over. 'Hi, Sandra.'

She rose from the seat, lay Anne-Marie in the pram, and turned around to hug me. 'Thanks for coming, Rachel. Sorry I've not been in touch.'

'That's okay. I understand.' I peeped under the pram hood. 'Bless her, she's fast asleep.'

'She wasn't ten minutes ago. I can tell you. She was screaming the roof off. I thought they were going to ask me to leave. Let's sit down.'

I slipped off my coat and placed it on the back of the chair.

Sandra picked up the menu. 'Shall we eat?'

I rubbed my brow. 'If you like.'

She glared at me. 'You look like you need to. Have you lost weight?'

'A little.'

'I'd say more than a little.' She studied the menu. 'What do you fancy? A cheese and pickle baguette?'

'Just a regular sarnie for me.'

'Is that going to be enough?'

'Yes, I'm not very hungry.'

Anne-Marie stirred.

'Is it all right if I hold her?'

'Of course. I'll go up to the counter and order our lunch. Coffee? Tea?'

'Coffee please.' I picked the baby out of the pram. She was getting big. I wondered what Linda would have made of her. She'd have been a brilliant mam.

On returning to the table, Sandra rested her hand on my shoulder. 'How are you really doing?'

I twiddled my hoop earring. 'Much the same. I miss her so much.'

'Yes, me too.' She perched on the seat. 'You know, Rachel, I was a total mess. It was my Keith who made me realise that I couldn't go on like that. He said I needed to make changes to be there for Anne-Marie. And he was right.'

'You talk about me losing weight but you've lost a lot too.'

'The difference is I could afford to.'

'Well, I am trying.'

'I know, love. It's tough. Keith found me a bereavement counsellor. She's really helping me. Up until a month ago, I couldn't even cope with seeing' – she stroked Anne-Marie's cheek – 'this little one, but Linda would've wanted me to be there for her daughter. It was wrong of me to miss out on almost the first two months of her life.'

'You've been seeing Anne-Marie for a month? Stu never mentioned it.'

'I asked him to keep it to himself as I wasn't ready to see anyone else.' She shrugged. 'You're the first person outside my family, apart from Stu, that I've seen. I had to pluck up a lot of courage to come into town today.'

'This counsellor, she's helped you then?'

'Yes, she has. It's a slow job as there's no magic wand, but yes, she's helping. I can give you her details if you like. The organisation is for families but Linda was like family to you. We need to bring back that beautiful girl with sparkling eyes. I know Joe's missing her.'

'Joe spoke to you?'

'No, Stu told me how concerned Joe is about you.' Sandra smiled. 'Anyway, from now on I've agreed to look after Anne-Marie three days a week while Stu's at work. Every Tuesday, Wednesday, and Friday, hence why I have her today.'

'I'm so pleased. She's such a treasure.'

'It wasn't right she was with a stranger all week. Sheila's nice enough but she's not family. Anne-Marie needs to grow up knowing her family cared.'

'What about your job?'

'I couldn't cope with going back to work' – she took a deep breath – 'and they needed to fill my position, and that's fine, as Keith said we can manage without my wage. Much better that I ensure Anne-Marie gets the attention she should from her grandmother and the chance to learn all about her mam.'

I glanced down at Anne-Marie. Her green eyes opened wide. 'She's so like Linda.'

'She is. I understand you bought the pram.'

'Yes. It's not the one she was supposed to have though. That was a navy and white Silver Cross which I'd promised Linda, but that was no good for Stu. This one's better because he can put it in the car, and Anne-Marie has plenty of room.'

'It's lovely to push too. And I love the maroon.'

'Yes, I think Linda would've approved.' I placed Anne-Marie back into the Tansad.

'I've ordered a cot so she can be more comfortable for stayovers at mine. She's staying with me tonight to give Stu a night off.' Sandra tapped the table. 'Look, I'd like us to make a pact. I'll try to be strong if you do the same.'

I shook my head. 'It's so hard.'

'I know, darling, but this isn't doing either of us any good. If Linda were here, she'd be horrified to see how we'd let ourselves go.'

'I thought I had a sign from her earlier.'

'Really? What was that?'

'It sounds stupid.' I bit my lip.

'Go on.'

'Coming through the park I thought I saw her, and then when I realised it wasn't her, this little golden and white spaniel with the most gorgeous floppy ears and brown eyes ran up to me.' I chortled. 'I thought it was Linda communicating to me through the dog. Mad, aren't I?'

'No, I don't think you are. And if it made you feel better, where's the harm? I have things happen like that too. The dog, it sounds like a Kings Charles spaniel.'

'I think it may have been.'

'You know that was Linda's favourite breed. Perhaps you're not as mad as you think and it really was a sign. A sign letting us know that she's still with us.'

A waitress with salt and pepper hair was at our table. 'Cheese and pickle baguette, cheese and pickle sandwich, two coffees?'

'That's us,' I said. 'Thank you. The sandwich is for me.'

The woman placed the tray on the table. She peeped into the pram. 'Aw, they're adorable at that age. Little girl?'

The pink pram set was a bit of a giveaway. 'Yes,' I answered.

'Yours?'

'No, not mine.'

'My granddaughter.' Sandra smiled.

'Grandkids are the best, aren't they? You can always give them back.' The woman chuckled. 'Enjoy your meal.' She hurried away to wipe down some tables.

I laid the serviette across my lap. 'I think that's one of the hardest things.'

'What? People asking if she's yours?'

'Yes. Do you think we should've said that her mam had died?'

Sandra shook her head. 'No. Too painful. Then you get those sympathy looks.'

'That's what I thought too.' I took a bite of the sandwich fighting the nausea.

Sandra watched me. 'Eat it up, love.'

I nibbled at the bread. 'I'm trying.'

She placed her hand on top of mine. 'I know.' She sipped her coffee. 'Now, has Stu mentioned the christening to you?'

'Christening?' I blinked. 'No.'

'Well obviously he wants you as Godmother and Joe as Godfather, not sure who he'll choose for the second Godmother yet, but he's speaking to the vicar sometime next week.'

'I'm surprised he didn't mention it as he's round ours most of the time.'

Sandra took a bite from her baguette, and pickle oozed around her mouth. I couldn't help but chuckle.

She joined in. 'Nice to laugh for a change.' She wiped the relish from her chin. 'He came around to mine last night and I think he wanted to clear it with me first. If he'd asked me a month ago, well, I was still refusing to see Anne-Marie, but I understand you've been supporting Stu right from the start.'

'Yes, I have. We went to register her birth together.'

'I'm glad you were there for him. I'm sure he'll come around to yours and chat about dates, and I'm presuming you'll be up for being Godmother.'

'Of course. Is he thinking before Christmas?'

'If the vicar has a slot, I believe so.'

I thought about Ben's christening when Linda and me had gone shopping together for a present. 'You know what, Sandra, I will take the number of that counsellor. You're right, we need all the help we can get.'

Chapter Twenty-Nine

Rachel

The oil in the chip fryer bubbled as the chips browned. I turned over the breaded cod in the frying pan.

'Mmm, what's cooking?' Joe said as he came into the kitchen freshly showered and changed.

'I thought I'd make a fish and chips supper as it's Friday.'

'Awesome.' He came up behind me, wrapping his arms around my waist. 'You're looking brighter, babe.'

I turned to him and kissed his lips. 'That's because I had a good day.' I served the food onto two plates.

'You did?'

'Yeah. I met up with Sandra and Anne-Marie.' I put the dinners on the table. 'Sit down and I'll get some cider.'

'Ooh, are we celebrating?'

'Not celebrating but a sort of thank you for putting up with me. I know I've not been the easiest person to live with.' I took the bottle of Woodpeckers from the fridge and poured a glass each before sitting down.

'I'm sure if it had been Stu rather than Linda then I'd have been exactly the same as you.' He tucked into his dinner. 'This is cool. We've not had fish and chips for yonks.' He stared at me.

I picked up my knife and fork and pushed a piece of fish onto my fork and into my mouth. My stomach screamed but

I had to try. 'Sandra gave me a telephone number today for a bereavement counsellor.'

Joe rested his cutlery down on the plate. 'Oh?'

'Well, I phoned the office and booked an appointment for next Tuesday evening.'

He stretched his hand across the table and squeezed mine. 'I'm really proud of you, and Linda would be too.'

The doorbell chimed. Joe looked at me. 'Stu maybe?' He rose from the table. 'I'll go. You eat.'

I pushed another forkful into my mouth. The more I ate the easier I found it.

'Look who's here,' Joe said, with Stu in tow.

'Hi, Stu.' I went to get up.

'Hi, Rach, don't get up. I didn't mean to interrupt your meal.'

'Have you eaten? I can easily make you something.'

Joe gently pressed my shoulders back down. 'Eat your meal. If Stu wants something then I'll get it.'

'Actually, I've eaten. Strangely enough I had fish and chips too but mine came from the chippie.'

Joe went to the fridge. 'Glass of cider, mate?'

'That would be cool. Cheers.'

Joe poured out a glass for Stu. 'We hadn't realised you were coming around this evening otherwise we'd have invited you to tea. And what have you done with Anne-Marie?'

'Sandra's got her for the night.'

Joe returned to his seat at the table. 'Sit down, Stu. You don't mind if we finish our teas, do you?'

'No, course not.' Stu perched on a chair next to Joe.

Joe scratched his head. 'Let me get this straight, Sandra's got the baby for the night?'

'Yep.'

Joe shook his head. 'Wow. Rach just mentioned Sandra had Anne-Marie today but for the night too. Will she be all right with her? I mean, you know, she's a stranger to her really.'

'Actually, she's been seeing her the last month and has built up quite a bond. I couldn't say anything before as she swore me to secrecy, but last night she said she was going to meet up with Rachel today and would tell her.'

'That's really good.' Joe patted Stu on the back.

'Anyway, the reason I turned up unannounced was I wanted to run something by you. Again, Rachel's already had the heads up about this from Sandra.'

Joe chortled. 'I see. I'm always the last to know. Spit it out.'

Stu took a gulp of the Woodpeckers. 'I want to get Anne-Marie christened and I'd like you and Rachel to be godparents.'

Joe's chocolate eyes twinkled. 'Ooh, we'd love that, wouldn't we, Rach? It would be an honour.'

'Yes, we would,' I said.

'I'm seeing the vicar next week and wondered if you'd both come with me.'

'Sure we will, won't we, Rach?'

'Of course. When?'

'Wednesday, seven o'clock at mine. Sandra said she'll keep Anne-Marie for the night again so I don't have to worry about getting her bathed, fed, and ready for bed before the vicar arrives.'

'We've got nothing on that evening,' I said. 'We'll be there.'

'Cheers. Why don't we all go down the pub for an hour after you've finished your tea?'

Joe glanced at me. 'Rach?'

'I think that's a lovely idea. We'll go to our local.' Linda had never been there so it wouldn't feel so strange without her. I was determined to try and move forward, for Joe's sake, Anne-Marie's, and mine.

*

My insides tore as I entered Linda's living room expecting her to come through the door. Thank goodness Stu had booked a different vicar than the one who'd conducted the funeral. The church was closer too, one of those modern ones rather than the old traditional type they were married in.

The vicar introduced himself. 'Pleased to meet you. I'm Reverend Nathan Peters.'

'Sit down, please, Reverend,' Stu said.

'Thank you.' The young minister sank into the sofa. He didn't look much older than me. 'Please accept my condolences on losing your wife. It must be difficult for you on your own but I see you have plenty of support.'

'Yes' – Stu took a seat next to the reverend – 'and my mother-in-law has started helping out with the baby now too. In fact, Anne-Marie's with her this evening.'

'That's pleasing to hear. Now, I'm required to ask you a few questions.' He took a notebook and pen from his briefcase.

Joe and I sat down.

'I've not seen you in my church, Stuart. Are you a regular churchgoer?'

Stu bit his lip. 'Well, no. I'm more of a wedding, christening, and you know...' His eyes filled.

'I'm sorry, Stuart,' the vicar said, 'I didn't mean to upset you. But if that's the case, why is it so important for you to have your daughter christened?'

Stu looked at me.

'It's what her mam would've wanted,' I said. 'Linda used to go to church. Not all the time but she did believe, and she'd want her daughter to be baptised.'

The vicar nodded. 'How about the godparents?'

Joe glanced at me.

I shrugged. 'Well, I did believe, but if I'm honest I can't help having doubts when if there is a god, why did he take my best friend away from her daughter, leaving Anne-Marie without a mam?'

'God works in mysterious ways. Rachel, isn't it?'

'Yes. And this is Joe.'

The vicar closed up the notebook. 'Look, forget the questions. I'm happy to conduct your daughter's christening. Do you have a second godmother?'

Stu gave a half smile. 'To be confirmed. I think I've made up my mind but still need to speak to the lady in question.'

'Fair enough. It's up to you how many godmothers or fathers you have, you don't have to go with tradition.'

Stu looked at us. 'I'd like to stick to tradition. I believe that's what my late wife would've wanted.'

The vicar smiled. He rooted through his case and brought out a black diary. 'Let's see where we can fit your little one in then.'

'Do you think you could do it this side of Christmas?'

The reverend raised his eyes. 'That may be tricky but let's take a look.' He flicked through the pages. 'The only slot I have is Sunday at half past two on the tenth of December. How does that sound? That's four weeks this Sunday. Does that give you enough time?'

'What do you think?' Stu said.

I blinked. 'If that's all the reverend has then you'll have to go for it.'

The vicar glanced up. 'Otherwise, we're looking at January at the earliest.'

Stu nodded. 'No, we'll take the December date. Thank you. Can I get you a cup of tea or something?'

Reverend Nathan packed his belongings into the case. 'No, I won't if you don't mind. I've a parishioner that I must see –' he chuckled – 'and believe you me' – he stood up – 'she'll have me drinking tea and eating biscuits for the whole time I'm there.' He patted his stomach. 'I'll need to do a few laps around the park tomorrow.'

'I'll see you out.' Stu got up and opened the front door.

Joe put his arm around me. 'Looks like we've a christening to go to. Are you all right?'

'Yes. It's what Linda would've wanted.'

Chapter Thirty

Peggy

The small number of guests congregated into the church but there was no sign of Sandra. Today would be hard for her, I was sure, but I hoped she'd turn up for Stu's sake, if nothing else.

Rachel looked glamorous in a mauve two-piece. The loose crepe fabric flattered her figure hiding where she'd lost weight, and the skirt flowed against her knee-high boots. The material was thin but the maxi coat she'd worn earlier would've protected her from the cold. Her brown eyes had lost their sparkle. Joe had said she was seeing a grief counsellor so hopefully we'd get our old Rachel back again soon. He stood handsome by her side in a navy suit with a light blue tie.

Mel and Phil joined them. I was surprised they were here. I thought it was family and close friends only. Stu hadn't even invited our Kate and David, or Rachel's sister for that matter.

Sheila came over to me. 'Hi, Peg.' She kissed me on the cheek. 'What a rush? Jacob tipped scrambled egg over his head and I had to bathe him again. Where's Adam?'

'Over there.' I pointed. 'Poor Adam's run ragged struggling to keep up with Ben. I offered to take over but he said it was okay. Where's Malc and Jacob?'

'Just coming. Malc said they'd follow me in.'

I wondered who the mystery godparent was. Was it Sheila? After all she'd been childminding Anne-Marie since almost newborn. 'So, tell me? Are you Godmother then?'

'No. Whatever gave you that idea?'

I fiddled with my pearl necklace. 'Because you've been looking after her since she was four weeks. You must've built quite a bond. If not you then' –I glanced across the room – 'it must be Mel.' But why had Stu chosen her? Was she even close to Anne-Marie? But then I supposed Linda and Mel had become good friends. Maybe that was why.

Adam and Malc came over to us just as Reverend Peters headed to the font.

'The service is about to start,' Adam said, 'we should sit down.'

We followed Adam into the pew behind Stu, Joe and Rachel. But where was the baby, and where was Sandra? The church door banged shut and she hurried down the aisle carrying Anne-Marie. She passed the baby to Stu before taking a seat. Keith lagged behind lugging a changing bag and dropped into the pew next to his wife. Anne-Marie must've stayed with them last night. Sheila had said the baby was now having regular stayovers with her grandmother. I was pleased. Sandra had aged, but Anne-Marie looked gorgeous in a white lace christening robe hiding her feet, and a beautiful matching bonnet. She gave a little cry letting everyone know she was the star of the show. I hoped I'd get a cuddle later as I hadn't seen her for a while.

The vicar coughed. 'Thank you all for coming. It's wonderful that you've been invited to Anne-Marie's christening today and by accepting Stuart's invitation you're supporting him.' The vicar continued to tell us what would be happening before inviting Stu and the godparents to join him at the font.

Ben wriggled and screamed. 'I'd better take him outside.'

'You sure?' Adam whispered. 'What about the christening? I don't mind taking him.'

'No. You stay.' I picked up Ben, slid from the seat and crept out of the entrance into the church garden.

Chapter Thirty-One

Rachel

Stu headed to the font with Anne-Marie and Mel. Joe took my hand and we joined them.

'Where's Mam and Aunty Sheila gone?' Joe whispered.

'The boys must've been playing up and your mam wouldn't have wanted to spoil the service. I'm sure they'll be back soon.'

Joe rested his hand on Stu's arm. 'You okay, mate.'

Stu nodded but looked anything but all right. In fact, he looked like he was about to spew up. Just like I felt. Linda should've been here holding Anne-Marie. How could there be a God when he'd left this little one without a mam and Stu without his wife? 'God acts in mysterious ways,' the vicar had said. Well, I wished someone would explain it to me. Stu was right though; Linda would've wanted Anne-Marie baptised.

The vicar spoke. 'Godparents are really important. Choosing them is one of the biggest decisions you'll ever have to make.'

I didn't see how that could be possible when I thought of the choices Stu would have to face on his own in the future. No one to share them with, although Joe and I would help in any way we could. Stu trembled.

'Let me take her,' I whispered.

He passed the baby to me and Joe put his arm around Stu.

The vicar turned to us. 'You're very important to your Goddaughter. Stuart's chosen you to be with Anne-Marie on an amazing journey of discovery that lasts a lifetime.'

For Linda, I'd do my best, although the faith bit would be rather testing. I looked down into Anne-Marie's little face. She opened her eyes and gazed up at me. My heart flipped. It was like Linda was staring at me. Was this what was meant by faith? That Linda was still here, her spirit coming through Anne-Marie? I'd heard that some religions reckoned God sent for you once you'd met your purpose on this earth. Was giving Anne-Marie life Linda's purpose? Tears pricked my eyes. What about Anne-Marie losing her mam? Stu losing his wife? Sandra losing her daughter. Me losing my best friend? How could Linda have reached her purpose when we still needed her here?

My attention was jolted when the reverend asked, 'Do you renounce the devil and all his works and all his ways?'

I joined in with Stu, Joe and Mel, 'With God's help we will.'

After we'd finished saying the Creed as part of the confession the vicar gestured to me to pass Anne-Marie. He moved closer to the font and poured the holy water over her head. 'In the name of the father.'

I glanced across at Sandra. She was dabbing her eyes with a handkerchief. Keith had his arm around her and was patting her arm.

For the second time the vicar poured water over Anne-Marie's head. 'The son...' I turned to Stu. His eyes filled. I gripped his hand.

Anne-Marie opened her eyes, gazed up and smiled at Reverend Peters as he poured water over her head for the final time. Afterwards he handed her to Stu and whispered. 'This one's a real cutie.'

'Thank you.' Stu cuddled his daughter.

Joe put his arm around me as we sauntered out of the church. 'You doing okay?'

I stared down at Anne-Marie in my arms. 'Yes. This is what Linda would've wanted. Stu's been amazing, hasn't he?'

'He has. But that's because he's had you to help him.'

Peggy came towards us. 'Hello you two.' She stroked Anne-Marie's cheek. 'She's certainly grown since the last time I saw her. Do you reckon Stu will allow me a little cuddle once we get to The Black Horse?'

Joe patted Peggy's shoulder. 'I'm sure he will, Mam.'

'You look nice,' I said, admiring her maroon pleated dress with its matching bolero under her opened coat.

'Thank you. As do you. In fact, Rachel, you look stunning and seem a lot brighter too. Are you feeling better?'

I positioned the lace shawl to shield Anne-Marie's face from the wind. 'I'm trying. Let's talk at the pub. It's too bloody cold standing here and I need to give this little one back to her daddy.'

'Yes, of course. I'll see you later then.'

I headed over to Stu and passed him Anne-Marie.

'Cheers, Rach. Are you sure you don't mind me going in the car with Sandra and Keith?'

'No, of course not. How you holding up?'

'You know.'

'I do. A day at a time, Stu. That's all we can do. Look, you'd better get Anne-Marie in the warmth.'

We were heading into the pub when Phil called, 'Wait up, Rachel.'

'You go on in, Joe,' I said. 'I'll be in shortly.'

'Don't be too long.'

'I won't. I just want to see what Phil wants.'

Joe went through the pub entrance and I headed towards Phil standing by his blue Ford Escort. 'Aren't you coming in?' I asked.

'Yes, but I wanted to show you something first.' He opened the boot and loosened a sheet of woven linen from a large painting. 'What do you think? Will he like it?'

'Oh my God, Phil. It's wonderful. Stu will love it. She looks…' I wiped my moist eyes. 'He's going to love it. 'Can you hang on to it for now though as Joe's got our car keys?'

'Sure. That was the plan but I couldn't wait to show you. Would you like me to get it framed?'

'Oh, yes please. Will you be able to have it done in time for Christmas?'

'Definitely do-able. The guy I use does my framings almost straight away. There's something else. I have yours in here too and you can take that home today.' He lifted the linen cloth from the painting of Linda and me down at the beach, now finished in an ornate gold frame.

'It's gorgeous. And I can take that home today?'

'Yes, it's all yours but I'll keep it in here for now.'

'Where's Mel?'

'She's gone in already.' He covered the pictures in the off-white fabric and packed them both back in the boot before locking up. 'Come on.' He linked his arm with mine as we wandered up to the entrance.

'Before we go in,' I said, 'are you and Mel okay?'

'Yeah, although we've decided to be just friends. A mutual decision.'

'Right, so you're both on the market again?'

Phil chuckled. 'I suppose we are.'

Peggy was cuddling Anne-Marie. I headed towards her. 'You're not getting broody, are you?'

'Give over.' She nudged me. 'I'm far too old. It was hard enough having Ben. At least I can give this one back. Poor Sandra's not looking too good, is she?'

I clenched my fists. 'What do you expect? She's not long lost her daughter.'

'I didn't mean it nasty. It was concern.'

'Sorry,' I said, realising I'd been far too judgemental, something I obviously hadn't grown out of. 'Actually, she's looking a lot better than she was.'

'It was kind of Stu to invite us. He's pretty amazing, isn't he? There aren't many men who've been able to go on as he has.'

'I was just saying the same to Joe. Mind you, poor Stu had a right battle with his mam when' – I signalled with my head to the baby – 'that one was born. She put so much pressure on him to call her Grace.'

'Is that why she isn't here today?'

'Not sure. Stu's not mentioned them but there again it's rather a long way to come for a christening and I understand he's going down there shortly to spend Christmas with them.'

Sandra came across. 'Sorry to interrupt you ladies but do you mind if I take Anne-Marie as she needs a feed?'

'No, of course not,' Peggy said, 'although I can feed her if you like?'

'No, you're all right. She wants her nanna.'

'Sure.' Peggy handed over the baby. 'Thank you for letting me have a cuddle. She really is a little darling.'

Sandra beamed with pride. 'She is. Our Lind would've been so proud.'

'She'd have been proud of you, too,' I said.

'Thanks, love. And you. How's it going?'

'Good. I've been seeing that counsellor you recommended and I'm determined to do everything I can to move forward. That's what Linda would've wanted.'

'Yes, it is. That's what she'd have wanted from us both.'

Anne-Marie gave a high-pitched cry.

'I'd best go and feed her.'

※

Stu passed Joe the packet of Embassy. 'Thanks for letting me crash here again. At this rate I'll need to start paying rent.'

'Don't be daft,' I said. 'You shouldn't be on your own tonight. Nice of Sandra to offer to take Anne-Marie back to hers.'

'Yeah, it was.' Stu puffed on the cigarette. 'Although, this may sound ungrateful, and I'm not, I promise, but I'm getting concerned that she wants Anne-Marie at hers a little too much. At the end of the day, she's my daughter and I don't want to give up my rights.'

I frowned. 'Why would you have to?'

'I dunno. Something she said about how she's got everything there now. Cot, highchair, equipped to have Anne-Marie full time if necessary.'

'Well, that's not on. I hope you told her.'

'Not really, I sort of laughed it off as I wasn't sure whether she was being serious.'

I placed a glass ashtray on the coffee table between Joe and Stu. 'It sounds to me that's exactly what she has in mind. Maybe cut her visits a little. Get them back down to three days a week while you're working and a maximum of two nights a week, enough to give you a bit of a break. Nip it in the bud.'

'You're right.' Stu stubbed out his cigarette and turned to Joe. 'You're quiet, mate. Something up?'

'Sorry, Stu, I was thinking about what you said and staying at your folks at Christmas seems perfect timing. It'll put a little distance between Sandra and Anne-Marie.'

'Yeah.' Stu sighed. 'Mind you, I haven't told Sandra yet.'

'Well, I'm sorry,' I said, 'Sandra will have to accept it. You're Anne-Marie's father and your mam and dad are her grandparents too. They deserve to see their granddaughter. They've not seen her for three months.'

'Yeah. You're right. I don't know what I'd do without you two. You're my rocks.'

I put my hand on his shoulder. 'That's what friends are for. Linda would've wanted us to look after you. I've got something to show you both.' I headed out of the lounge into the hallway and picked up my gift from Phil and returned to the room. 'Look what I've got.'

Joe gasped. 'It's Linda and you.'

Stunned, Stu got up and stared at the picture.

'Phil painted it as a surprise for me and had it framed.'

'He's got Linda's likeness so well,' Stu said. 'Where's it going?'

'Hmm, I'm not sure. In this room somewhere. Where do you think?'

'How about up there?' – Stu pointed over the fireplace – 'or is that too intrusive?'

'Not for me, it's not. What do you think Joe?'

'I think that will be perfect, babe.'

I smiled at Stu. 'We've got something special lined up for you. I should have it in a few days. It's your Christmas present but I don't see the harm in you having it a week or so early.'

Stu's eyes lit up. 'Has Phil done a painting for me too?'

'Not the same as this one but' – I grinned – 'you're going to love it. I'm not saying anymore, you'll just have to wait.'

Chapter Thirty-Two

Rachel

Stu loaded the car boot.

'Is that it?' I asked still holding Anne-Marie.

'Yeah. The pram's in the car ready so I just need to put my little darling in and then we're good to go.' He took Anne-Marie and laid her in the soft detachable carriage.

'I made you something to eat.' I passed him a Tupperware box from my bag.

'That was kind, Rach, but you didn't need to. I'll have to stop at the services anyway.'

'I know but you should save your pennies. Joe, did you get Stu's present from out of our car?'

'Oops, no. It's still in the boot. I'll do it now.' He headed to the Triumph and returned moments later with the large gift.

'Go on,' I said to Stu, 'open it.'

He licked his lips smiling in anticipation as he ripped off the wrapping. 'Oh my God. Rachel, Joe, this is such an awesome gift. Anne-Marie will be able to grow up seeing what her mam looked like.' His eyes misted up. 'And you expect me to drive now?'

'You'll be fine.' I hugged him tightly. 'Have a wonderful time' – I took a deep breath – 'and no arguments with your mam.' I chuckled.

Sandra put two mugs of black coffee onto the table. 'Did you know he's taken Anne-Marie away for two weeks?'

'Yes, I did. He was dreading Christmas and felt it would be easier if he was with his family. Seems fair enough to me.'

Sandra blinked. 'But that means I won't get to see her and we've got all these for her.' She signalled to the pile of presents stacked under the tree. 'I even put lights on there especially.'

'She'll have the presents when she gets back and you'll still have the tree up. Anyway, it's not like Anne-Marie will know it's Christmas. She's too young. And hasn't Stu said you can have her for a few days once he gets back?'

'Yes, it's just that I've got so used to her being here. Between you and me, I reckon she'd be better off here with me. What do you think?'

I put my coffee down. 'Are you suggesting you have her full time?'

'Yes. Stu's still a young man and being a single parent isn't easy, I can tell you. If she lives with us then he can get on with his life. Obviously, he can still visit.'

I shook my head. 'Let me shut you down on that idea, right now, Sandra. That's not what Stu wants and that's not what's right for Anne-Marie. She needs to be with her father and he needs her.'

Sandra dabbed her eyes, sniffling. 'But I need her more. I've lost my daughter and bringing up her child will help me. It's what Linda would've wanted.'

'No, Sandra, it's not. Linda would've wanted Stu to bring up Anne-Marie.' I took her hand. 'I'm sorry but this isn't going to happen. You need to speak to your counsellor to help you through this. Look, why don't you get Keith to take you away for a few days? Have Christmas somewhere away from here?'

She shrugged. 'Do you think it would help?'

'Yes, yes, I do. My boss has a lovely place just outside of Southport. He's let me and Joe use it a couple of times, and my folks stayed there after Dad's heart attack. I'm sure if Mr Strange isn't staying there himself and it's empty, he'll let you have it. I'll have a chat with him.'

'Oh, would you? We'd pay rent. We wouldn't expect it for nowt.'

'Speak to Keith this evening and give me a ring. If he's up for it then I'll have a word with my boss tomorrow.'

Sandra hugged me. 'Thanks, love. What are your plans?'

'We're spending Christmas at Lytham St Annes with my parents as I think it will be easier with no memories of Lind there. Jen's going down there too. It'll be great to see her as we've not seen each other for ages.'

'What does Peggy say about that?'

'She's not going to be happy but we'll spend New Year with her.'

Thank goodness it had stopped snowing. It was a relief yesterday to watch the rain finally flush the white stuff away but the overnight freeze had left dangerous ice on the road so we waited until after lunch before setting off. The boot was loaded to the brim with presents to each other and gifts for my parents and sister. Then we had a bag each for clothing. It had been at least a couple of years since I'd last spent Christmas with my family and this was our first time visiting Mum and Dad's new home so part of me was a little excited.

I turned into the cul-de-sac and pulled up outside Coral Cottage. It looked inviting with its climbing winter clematis blooming pink up the wall beside the leaded bay window, and Mahonias with dark green foliage bloomed yellow clusters either side of the footpath. A holly wreath boasting red berries hung from the light blue cottage style front door.

'This place looks gorgeous,' I said stepping out of the car. 'And wow, I can hear the sea.'

'Me too' – Joe opened the boot – 'but can we see it from here?'

'Apparently not but Mum says we'll be able to see it from our bedroom window.'

'Cool.'

Before we were fully down the footpath, Mum had the front door open. 'They're here,' she shouted to Dad who appeared on the doorstep and hurried outside. 'Let me help with your stuff,' he said.

'Are you sure you're up to it, Mr Webster?' Joe asked bundled up with plastic sacks of presents and a suitcase.

'Good lord, son, I'm not an invalid just yet. I can carry a few things.' He relieved Joe of two plastic sacks.

I hugged Mum. 'Is Jen here yet?'

'Not yet but we're expecting her anytime now and she's bringing a friend.' Mum beamed. She couldn't wait for one of us to get married so she could sport a fancy outfit and big hat.

'I look forward to meeting him,' I said lugging the bags inside where we were greeted by a sandalwood smell from the burning joss sticks in the hallway.

'Come in.' Dad ushered us into the lounge which was probably half the size of the one in the old house.

'This looks pretty,' Joe said, settling the presents down by the six-foot tree in the corner.

'Yes' – Dad fingered the ornaments – 'Rosalind decorated it earlier today. We considered getting an artificial one this year but then we spotted this wonderful specimen and couldn't resist it. Nothing like a real tree.'

Silver and gold-glittered baubles hung from the branches with velvet red bows positioned evenly all over, everything colour co-ordinated. On the top was a huge silver star. Gifts wrapped in red, silver and gold paper were piled either side of the tree. Underneath a little train chugged on a track. Mum and Dad always did go all out with the decorations.

'It looks lovely,' I said.

'Wait until you see it with the flashing lights.' Mum hovered by the door. 'I've put the kettle on. Shall I make you a sandwich. You must be hungry.'

'The journey wasn't that long, Mum, and we had something to eat before we left. I'm more interested in where we'll be sleeping tonight and I'm dying to see the sea.'

'Have a cup of tea first and then I'll show you around. The water should be boiled by now.' Mum left the room.

Dad sank into a deep rose Parker Knoll armchair. 'Sit yourselves down. Don't stand on ceremony.'

Joe and I took the sofa leaving the other Parker Knoll for Mum. The sofa was from the old house and ample enough to seat four people comfortably.

'Here we are.' Mum returned with a tray and passed each of us an Earl Grey in Royal Albert china. She placed a plate of Jaffa cakes onto the occasional glass table.

'Thanks, Mum.' I peered around the room. The bay-shaped glass cabinet inherited from Dad's mum was in the opposite corner from the tree, and the oak sideboard which had been in the old lounge dominated the back wall. Rose velvet drapes hung from the window with an eight-inch valance. 'It's really cosy in here.'

'We like it.' Dad took a sip of tea. 'And because it's smaller than the old place it'll be easier to maintain.'

The doorbell chimed. 'That'll be your sister.' Mum hurried out of the room. 'Jennifer,' she said, and the next thing Jen and a bloke over six foot tall entered the room.

I got up from the sofa and hugged her. 'How are you? It's been so long.'

'I'm good. How about you?'

'You know. Getting there. Are you going to introduce us?'

'Sure. Richard, this is Rachel and her fiancé, Joe.'

Richard leaned forward to shake my hand. 'Pleased to meet you.'

'And this is Dad,' Jen continued, 'and you met Mum at the door.'

Richard turned to Dad and shook his hand. 'Pleased to meet you, sir.'

'And you too, son. Take a pew. Rosalind's just made tea.'

'Cool. I'm gasping.' Richard chuckled.

He must've been in his thirties. I wondered why I'd not heard anything about him but then I supposed I'd been preoccupied since Linda had died.

※

Dad placed a platter of beef surrounded by huge Yorkshire puddings onto the table. Mum brought in a spinach quiche.

I inhaled the aromas. 'Smells delicious, Mum, but quiche with a roast?'

'Oh, that's for your sister and Richard as they're vegetarians.'

'Since when?' I asked.

Jen glared at me. 'If you'd bothered answering any of my calls you'd have known.'

She was right. I'd ignored all her calls, even her letters. I'd no idea what she'd been up to or how her course was going. I'd been too wrapped up in grief to care about anyone else. 'I'm sorry. You're right. I've been an awful sister.'

Jen smiled. 'It's okay. I understand. You've been hurting.'

I nodded. 'Yes. Yes, I have. Still am, but I'm trying.' I took a slice of beef and one Yorkshire pudding.

'Richard and Jennifer' – Mum pointed to a dish of Yorkshire puddings and roast potatoes – 'these have been cooked separately just as your instructions. I made sure they didn't touch any of the meat products and used different utensils.'

Jen tossed her hair away from her face. 'Thanks, Mum. We really appreciate it.'

Joe focused on my plate.

'It's okay,' I whispered, 'I've not finished serving out yet.' I added a roast potato and a spoonful of carrots and peas. 'Can you pass the gravy please, Dad?'

Dad poured some over his full plate before pushing the boat across the table.

'Thanks.' I poured the thick sauce over my dinner. 'So how did you two meet?'

'In Richard's restaurant.' Jen served a slice of quiche onto her plate. 'About six weeks ago I got a placement. Richard's the owner as well as the chef and he's been teaching me a lot.'

'This is my first attempt at a vegetarian quiche,' Mum said, 'so I hope it's up to your standard, Richard.'

His blue eyes sparkled through his glass lenses. 'It's delicious, Mrs Webster. Thank you for going to so much trouble.'

I couldn't help but stare at his loaded plate. More than a quarter portion of the quiche, four Yorkshire puddings, six roast potatoes and piles of veg. Goodness, where did he put it? He was so lanky, his bones almost showed through his skin. What I really couldn't understand was what Jen was doing with him. He didn't seem her type at all. 'That must be difficult being a vegetarian and a chef,' I said. 'How do you cope with cooking meat?'

'I don't,' he said, 'my restaurant's vegetarian.'

'I see.' I vaguely remembered Jen saying something about wanting to open a vegetarian restaurant of her own which is why she went back to college. 'So, is it serious between you two?' I asked.

Joe glared at me.

Richard peered over his round metal glasses. 'It's early days.' His face flushed.

'Rachel,' Mum said, 'leave your sister alone.'

'Yes, leave your sister alone,' Jen repeated.

Dad rested his knife and fork on the sides of his plate. 'I see normal service has resumed with our daughters squabbling over the dinner table.' He sighed. 'I thought now you were past teenage years we'd had the last of that.'

I gazed into space. 'Sorry, everyone. I was out of order. I've no idea what came over me.'

Dad picked up his cutlery. 'Very well. We know things haven't been easy for you so we'll make an exception.'

'I really am sorry.' I sensed my eyes filling up. 'Please, would you excuse me. I think I'd like to go to my room.'

Joe glanced at my plate. 'But, babe, you've hardly eaten anything.'

'Sorry. I'm not hungry. Please may I leave, Mum?'

'You're obviously tired, darling.' Mum said. 'Do you remember which room you're in?'

'Yes, thanks.' I got up from the table and kissed Joe on the cheek. 'Sorry, babe,' I whispered, 'I need to get out of here.'

I opened the French doors and stood on the balcony. Mum had given us a wonderful room. Other than theirs it had the best view. Tomorrow I'd rise early and go for a walk before everyone was up. Maybe Joe would like to come with me. I wished we could have gone this evening but he was likely to have been too tired. Instead, I'd have to make do with the scene from the veranda. I lowered myself onto one of the two wicker chairs, wrapped a blanket around me, closed my eyes and listened to the waves crashing on the sandbanks.

Joe shook my shoulders. 'Rach.'

I jolted. 'I must've fallen asleep.'

'You did. You're freezing and so is this room.' He guided me back inside. 'Get into bed. Your mam gave me a hot water bottle so I've put it under the covers.'

'Sorry.'

'What for?'

'Everything.' I sobbed.

'Hey.' He held me in his arms. 'Nothing to be sorry about. Come on, get undressed.'

'I'm trying. Really, I am' – I sniffled – 'but I feel so guilty being here when Linda isn't.'

'You're just overwhelmed. You've not seen your folks or sister for ages and what with Christmas, it makes everything worse. Things will seem better in the morning.'

We bundled up and headed outside, down a little cut-through, and came to the promenade. The waves lashed high.

I shivered. 'It's a bit rough out there.'

Joe put his arm around me. 'Yep, wouldn't fancy a swim in that.'

'It's lovely though, isn't it?' Salt from the sea itched my eyes.

Joe picked up a pebble. 'Look, a wishing stone? Remember you found one in Southport straight after Linda died, well maybe this is a sign?'

'How so?'

'She wants you to make another wish. Go on?'

'No. You make a wish this time.'

'Okay.' He closed his eyes, blew on the stone, and catapulted it into the waves.

'What did you wish for?'

'I can't tell you otherwise it won't come true.' He returned his arm to my shoulder. 'Come on, let's go back. The others will be up now and waiting for us.'

⋆

Dad ripped the snowman wrapping paper from his present and held up a stripey dressing gown. 'Thank you, Rachel and Joe. It's lovely.' He turned to Mum. 'Rosalind, open yours.'

Mum gently tore away the paper trying to keep it intact. She held the red box. 'What is it?'

I grinned. 'Open it and see.'

She lifted the lid and stared. Eventually she said, 'A locket. This is beautiful. You shouldn't have spent all that money on me.'

'Look inside,' I said.

She unclasped the gold-plated heart revealing a photo of her and Dad on their wedding day. 'I shall treasure it.'

Dad chuckled. 'I see your mother gets jewellery while I get a dressing gown and slippers. I just need the pipe now. Oh wait. I had to give that up.' He chuckled. 'My daughters are making me feel like an old man.'

I fiddled with my fingers. 'You do like your gifts though? It's easier to buy for Mum than you.'

Dad smiled. 'I love all of them. Thank you. I'm just teasing.'

Joe nudged me. 'Put your dad out of his misery.'

'We don't see you as an old man, Dad.' I passed him a small gift. 'Here open this.'

He beamed and tore off the wrapping with speed. 'What's this?' he asked while holding the small blue box.

'Open it and see,' Joe said.

'Now this is more like it.' Dad slipped the silver-plated watch onto his wrist.

'I'd better give you my proper present too.' Jen passed him another parcel.

Out of nowhere I started thinking about Linda. My eyes filled. I was never going to feel this joy of watching my friend open a gift ever again.

Joe rested his hand on my wrist. 'You, okay?'

I shook my head.

'You want to go for a walk?'

'Please.'

Joe rose from the carpet and helped me up. 'Hope you don't mind, Mr and Mrs Webster, but we're going to pop out for some fresh air.'

'Be back for lunch,' Mum said, 'and wrap up warm, it's freezing out there.'

I slipped my feet into faux fur lined boots and shoved my arms into my maxi coat. As we stepped outside my tears flowed. 'Sorry, Joe, I don't know what came over me.'

He cuddled me into his chest. 'It's okay. You've been amazing. It's understandable you're going to be emotional. Come on, let's take a stroll along the seafront.' He took my hand in his.

'I suppose so.' I sniffled. 'I wonder how Sandra's getting on. She doesn't even have Anne-Marie to help her through it.'

'Keith will look after her. Stu needed the baby with him. Goodness knows how he's feeling right now. I just hope his mam's not giving him a hard time.'

'I think she'll be too busy monopolising Anne-Marie.'

'If your folks don't mind, maybe I could give Stu a ring after lunch.'

'They won't mind at all. I'd like to say hi too.'

Suddenly the wind picked up and Joe's hat flew off his head. He charged after it but the wind carried the woollen garment into the swelling waves, washing it out to sea. 'I knew it was rough but... That was my best hat too.'

I laughed. Maybe Linda was here. That was just like her sort of humour. 'I'll buy you a new one when the shops open.'

He huddled up close to me. 'Smell that salt. I'm glad we both feel so at home by the sea. When we retire, I reckon we should move somewhere like this. What do you think?'

'I'd say that's an awesome idea.' I touched Joe's face. 'I love you.' Shivering, I kissed him hard on his lips. 'You know about us setting that date?'

'Yes?'

'I'm ready. We'll tell Mum and Dad after lunch. My Christmas present to you.'

He kissed me back. 'And they say wishes don't come true. That's the best present in the world. I love you, future Mrs Davies.'

The table was covered in a strawberry-red tablecloth and amber flames flickered from tall white candles standing in holly and pinecone circles. 'Where did you buy these?' I asked. 'They're rather quaint.'

Mum grinned. 'I didn't. I made them. I went to a Christmas craft class at the village hall, and I made the wreath on the door too.'

'Awesome. Can you teach me?'

'And me,' Jen said.

Mum laughed. 'Not sure about that, girls.' She sliced a nut roast while Dad carved the huge turkey.

'What's the nut roast like?' I asked Jen. 'Have you tried it?'

'It's yummy. Richard showed me how to make it and then I made a couple to bring down here. Why don't you try a bit?'

I screwed up my nose. 'I'm not sure.'

'You never used to be so close-minded about trying things.'

'Now, now,' Dad said as he cut through the bird, 'you girls aren't going to start arguing again, are you?'

'Of course not,' I said, 'we're not arguing, it's called a discussion.'

Joe smiled. 'I'll try a small slice if there's enough.'

'There's plenty,' Richard said. 'We brought extra in case you folks fancied a meat free Christmas.'

'We're all for trying something new' – Dad passed Joe a plate of sliced turkey – 'but don't expect to convert us to vegetarianism. Do you get many covers in your restaurant, Richard?'

'Actually, yes. We're booked up most lunchtimes and evenings. If you and Mrs Webster decide on a visit to

London sometime you must come and eat at my restaurant. Complimentary of course.'

'Now there's an offer we can't refuse. How about you, Jennifer, have you thought where you'd like to open your restaurant?' Dad got up, placed the platter with the remainder of the bird onto the pine dresser, and returned to his seat.

Jen twiddled the opal ring on her right hand. 'At the seaside somewhere. Maybe here. It's seems a nice enough place.'

Mum's eyes lit up. 'You could live here with us.'

Dad shook his head. 'Let your babies fly, Rosalind. Jennifer won't want to return to her parents after having her own place.'

Jen helped herself to three golden roast potatoes. 'Dad's right, Mum, but I'd be able to visit lots.' She shrugged. 'I've still a year's training to do so who knows where I'll decide to end up.'

I coughed to get everyone's attention. 'Joe and I have an announcement to make.'

'You do?' Jen glared at me. 'You're not...'

'Don't be stupid. Actually' – I turned to Mum – 'you'd best start looking for a mother of the bride outfit.'

Jen clapped. 'That's really good news. When's the big day?'

'March but we need to confirm dates once we get back home.'

Mum cut into her turkey. 'In a church, I hope?'

'No. I don't want all that fuss but I do want my family around me.'

'That's wonderful news, darling.' Dad picked up his glass. 'A toast to the happy couple. We couldn't be more delighted.'

Chapter Thirty-Three

Rachel

When I came out of work Phil was huddled against the shopfront window.

'Thanks for meeting me.' I buttoned up my coat and put a purple woolly hat on that Jen had bought me for Christmas. 'It's bloody freezing. Where shall we go?'

'How about Elmo's? It's always nice and toasty in there.'

The last time I'd been in there was with Linda but I couldn't avoid the place forever and who better to go with than someone I trusted. 'Okay.' I hooked my arm in his and we hurried down the road.

'What was it you wanted to chat about?' Phil breathed out cold air.

'I'll tell you when we get there. Did you have a good Christmas?'

'Not bad, thanks. Went to my folks, and Jan came home for a few days too.'

'That must've been nice.' I pushed open the café door and was greeted by Elmo.

'Rachel, darling.' He hugged me. 'How's it going? Long time no see.'

I squeezed my eyes shut, and shrugged. 'You know.'

'I do, darling.' He released me from his hold. 'Come and sit by the heater. Whatever you want is on the house.'

'You don't have to do that.' I took off my hat and perched on the red plastic chair.

'I know I don't have to but I'd like to.' He turned to Phil. 'And how's our local artist?'

'Good thanks, Elmo.' Phil took the seat opposite me.

'I'm glad you've come in, Phil, because I've been meaning to get in touch with you.' Elmo rubbed his moustache. 'How do you fancy having a small exhibition here one weekend. Help us both. Hopefully get me more punters in to eat and with any luck some sales for you. Been really quiet in here of late so I've been thinking of ways to pick up trade. And if you fancy bringing half a dozen or so of your smaller pictures in as a taster, I can display them at the back.'

'Cheers, Elmo,' Phil said. 'I'll drop some round to you.'

'Cool.' Elmo passed each of us a menu.

'That's a brilliant idea,' I said, 'and I could do an article to promote it.'

'That would be ace, Rachel. Sorry, I didn't mean to gatecrash your meeting. Give me a yell when you're ready.' Elmo headed over to the counter.

Phil scanned the menu. 'That was kind of him.'

'Yeah, it was.' I slipped off my coat and laid it on the chair next to me.

'So, are you going to put me out of suspense?'

'I suppose I should.'

'Go on then.'

I gave a little laugh. 'You know how you encouraged me to think about setting a date?'

'Yes.'

'At Christmas when we were away at my parents, it suddenly felt right.' I chuckled. 'Joe threw out a wishing stone to sea and reckoned his wish came true.'

'So?'

'We've set a date for 17th March. It'll be just a small do with friends and family and' – I smiled – 'Joe and I would like you to be our second witness.'

Phil pointed to his chest. 'Moi?'

I nodded. 'Obviously my first choice would've been Linda but as she's not here it has to be you because you're my best friend alive.'

He reached for my hand and twisted my engagement ring. 'I shall be delighted to accept, dear lady. It will be an honour. Merci.'

I pulled back my hand and checked the menu. 'Now what are you eating?'

'Hmm' – he perused the offerings – 'quiche and chips. And you?'

'I'm not that hungry. I've a sarnie at the office so just a coffee for me.'

He stared at me.

'Honestly, I am trying to eat. There's a cheese and pickle sandwich sitting on my desk. You wouldn't like me to waste it would you?'

'If you say so.' Phil signalled to Elmo and he hurried over.

'Ready to order?' He took a pencil from behind his ear and held his pad in place.

'Quiche and chips for me.' Phil glared at me. 'And a small bowl of fries for Rachel because she won't be able to resist them once she sees and smells mine.' He laughed. 'Oh, and two black coffees.'

Debs brought over a pint of bitter to Joe and half a cider for me. 'There you go, ducks. Now what is it you wanted to discuss?'

'We'd like you to do a small buffet for our wedding,' Joe said.

'Wedding?' She put an arm around each of us. 'Now that's the best news I've heard in a long time.' She pulled out a chair and sat down at the table with us. 'You've set a date then?'

'Yep,' I said. 'Nine weeks tomorrow. 17th March.'

'I couldn't be more pleased. You've waited so long. If anyone deserves this it's you two.'

'Thanks.' I took a sip from my drink.

'Cheers, Debs' – Joe winked at me – 'Rach has made me the happiest man alive.'

'Let me just grab a notebook.' Debs hurried over to behind the bar and returned with a pad and pen. 'Now, how many at this do then?'

'Not many.' I visualised in my head and said out loud, 'Mum, Dad, Jen and her new man for starters, then there's Peggy, Adam, Kate, David.' I took a breath. 'Stu and Phil who are our witnesses, Mel and Betty from work. How many is that?'

'And what about Teresa?' Debs asked.

'Oh, didn't we say? She decided to stay out in the States. Thank goodness.'

'Meow.' Debs laughed.

'Not really. She had it in for me.'

'Never mind that now.' Joe lit up a cigarette. 'Let's get back to sorting out the arrangements. Don't forget Aunty Sheila and Uncle Malc.'

'So, with Joe and me, you and Harry, Debs, I think that gives us eighteen. Is that right?' I counted on my fingers.

'You mean we're invited?'

'Naturally,' I said. 'You two have been bricks over the years.'

Joe flicked ash into the ashtray. 'Oh, we've forgotten about Sandra and Keith.'

'Oh yes, although I think it may be too difficult for Sandra, but we should invite her anyway, giving us a nice round twenty.'

'I tell you what, love' – Debs picked up her pen – 'I'll add in enough just in case she says yes but only charge for eighteen.'

'Cheers.' Joe's eyes twinkled. 'We really appreciate that.'

She squeezed Joe's fingers. 'I'll book a couple of casuals to work so Harry and I can take the time off. Now, the menu. How about sausage rolls, cheese and pineapple on sticks, cocktail sausages, hard-boiled eggs, sardines on toast fingers, chicken and mushroom vol-au-vents, twiglets, crisps, and sandwiches with a few different fillings?'

I glanced at Joe. He nodded. I turned back to Debs. 'That sounds awesome.'

'And your cake?'

I shook my head. 'We weren't going to bother.'

'Nope' – she slammed her hand down on the table – 'I'm not having that. I'm putting my foot down. You can't have a wedding without a cake. Leave it to me. That'll be mine and Harry's wedding present to you.'

'Thanks. Debs.' I put my arm around Joe.

<hr />

Peggy opened the door. 'What a wonderful surprise. Come in. Have you eaten?'

'Yes, Mam. Don't worry about food.' Joe kissed Peggy on the cheek. 'Is Dad in? Only we've got something to tell you.'

'He is. Go through.'

We strolled into the lounge. Adam turned his head from the television. 'Hi guys, this is a nice surprise.' He got up to turn the TV off.

'Sorry,' I said, 'we didn't mean to interrupt your programme. Would you like to finish watching it?'

'Nah, you're all right, it's just a new crime drama series. I reckon it'll be easy enough to fill in the gaps.' Adam sat back down. 'Great to see you both. You're looking better, Rachel.'

'Thanks.' I perched on the arm of the sofa next to Joe.

'Is your mam making a cuppa?'

'Probably.' Joe took out a packet of Embassy and passed it to Adam. 'Cig, Dad?'

'Cheers, son.' Adam flicked his lighter and lit a cigarette. 'You not having one?'

'Not for the moment. Mam,' he yelled, 'you coming? Only Rach and I haven't got long and we need to speak to you.'

Peggy rushed in. 'The kettle's boiling.'

'Don't worry about that,' Joe said, 'come and sit down.'

Peggy's eyes narrowed. 'What is it?'

'You're all right, Mam. It's good news. Rach and I have set a date.'

Peggy beamed. 'A date for the wedding? You're finally getting married.'

Joe grinned. 'Yeah. We are.' He clutched my hand. 'Keep 17th March free. Two o'clock at Woodhaerst Register Office. Just a small do. Family and a couple of close friends.'

Peggy hugged each of us in turn. 'I couldn't be happier. This is wonderful news. Now how can we help? Catering?'

I shook my head. 'All sorted.'

'Outfits?'

'Well,' I said, 'you can probably make do with the same outfit you wore to Kate's as you've not worn it anywhere else.'

Peggy frowned. 'Absolutely not. I've waited too damn long to see you two wed.'

'As long as you don't outshine the bride then.' Joe slapped his thighs before standing up. 'Right, we need to be off. Early start tomorrow and Rachel's still got to ring her folks and sister to let them know the date.'

Peggy stood up. 'I take it Kate and David are invited?'

'Yes, of course,' I said, 'Sheila and Malc too.'

'Wonderful. I'll ring them tonight.' Peggy's brown eyes sparkled.

Adam rose from the chair. 'Great news, kids.' He patted Joe on the back. 'I'll see you out.'

'Cheers, Dad. You can get back to the telly then.'

Adam glanced at the clock. 'Yep, I'll only have missed a few minutes. Are you two coming over for tea next week?'

Joe looked at me.

'We can do,' I said heading out into the hallway.

Adam opened the front door.

Peggy kissed Joe and me on the cheek in turn. 'I'll make something special.'

Joe held my hand as we stepped outside. 'Thanks, see you then.'

Adam closed the door behind us and I brushed my lips against Joe's. 'That went well.'

Chapter Thirty-Four

Rachel

Sandra crashed the dishes into the sink. 'I can't believe you knew.'

I touched her arm. 'I'm sorry.'

'But to restrict me to two days a week and only one overnight a fortnight. It isn't right. Or fair.'

'It's right for Anne-Marie. You're getting too attached and all that talk about bringing her up full time, you can't really blame Stu for taking action.'

'Well, I'm going to bloody take action.' She rinsed the mugs and slammed them onto the draining board.

'What do you mean?'

'I'm going to see a solicitor and I'll take Stu to court for full custody.'

I shook my head. 'You've got to be joking.'

'Why?' She raised her voice. 'Why shouldn't she live with me? She's mine. She needs me, not left with a childminder for half the week while he's at work. It makes sense.'

'Are you still seeing the counsellor?'

'No. There's no need. My baby's all I need.'

Her baby? She was clearly deluded. 'If I were you,' I said, 'I'd have a re-think, otherwise you're going to have a fight on your hands. Stu's not going to let his child go and no court in the land would make him. He's a good dad.'

She untied her apron and threw it onto the back of a chair. 'Why aren't you on my side?'

'It's not about sides. Stu's her dad. Don't you think he's gone through enough with losing his wife without all this extra nonsense? You carry on like this and I wouldn't mind betting he'll stop you seeing her at all.'

'He can't do that. She's my daughter.'

'Sandra, she isn't your daughter. She's your granddaughter.'

'That's what I meant. You're just trying to trick me. Stu's sent you here to spy on me, hasn't he?'

'What? Sandra, you do realise Anne-Marie isn't your daughter, don't you?'

She gritted her teeth. 'Of course I do, you stupid woman. Now get out. Just get out. You're no longer welcome in this house. And don't expect to see us at your wedding. It's all right for you getting your happy ending but what about my Linda and what about me?'

I squeezed my eyes shut. 'That's unfair, Sandra. You've no idea how hard this decision to go ahead with our wedding has been. But I believe it's what Linda would've wanted.'

She prodded my arm. 'You keep telling yourself that, girl. You keep telling yourself. Now if you don't mind my husband will be home shortly and I need to get his tea.'

'Please, Sandra, don't leave it like this.'

She thrashed her arms. 'I'll leave it any way I bloody well like. Now leave my house. Now.'

'All right, I'm going, but Sandra, please, make an appointment with your counsellor. You need help.' I picked up my handbag from the shag pile carpet, opened the front door, stepped outside, and burst into tears.

'I'm not kidding you, Joe. She's deranged. We need to tell Stu.'

'Are you sure it's that bad, Rach, and you're not overreacting?'

'Yes, I'm sure. I'm not overacting. I'm telling you, Joe, I don't trust her. She thinks Anne-Marie's hers. Talk to Stu and perhaps he should speak to Keith. If it were me, I'd only allow her supervised visits.'

'Don't you think you're getting everything out of perspective?'

'No, I don't. I've a good sense about these things. Was I wrong about Miranda? Was I wrong about Teresa when she took Ben? No. And I'm not wrong now. Sandra's not a bad person but she's ill. She needs help. Who knows what she might do?'

'Calm down, Stu. Tell us what's happened?'

'I went to get Anne-Marie but she wasn't there. Sandra had taken her. Keith had no idea where they'd gone. He checked upstairs and discovered a suitcase missing with lots of Anne-Marie's stuff. Stu put his hands across his face. 'Supposing something has happened to her.'

Joe patted Stu's back. 'It's all right, mate. We'll get her back. Sandra won't hurt Anne-Marie. She loves her.'

'This is what I was talking about,' I said. 'I knew something like this was going to happen.'

'You knew, Rach? Why didn't you tell me?'

'Joe was going to talk to you tonight.' I shook my head. 'I must admit I'd no idea she'd do something so stupid this quickly. She practically kicked me out of the house earlier today.' I took a deep breath. 'I think you should call the police.'

'Rach' – Joe frowned – 'don't you think that's a bit much?'

'No. No, I don't. She's clearly disturbed and who knows what she might do in that state of mind? Not intentionally but she's sick, Joe. I told you that.'

'I'll call them now.' Stu dialled 999.

※

Stu shot up from the sofa. 'I can't just sit here.' He brushed hair away from his forehead. 'It's no good. I need to do something. I need to be out there searching for my daughter.'

'You need to be here, mate' – Joe rested his hand on Stu's shoulder – 'in case the police call with news. I'll put the kettle on.' Joe headed towards the kitchen.

'I don't need any more tea, Joe. I've had enough to last me a lifetime.' Stu grabbed his jacket from the back of the chair. 'I'm going to find Anne-Marie. Don't try and stop me.'

'Stu's right, Joe. We can't just sit here. We should be out looking.'

'All right but I'll drive.' Joe picked up the car keys from the trinket tray on the sideboard. 'Where do we start?' he asked.

I slipped on my maxi coat and followed the boys out, slamming the door behind me. 'The graveyard. She might have gone there to be with Linda.' I opened the back door to the Triumph. 'Stu, you sit in the front with Joe.'

※

'You two wait here,' I said getting out of the back passenger door.

'No way.' Joe slid out of the car. 'We're coming too. There's no way you're going into a graveyard when it's turning dark.'

'All right, but you two stay back if she's there and let me speak to her first.' I traipsed through the graveyard with Stu and Joe close behind. As we got closer to Linda's grave, I could see there was no sign of Sandra.

Stu sighed. 'Where now? Where would she go, Rach?'

I flicked my fingers. 'The park. She always liked to meet me there. Said she felt close to Linda. Yes, that's where she'll be.'

※

We crunched across the gravel path and headed towards the duck pond.

'Look' – Stu pointed – 'there's someone on the bench and that looks like a pram.' He sped across the grass.

'Come on.' Joe took my hand.

'Stu,' I shouted, 'if it is her then don't get too close. Let me speak to her first.'

He stopped running. 'Okay. You're right. She might do something stupid and being that close to the water I shan't risk it.'

As we got nearer, I was able to make out Sandra's silhouette. 'It's her,' I said. 'Leave this to me.'

I crept closer. Sandra was staring into space, oblivious to the fact that I was even there. I peeped into the pram. Anne-Marie was sleeping. I touched her face. The blankets and pram apron had kept her warm. I released the brake and pushed the pram over to Stu. 'Anne-Marie seems okay but maybe we should get her checked over by a doctor, just in case.'

Stu let out a sigh of relief before scooping up his daughter. 'It's all right, little one, Daddy's here.'

Anne-Marie gave a small cry before closing her eyes and going back to sleep.

'Get her in the warmth, Stu' I said. 'Joe, give him the keys, and Stu put the car heater on while you wait for us. Joe, phone the police from that phone box just outside the car park. And then phone Keith.'

Joe put his arm around me. 'But I don't want to leave you here on your own.'

'I'll be fine. Once you've made the phone calls you can come back.'

'Okay, babe. I'll be as quick as I can.'

Stu returned Anne-Marie to the pram. She gave a small murmur. Stu and Joe hurried away disappearing from sight.

I moved closer to Sandra, took a seat next to her on the bench, and put an arm around her. 'Sandra, it's Rachel.'

She continued to stare into space.

⇜

Joe parked the car and we hurried into the hospital entrance, through some double doors and down a corridor towards the mental health unit. Keith had his head down.

'How is she?' I asked. 'We got here as quickly as we could.'

He lifted his head and shrugged. 'She's being assessed. How's Anne-Marie?'

'She's fine,' I said. 'Back home with her daddy after the doctor gave her a good once over. It's lucky we found Sandra when we did.' I shivered. 'Imagine if she'd stayed outside in the park all night. Goodness knows what was going through her head.' I clenched my fists. 'It doesn't bear thinking about.'

Keith put a hand to his forehead, pressing his temple. 'It's my fault. I should've spotted something.'

'You weren't to know, mate.' Joe patted Keith's shoulder.

'I should've known. I live with her for God's sake. Rachel realised something was wrong.' Keith glared at me. 'But what happened? Did you say something to make her snap?'

'Now, mate,' Joe said, 'don't go blaming Rachel.'

'Sorry, I wasn't. I'm just trying to make sense of things. It's just she seemed fine when I went off to work this morning' – he took a deep breath – 'and then when I got home loads of stuff had gone. She obviously left in a hurry as the wardrobe door was left wide open.'

Joe frowned. 'It sounds like you're blaming her to me.'

I blinked. 'Maybe it was my fault. We argued. It wasn't an easy visit. She seemed to be under the impression Anne-Marie was her baby. It was like she'd gone back in time.'

Joe took my hand. 'That doesn't make it your fault. She was already in a bad place and should've been getting help.'

'You're right, Joe, it's not Rachel's fault.' Keith blinked. 'I should've done more.' Keith sniffed. 'I've lost one wife; I can't lose another.'

I put my arm around him. 'You're not going to lose Sandra. The doctors will make her better, you'll see. She just needs the right help. Goodness knows how she felt after losing her daughter. No wonder she snapped. Losing my best friend was hard enough. None of us could have foreseen that this would happen.'

A door swung open and a young nurse came out. 'Mr Rodgers, we're ready for you now.'

Stu hugged me. 'How is she?'

'She's been sectioned. Not the best thing to have happened to her but at least now she'll get the help she needs.'

'It's poor Keith I feel sorry for.' Stu went to the fridge and took out a couple of beers and passed one to Joe. 'How about you, Rach, want one?'

'No, I'd better not as it looks like I'll be driving.' I sighed. 'You do know Sandra didn't do any of this deliberately, don't you?'

Stu rubbed his nose. 'If you say so.'

'Seriously, Stu. She's ill. Losing Linda has thrown her over the edge.'

'What does she think it's done to me? And then this?' He flicked off the lid of the can and took a gulp.

'She's not responsible, mate.' Joe took a sip of his drink. 'Like Rach says, she's sick and we need to support her.'

'You will let her see Anne-Marie once she's better?' I asked.

Stu slurped from the can. 'I'm not sure.'

'You've got to,' I said. 'It'll break her again if you deny her access.'

'We'll talk about it once she's better. I'm not in a rush to put myself through that again thanks very much.'

I glared at Joe. He shrugged.

'Is it okay if I pop up and see Anne-Marie?' I asked.

'Sure. You know where she is.' Stu plonked down on a chair at the table with Joe.

I crept upstairs and into the nursery. Anne-Marie was on her back fast asleep. 'Hi, little one.' I stroked her cheek. 'You had a bit of drama today.' She'd miss her nanna but surely they wouldn't keep Sandra in the unit for too long and at least she'd be getting the medical help she desperately needed. Hopefully once she was better Stu would relent and allow her to see Anne-Marie. 'Oh, Lind,' I said out loud, 'your poor mam.'

'And there you have it,' I said to Peggy.

'So, they think they can keep it out of the newspapers?'

'With any luck. That's the last thing Keith needs. Poor bloke.'

Peggy poured water from the kettle into the pot. 'How's he doing?'

'Broken. As you might expect. I've never seen a big bloke like him cry before.'

'And how about you, love' – she passed me a mug of tea – 'how are you coping?'

I shrugged. 'You know. I keep wondering if it was my fault.'

'Hey, you can stop thinking like that for a start.' Peggy pulled a chair out from the table and perched next to me. 'Why would you even think that?'

I took a sip of the strong tea. 'Keith said she was fine that morning, then I go round there, we argue, and the next thing she packs up some bits and runs away.'

Peggy patted my arm. 'It wasn't your fault. Anyway, Sandra will thank you in the long run. This way she's getting the care she needs.'

'That's what I'm hoping.'

Peggy shoved the plate of Jammie Dodgers in front of me. 'Your favourite. Go on, eat one.'

'I'm not hungry.'

'I bought them in especially. We need to build you up for your wedding day. Less than four weeks now.'

'I'm feeling kind of guilty about that now.'

'We'll have none of that, thank you. Now eat.'

I took a biscuit from the plate and forced myself to take a bite.

'Are you going to let me see your dress?'

'It's nothing special. Ivory, pleats from the bodice falling to the ankles, and strapless. Nothing expensive. Got it off the peg in that new dress shop in Woodhaerst. Forget what the name is. On the corner next to the chemist.'

The front door slammed and Adam came in with Joe. 'You girls okay?'

Peggy got up from the table and flicked the switch on the kettle. 'We're fine. Tea?'

'Cheers.' Adam pecked Peggy on the cheek. 'We'll just whip upstairs and wash up.'

'Did you manage to fix it?' I asked.

'Yeah, it was the alternator,' Joe said heading upstairs to the bathroom after Adam.

'Malc will be pleased.' Peggy refilled the pot and gave it a stir. 'He was worried he'd have to take it into a garage, which they couldn't afford.'

'It's good our menfolk were able to help out then. I think they quite like working together.'

'Yes, I do too.' She chortled. 'They've been working on motors together since Joe was around three. No wonder he grew up wanting to be a mechanic.'

'Right' – Joe peeped his head around the door – 'you ready, Rach?'

I rose from the table and picked up my handbag. 'Yep.'

'You not staying for a cuppa?' Peggy held out a mug of tea.

'Nah, I won't, thanks, Mam. I'd like to get back home and have a bath as we've promised Stu we'll pop round to his this evening.'

'Oh, right.' She put the mug down on the side. 'We'll see you soon then.'

Chapter Thirty-Five

Rachel

17ᵗʰ March, 1980

Mel piled my hair into a bun and using heated tongs, she teased the loose strands into spirals.

'It suits you,' she said.

I glanced in the mirror. 'Yeah, it looks all right.' I passed her a plastic bag. 'Can you put these in for me?'

'Sure.' She clipped the ivory silk roses around the chignon. 'You look lovely.'

'Ta. You do too,' I said. 'That blue suits you.'

'Cheers. I love the crepe fabric. Right, you'd better get into your frock.' She passed me my outfit. 'This is gorgeous by the way. Where did you get it from?'

I stepped into the dress and smoothed it down. 'That new shop in town.'

Mel rubbed my arms. 'Hope you're not going to be too cold.'

'It's okay, I have a shawl.' I took the lace wrap from the ottoman and wrapped it around my bare shoulders. 'There' – I swayed from side to side – 'what do you think?'

'Stunning. You may not have a hundred-pound wedding gown but boy you look a million dollars.'

'Thanks.' It should've been Linda standing here with me, doing my hair, helping with my dress and make-up. *Oh Lind, I miss you so much*. I dabbed my eyes.

'You okay?'

'I miss her.'

'I know.' Mel put her arms around me. 'Don't cry though, otherwise your mascara will run. Here.' She passed me a posy of lemon roses and purple iris. 'I'm sure she's up there somewhere watching.'

And what of Sandra? She was being discharged from the unit today but had agreed to go into a private clinic that Keith had found. I hoped she'd get better soon. Anne-Marie needed her. Keith needed her. I needed her. I lifted my small purple purse from the dressing table and placed its gold chain over my shoulder. 'Let's do this.'

※

Mel pulled up in Woodhaerst Register Office car park.

'Right,' I said, picking up the posy, 'let's go and find my man.'

Joe was standing near the entrance with Stu. They looked like twins in burgundy suits with yellow rose boutonnieres. My heart skipped a beat at how handsome Joe was. I glanced around. Where was Anne-Marie? But then I spotted Peggy holding her. Anne-Marie was dressed in a gorgeous lemon and purple outfit matching my bouquet. Peg looked good too in an apricot suit finished with a cream floaty hat. She waved.

Mel linked her arm in mine as we took the four steps to meet the men. Joe brushed his lips against mine. 'Ready?'

I nodded. And yes, I was ready. I wished Linda was here but this was the right thing to do. Joe and I had been pulled through the wringer on so many occasions. This was our time. Time for me to become Mrs Joe Davies.

'Wait,' I said. 'Where are my folks and Jen? And Phil? Phil's got to be here because he's our second witness.'

Joe squeezed my fingers. 'It's all right. Everyone's inside. Phil and Dad are looking after everyone. Mam only came out because Anne-Marie decided to have a screaming match.'

'Really? She looks happy enough now.'

'Yes, really. Come on. Let's do this before you change your mind.' Joe took my hand.

'I'm not going to change my mind.' I glanced at Peggy. 'We're going in now.'

She signalled okay with her head and followed us in.

My parents came over. 'You look beautiful, darling,' Mum said.

'Your mother's right.' Dad kissed me on the cheek. 'We're very proud of you.'

'Thanks, Dad. Mum. Thank you for everything.' I gazed around the waiting room. 'Is everyone here? Sheila? Kate?'

'They're all here, darling.' Dad held my arm. 'Now get in there and marry your man. He's waited long enough.'

A woman aged around forty came out of the ceremony room. 'Joe Davies and Rachel Webster?'

Joe led me over. 'That's us.' He beamed at her.

'Would you like to come through.' She turned to our guests. 'The registrar just needs to go through a few things with the bridal couple and then we'll call you in.'

My legs felt like jelly as we headed over to the registrar's desk. I didn't understand why though because I wasn't nervous.

Joe held my hand and whispered. 'It's all right, babe. This is the right thing for us to do.'

'Yes, I know.' I sneezed, most likely from the lemon roses around the room and in my posy.

The registrar asked a few questions and told us what was going to happen before signalling to her assistant to invite our guests in.

Mum, Dad, Jen and Richard sat on the left, with Peggy, Adam, Kate, and David on the right. Mum and Peggy smiled at me.

It had been a long pathway for Joe and me to get here. So many times I thought we never would. Especially when told we were brother and sister. Then when he married because he thought there was no hope for us, the stabbing, waiting for the divorce, Linda's death. Yes, it had been a long, tough road. I squeezed Joe's hand.

The registrar coughed. 'Good afternoon, ladies and gentleman, on behalf of Joe and Rachel I'd like to extend a warm welcome to you all to Woodhaerst Register Office. My name's Joan Southern and I'll be conducting the ceremony while my colleague, James Stevens here, will complete the schedule to record a legal record of the marriage.'

Joe and I stared into each other's eyes.

'This ceremony will be in accordance with the civil law of this country,' the registrar continued.

To think within fifteen minutes, we'd finally be married and get our happy ever after. How I longed to have my best friend by my side like we'd always planned. Life could be so unfair.

The registrar smiled. 'This place has been duly sanctioned, according to law, for the celebration of marriages, and we are here today to witness the joining in matrimony of this couple and to share in their happiness.' She paused before saying, 'If there is any person here present who knows of any lawful impediment to this marriage, then they should declare it now.'

Anne-Marie let out a high-pitched scream.

Stu put a hand over his mouth. 'Sorry.'

Sheila got up from her seat and hurried over to Stu. 'I'll take her.'

'Thanks.'

Sheila hurried out of the room with Anne-Marie still screaming.

'You don't think Linda's behind that, do you?' I gave a quiet laugh.

'No.' Joe stroked my cheek. 'If Linda were here, she'd be willing you to say *I do*.'

The registrar gave a little chuckle. 'I shall continue. Before you are joined in matrimony...'

I wished she'd hurry up and get to the vows. I was terrified that something was going to stop this wedding. I realised then that's why I'd been shaking, not because I was nervous of marrying Joe but nervous something would stop it from happening.

The registrar faced us both. 'I'm now going to ask each of you in turn to declare that you know of no legal reason you may not be married to each other.' She turned to Joe. 'Are you Joe Neil Davies free lawfully to marry Rachel Julie Webster?'

Joe smiled at me. 'I am.'

'And are you, Rachel Julie Webster free lawfully to marry Joe Neil Davies?'

Butterflies fluttered in my stomach. 'I am.'

'You've both declared that you're free to marry. Now it's time to take each other as husband and wife. Repeat after me. 'I, Joe Neil Davies, take you Rachel Julie Webster, to be my wedded wife.'

Joe coughed to clear his throat. 'I, Joe Neil Davies, take you Rachel Julie Webster, to be my wedded wife.'

'Rachel. Your turn now. Repeat after me. 'I, Rachel Julie Webster, take you Joe Neil Davies, to be my wedded husband.'

Smiling, I gripped Joe's hand. 'I, Rachel Julie Webster, take you Joe Neil Davies, to be my wedded husband.'

When it was time for us to exchange rings, Joe slipped a gold band on to my finger and I followed suit.

'Joe Neil Davies and Rachel Julie Webster you have now both made the declarations required by law and have made a solemn and binding contract with each other in the presence of your witnesses, guests and the registrar of marriages.'

A kaleidoscope of butterflies partied inside my stomach.

'It's my pleasure to pronounce you now as husband and wife. Congratulations.'

We smiled at each other.

'It's normal,' the registrar said, 'for the groom to kiss the bride.'

Joe took me in his arms and kissed me long and hard on the lips. I couldn't believe we'd actually done it. We were now finally husband and wife. I was Mrs Rachel Webster.

Our guests clapped.

After I'd signed the register as Rachel Julie Webster for the last time the registrar prompted Phil and Stu to sign as witnesses. Stu appeared to be holding up well. He patted Joe on the back and said, 'About time, mate.'

Out of nowhere Alan, the photographer from *The Echo*, appeared. 'If you can just look like you're doing that again, please. Joe and Rachel first.'

What? Who? How come? I hadn't invited Alan to take photographs as Adam had agreed to take some snaps. Was it Joe? I smiled as Alan clicked.

'Now can we have a shot with the witnesses.' Alan positioned the camera.

Next up he took photos with Mum and Dad on either side of us then Adam and Peggy. 'I'll take some more shots once we get outside. There's a lovely little garden and the sun's shining.'

⊱

I couldn't believe how warm it was for March. I slipped my shawl from my shoulders and placed the lace garment on the nearby wall. 'Did you arrange for Alan to do the photos?' I asked Joe.

'Nope. I was as surprised as you. Maybe Mel?'

'Oh yes of course. It had to have been Mel.'

Joe rested his hand on my arm. 'Are you okay?'

I kissed him softly. 'Yes, yes, I really am. This is what Linda would've wanted. She wouldn't have wanted me to stop living, no more than she'd want that from Stu or Sandra.' Sandra. I wondered how she was coping. I glanced around at the smiling faces of my guests.

Without warning Kate and Jen sprinkled confetti over us like coloured snow and Alan snapped the camera. Joe leaned into me. 'I love you, Mrs Davies. We got there in the end.'

'And I love you too, Mr Davies. Yes, we were certainly tested along the way. Something to tell our children.' I held my stomach.

'You're not?'

I nodded. 'I think so. Come end of October I believe we may have a mini-Joe or Rachel.'

Joe hugged me closer. 'You've made me the happiest man alive.'

⊱

Debs and Harry had hired in four members of staff, two blokes and two girls who took turns serving at the bar or acting as waiters and waitresses offering out the food. Tables had been joined together in an 'L' shape to accommodate our small number of guests with Joe and me positioned at the head. This was more than I'd expected but I was glad. It was our wedding and it should be celebrated.

Dad coughed as he rose from his seat. 'Welcome everyone and thank you for joining us today to celebrate the wedding of Rachel and Joe. My wife, Rosalind, and I are proud to welcome Joe as a son into our family. I'd always wanted a son...'

Everyone laughed.

'And I couldn't have done better if I'd chosen him myself.'

Joe turned to Dad. 'Thanks, Mr Webster.'

'You can call me Dad now, son.'

'Cheers, Dad.' Joe took out a hanky and blew his nose.

'I'd also like to welcome Joe's family into ours, although truth be told I think we've all felt like family for a long time. This wedding's been a long time coming and I'm glad this wonderful couple have finally got there.'

'Yes.' Peggy and Adam called out in unison.

'I couldn't be prouder of my eldest daughter, Rachel. Not only is she beautiful but she's an intelligent, generous and kind woman. I won't say we didn't have our problems with her as a teenager while she found herself but that just made her stronger.' Dad winked at me.

I smiled. 'Thanks, Dad.'

'I think now's the right time to have a special moment for Rachel's best friend, Linda, who's no longer with us, but I'm sure she's up there somewhere watching Rachel and Joe's special day.'

Tears pricked my eyes. Joe gripped my hand.

'And looking at Anne-Marie, Linda and Stu's daughter, I believe Linda's living through her. I don't think I've ever seen a child so like their mother.'

Dad was right. Anne-Marie not only shared Linda's looks but already she was showing the same mannerisms.

'Please join me in toasting the bride and groom.' Dad raised his glass. 'To the bride and groom.'

'To the bride and groom,' our guests echoed.

I clinked my glass with Joe's. 'To us.'

'And now I'll hand you over to my son-in-law.'

Joe and I clapped as did our guests. He patted my hand before rising from his chair. 'Well, what can I say? Thank you to my father-in-law for the welcome. I can't find the right words to express how happy I am to be part of your family and to have Rachel' – Joe turned to look at me – 'finally as my wife. She's made me the happiest man alive. Thank you to everyone for coming and for the wonderful gifts.' He signalled to a table piled up with presents. 'Even though we said don't worry, but thanks. Really appreciated.' He took a sip of champagne and put the glass back down. 'Just a few words of thanks. To my mam and dad for putting up with me all my life...'

'It's been hard, son.' Adam laughed.

Peggy jabbed him with her elbow. 'The pleasure was all ours, Joe.'

'And to Rachel's mam and dad. To my best friend Stu. I know how tough today was for you, mate. Rach and me really appreciate you being here by our side.'

Stu playfully thumped Joe on the arm. 'I wouldn't have missed it.'

'To Debs and Harry for organising this, to Alan for taking photos, and to Phil for acting as our second witness.' Joe picked up his glass. 'To my gorgeous wife, Rachel.'

'To Rachel,' our guests echoed.

I sensed myself blushing. 'Cheers, babe.'

'And now I believe it's time for me to hand over the reins to my best friend.' He smiled at Stu. 'And no wild stories.' Joe took his seat and kissed me on the lips. 'Was that okay?'

'It was awesome.'

Stu coughed as he rose. 'I'll keep this brief as I'm not a great speaker. Now, where do I start?'

And I couldn't resist springing into song with, 'Start from the very beginning...'

Everyone laughed.

'Er yes. Okay. Congratulations to my very best friends as although I've not known Rachel quite as long as I've known Joe, I love her just the same. Their fairy tale began in Elmo's.' Stu's eyes filled.

I whispered to Joe. 'Check he's all right.'

Joe leaned up to Stu who was next to him and whispered, 'You cool, mate?'

Stu nodded before turning back to the guests. 'Doesn't Rachel look stunning today? I mean she always does, but today, wow. You're a lucky bloke, Joe.'

'I know.' Joe beamed.

'Now it wouldn't be a proper best man's speech if I didn't spill a bit of dirt on Joe. Hmm. I suppose the biggest thing was how he managed to fool Harry and Debs that he was eighteen from around fifteen.'

'Oi' – Debs cackled – 'don't give out stories like that.'

'No, seriously, Joe's always been a good bloke. He's been the best friend in the world and has never let me down. Always been here for me. And since losing Linda, my wife and soulmate, both Joe and Rachel have been my rock. I couldn't have got through without them.'

Joe reached up and patted Stu's arm. 'Always, mate.'

'Let's take a moment,' Stu continued, 'to remember absent friends. Sandra, Linda's mam who's recovering from a breakdown, and my dear late wife, Linda. Although I'm sure she's here watching. Let's face it why else would Anne-Marie decide to have screamed when asked if anyone knew any reason why the marriage shouldn't go ahead?' Stu laughed. 'Not that Linda wouldn't have wanted this to go ahead as it was her dream to see Joe and Rachel tie the knot.' Stu picked up his glass. 'Please join me in toasting the bride and groom.'

Everyone raised their glasses and echoed Stu's words, 'To the bride and groom.'

※

The tables had been pushed to the side to make a small dance floor and over in the corner Dark Chaos were setting up their band. How? I hadn't asked them. I turned to Joe. 'Is this you?'

Joe grinned. 'This I am guilty of. Sorry, babe, but it's our wedding day so I thought we should at least have a party.' He kissed me briefly. 'I've invited a few more friends along too. Hope that's okay.'

'It is, thanks.' And it was. I was glad Joe had done that. Mind you Steve and the band were under the impression Joe and I had married years ago. Maybe they thought it was just a party. I shrugged. I didn't care what they thought.

Harry took the microphone. 'The happy couple will now have their first dance.'

Joe led me to the centre of the room and took me in his arms as we smooched to a slow dance that must've been Dark Chaos' own composition as I hadn't heard it before. It had some tender words though like *a couple getting there in the end* and *how true love always finds a way*.

Mum and Dad surprised me by being the first couple up to join us. Peggy and Adam followed. Kate, David, Jen and

Richard didn't take long to be on the floor too. I glanced across at Stu. He joined the dancers with Anne-Marie in his arms. He winked back letting me know he was cool.

After our dance I said to Joe, 'I think we should mingle. I've not had a chance to speak to Betty yet, or your Aunty Sheila and Uncle Malc.'

'You're right, we should.'

We headed over to Betty who was with Mel and Phil. I pecked Betty on the cheek. 'Thanks for coming.'

'I wouldn't have missed it for the world, pet. You make a wonderful bride. There's not many that could have carried off a dress like that and look a million dollars.'

I laughed. 'That's what Mel said.'

'Well she's right.' Betty tapped my upper arm.

I turned to Mel. 'Was Alan's presence your doing?'

She shrugged. 'Nope I had no idea until he turned up.'

'Then who?'

Betty beamed. 'Guilty as charged, pet. You couldn't have a wedding without some proper photos. You'll thank me in your old age.'

I kissed her. 'I'm thanking you now, Betty. It was an awesome idea.' I'd been so set on keeping everything low key that I'd have spoiled the day not only for Joe but for me too.

Phil tapped my shoulder. 'Happy?'

I turned around and put my arms around his neck. 'Gloriously happy. Thanks, Phil, and thanks for pushing me to set the date.' I gazed around the room. 'Anyone take your fancy?'

He searched the area. 'Well let's put it this way, I've been out with your sister, out with Mel, not Kate but then she has David. I reckon I'm going to be a bachelor for a while yet.' He laughed. 'So, look at you with two of your old flames in the room. Steve and me. Good job your Joe's not a jealous man.'

'He knows there's nothing to be jealous of. I love you as a friend and Steve, well, okay he's here playing the band, but I still reckon he's a plonker.' I giggled. 'Come on, dance with me.' I dragged him up to the makeshift dance floor and he led me into a jive.

Chapter Thirty-Six

Rachel

19th September 1980

I gasped on entering the office. Pink and blue balloons bobbed on my desk in an arch shape. This was so touching and unexpected. Good luck banners hung on the wall and a pile of presents wrapped in baby wrapping paper along with a stack of white envelopes covered the desk.

'Surprise.' Mel and Betty jumped out from the stationery cupboard.

'Wow. Thanks. This is amazing. It must've taken you ages.' My eyes filled.

'Mel did most of it,' Betty said. 'She came in at seven.'

'You're joking.' I flopped down into the typing chair.

Mel touched my stomach. 'You're so lucky hardly showing. My cousin's due around the same time as you and she's huge. You only look about four or five months.'

'That's what the other mums at the clinic say, but apparently, some women pop in the last few weeks. That could be me.' I laughed. 'My midwife's not concerned. She said my baby's got a good heart rate and is developing well.'

'Here you go love.' Betty passed me a glass of milk. 'Get this down you.'

'Must I, Betty? You know I don't really like milk.'

'And like I tell you every day, it's good for the babby.'

Betty had brought in an extra pint of gold top milk each day since I'd first announced my pregnancy. She insisted my baby needed it. I was looking forward to not having it pushed on me.

Mr Strange and John came through the door. 'Good morning, Mrs Davies,' Mr Strange said. 'Mr Smythe has cleared your diary so we don't expect any work from you today.'

I frowned. 'Sorry? Why?'

'It's your last day.' John grinned. 'No one ever likes working on their last day.'

'I do.' I'd been looking forward to doing a last story before my maternity leave. Thankfully, Mr Strange had agreed I could return to work part-time after the baby was born. 'I was hoping to cover the story for that new florist in town.'

Mr Strange looked at John. 'What do you think, Mr Smythe, are you happy for Mrs Davies to do this?'

John shrugged. 'If that's what Mrs Davies would like to do then it's all hers. I can't say I was too enamoured about doing it myself.'

'Great.' I rubbed my hands. 'What time's the meeting?'

'Not until after lunch,' John said, 'so you have plenty of time to enjoy coffee and cake as well as opening your presents.'

'You want me to open them today?'

'Yes,' Betty said, 'and this morning, please, so I can see your face.'

'Oh right.' I smiled.

⋆

After drinking coffee and eating far more chocolate cake than I'd have liked, Betty prompted me to open the gifts. One by one

I tore off the wrapping. White nightgowns with lemon teddies across the bodice, a lace shawl, bodyvests, a dozen terry nappies, and three matinee coats in blue, lemon and white, handknitted by Betty.

'Thank you so much,' I said. 'I'm overwhelmed by all your generosity.'

Mr Strange returned with a huge wrapped box. 'You're not finished yet. This one's a collective gift from us all.'

I ripped the paper and opened the box.

'Dig in,' Betty prompted.

One by one I pulled out the items. A Fisher Price activity centre, a Peter Rabbit cot mobile, three different rattles, a steriliser, two Tommy Tippee plastic bowls with cutlery and two trainer beakers. 'Wow, thank you. This is incredible. It looks like you bought half of Mothercare.'

'You deserve it.' Betty hugged me.

'And make sure you rest for the next six weeks,' Mel said.

'Well, I don't plan to rest all the time and at least I have my antenatal classes starting Monday.' I was sad to leave, even if I would be coming back. This place had been like a second home to me for so many years now. It was the best decision I'd ever made to resign from Woolworths, even if it had caused that rift with Linda for a while. 'I'm going to miss you all so much.' I dabbed my eyes.

'You can pop in whenever you're passing,' Mr Strange said. 'And after the birth I'm sure Mrs Jones and the office girls would love a cuddle with the new little one. And you'll be back here again before you know it.'

I got up and hugged Mr Strange. 'You've been so good to me.'

He backed away putting his hands up. 'Now, now, Mrs Davies' – he chuckled – 'don't get carried away. I'd hate for Mr Davies to get jealous.'

'Seriously, thank you' – I sniffled – 'thank you all. I'm going to miss this place so much. I won't know what to do with myself before the baby's born.'

'Sounds like a bit of daytime television for you.' John laughed. 'My wife vows by *General Hospital*.'

I chuckled. 'I'll look forward to that.'

'You could always start that novel' – Betty winked – 'after all, you've been talking about writing it for years.'

'Betty, that's a brilliant idea. Maybe I should. Right, I'd better go to the loo and get myself down to that florist.'

⚜

After interviewing the florist in town, I headed to Phil's gallery. I pushed open the entrance. 'Hiya,' I called out as I wandered in towards the latest art exhibition.

'Hello, stranger.' Phil hurried over to me. 'You look positively blooming. Pregnancy suits you.'

'Thanks. I've been lucky. I've just been interviewing the new florist around the corner and thought I'd take the opportunity to see how you are.'

'Cool. I'm well.'

'Joe was saying last night how we haven't seen you for ages. What gives?'

Phil grinned.

'What?'

'If you must know, I've met someone.'

'You have?'

'Yeah. If you come through to the staff room, I'll introduce you.'

'Is she working here then?'

'Nope. She's just popped in for lunch. Come on.' He took my hand.

A woman with auburn, curly hair turned around as we headed in.

'Isabella, darling, meet Rachel, one of my closest friends.'

Her light brown eyes twinkled. 'Pleased to finally meet you. I've heard so much about you.'

'You have the advantage over me then.' I laughed. 'So, when did this happen?'

'5th July, wasn't it, Phil? The first day I walked in here.'

'Indeed, it was. And it was love at first sight, so I'm sorry, Rachel, I really should've been around to yours but to be honest I've been swept off my feet. Izzy and I have spent every moment together that we can.'

'Every moment?'

'Well almost. Izzy moved in with me after only one week.'

'What?' What was going on? One week and he'd moved this girl in with him. She appeared nice but even so, he didn't know anything about her.

'So, I'm truly off the market.' Phil winked at Isabella.

She glanced at my stomach. 'When's it due?'

'End of October.'

'Your first?'

'Yep.'

'I love babies. I can't wait to be a mum.'

'Izzy and I have been talking about getting married. Isn't that right, darling?'

'Yes, it is.' She beamed. 'Actually, Phil asked me last night and I said yes. When you know you know, why waste time?'

'Marvellous,' I said, 'congratulations.'

'I should go. Hope I'll see you again soon, Rachel, and good luck.' Isabella kissed Phil. 'See you just after five.'

'Catch you later, gorgeous.' Phil tapped a chair as Isabella left. 'Sorry, Rachel, I've been neglecting you. Sit down and tell me what's been happening in your life.'

'Well, this is my last day at work before I go on maternity leave.'

'Goodness, that's come around fast.'

'For you maybe.' I laughed.

'What do you think of Izzy?'

'She seems nice enough.' Everything had happened so quickly with them. I hoped she wouldn't hurt him. 'Tell me about her. What does she do?'

'She's a secretary for the solicitor across the road, but she's really interested in art. Come and look at my latest masterpiece.' He headed out into the gallery. 'What do you think?'

I looked up on the wall at the oil painting of Isabella. 'Striking.'

'She's such a good model. So gorgeous. I'm hopelessly in love with her. I've never felt like this about anyone before. She makes me giddy with excitement. I feel like a schoolboy again.'

'You thought you were in love with me, remember?'

'Rachel, that was nothing like this. This is something else. I can't bear to be apart from her.'

I squeezed his hand. 'Phil, are you sure it's not just infatuation?'

He scowled. 'No, it's not. I'm in love with her and she's in love with me. Please don't spoil this. Don't be a dog in a manger. You didn't want me, but now I've found someone...'

'Phil, stop. It's not like that at all. Of course, I want you to be happy but what do you know about this girl?'

He pushed my hand away. 'I know everything I need to know. I thought you were my friend.'

'I am. Sorry, I didn't mean to upset you. I'm just being overprotective.'

'Well, there's no need.'
'Then I'm very happy for you.' I hugged him. 'Friends?'
'Friends.' He smiled.

Chapter Thirty-Seven

Peggy

12th November 1980

Joe lit a cigarette and took a puff. 'Anyway, I thought I'd pop in and let you know what's happening.'

'So, you say they've taken her in to be induced? How does Rachel feel about that?'

'She's so fed up that she doesn't care. She just wants the baby to be born. I've come straight from the hospital. It was hard leaving her but she seemed happy enough. Anyway, I can't stay as I need to get home for some kip. The midwife suggested I may like to be back in the ward before seven tomorrow morning.'

'What about work? Do you need me to ring them?'

'No, you're okay. I popped in there before I came here and left a message to say I won't be in.' His eyes twinkled. 'Can you believe it, Mam, I'm going to be a dad?'

'It's wonderful news, love. Is there anything you need me to do? Does Rachel need her bag?'

'All sorted, thanks. Tonight's going to be a tough one as this will be our first night apart from each other for a long time. The house will seem quiet.'

'You can always stay here.' I rose from the sofa. 'It won't take me five minutes to get a bed ready for you.'

'Nah. You're okay. I need to be home in case they ring me. Where's Dad?'

'Gone for a pint down the local. He should be home soon if you fancy waiting. I could put the kettle on?'

'No, I won't thanks. Didn't you fancy going with him?'

'Not really. To be honest I couldn't be bothered getting a babysitter.'

Joe stubbed out his cigarette. 'So just the three of you here now. That must be strange.'

'It is. Too quiet. You sure you don't want to stay this evening?'

'Positive. Look' – he got up from the armchair – 'I'd best be off.' He pecked me on the cheek. 'I'll be in touch tomorrow.'

'Yes, do, please.' I stood up, followed him out into the hallway and opened the front door. As he strode down the footpath I said, 'Take care, son. Three rings when you get in.'

'I'll try and remember.'

I closed the door, headed back into the lounge and sank into the sofa. Should I carry on with my knitting? I picked it up to do a couple more rows. The pram set was coming on well. The leggings were finished. They looked smart knitted in stocking stitch with a moss stitch rib. I was rather proud of them. Mittens and a bonnet too. This set was white but once we knew the sex, I'd make another in pink or blue. The matinee jacket fell into my lap as I drifted in thought. Me becoming a grandmother again. Two grandchildren in such a short time. Kate made a smashing mum to Teddy who was now two months old. He'd been three weeks early but still a good weight at over six pounds. Poor Rachel thought she'd be early too but these babies don't always come when you want them to. Joe had been late. Less than a week though, unlike this baby, he or she should've been born twelve days ago.

Kate was doing well. I'd been concerned when she was first pregnant and being sick that the anorexia nervosa had returned but she assured me she was fine, just pregnant, and even though no longer working at the hospital she continued running the support group.

News at Ten chimed out of the television. I got up and switched it off as I didn't fancy hearing anything bad this evening. I flopped back down on the sofa.

How things had changed since Rachel first came into our lives nine years ago. She'd been a fiery teenager that's for sure. Strange how we'd bonded so well just like we were mother and daughter. On discovering that wasn't the case I'd had mixed feelings. Glad because it meant she and Joe weren't related but sad because she was so like me that she should've been my daughter.

Teresa on the other hand, well, I'd had to work hard to build up a bond with her, unlike Mike, whom she'd made a connection with almost instantly. So much so she decided to stay out there after meeting some guy.

Adam had promised we could visit Teresa in the spring. He'd started saving like mad. 'We need money for the tickets and somewhere to stay,' he'd said. 'There's no way we're kipping under that yank's roof.

Then there was our Ben. How quickly he'd grown. Three in July and had started play school in September three mornings a week, which he was loving. Maybe I'd see if Rachel needed me to help out with childcare for the new baby. Sheila had offered as she was now a registered childminder and was still looking after Anne-Marie. I wouldn't mind betting that Kate would be offering her services before long too. She was so good with Teddy. The other day she mentioned she couldn't wait to be expecting again. I could see her in the future with a hoard of kids around her. She'd always loved looking after children, even as a young child herself.

I sighed. I was blessed having such a wonderful family and I was so lucky with Adam. He was such a loyal, loving husband. He really was the best. He'd stuck by me through everything. At one time in our lives, we were in pieces. Mike had caused problems and for a moment I'd lost my head. Our relationship was certainly tested but that was behind us now. We were whole again and our family was growing.

The door slammed shut. 'Hi there, love.' Adam came into the lounge.

'Hi, sweetheart.' I got up and kissed his lips. 'Our Joe's been around. They've taken Rachel in to be induced. Looks like we'll have another grandchild by tomorrow.'

Adam rubbed his hands. 'How exciting, although I still think we're too young to be grandparents.'

I put my arms around him. 'I love you, Mr Davies.'

'What was that for?'

I shrugged. 'I've just been thinking how lucky I am. How lucky we are to have each other and fortunate to have our wonderful family.'

'We are.'

'I love you, Adam. I don't tell you often enough, but I really do.' I kissed him hard on the lips.

'And I love you too, Peg. Want to show me how much you love me?'

'You bet.' I took Adam's hand and led him upstairs.

Chapter Thirty-Eight

Rachel

Joe arrived at the hospital.

'Thank goodness you're here.' I put the knitting down on the side of my chair.

'I came as soon as they called me.'

'Well, I've been having contractions all night. I think they're taking me into the delivery room soon.'

'Sorry, babe, but I'm here now. Mam sends her love. I popped round there last night to put her in the picture.'

'What did she say? Oh no, here it comes again.' I took breaths to control my breathing like I'd been shown at the antenatal class.

A doctor tapped on the open door before strolling in. She smiled, picking up my chart. 'Hello, Rachel, do you mind if I take a look to see how you're doing?'

I shook my head. 'No, that's fine.'

She washed her hands at the sink. 'Can you manage to pop yourself up on the bed.'

'Yep.' I climbed up and laid my head on the pillow.

'The doctor placed a sheet across the bottom half of me. 'I see your waters have broken. Looks like we should've had you wired up to a monitor but you've been so quick. Don't worry though.

We'll get you wheeled into the delivery room and sort you out.' She washed her hands again at the sink.

※

'Stop pushing for a minute,' the midwife said.

'Is something wrong?'

'Nothing to worry about. The cord's around your baby's neck so I just need you to do your breathing exercises while I sort things.'

I squeezed Joe's hand. 'What does she mean? Is that dangerous? Is our baby going to be okay?'

'Shh, babe. The midwife said not to worry.'

'Okay,' the midwife said, 'you can push now.'

With three big pushes I managed to push our baby into the world but he or she didn't cry. 'Is my baby okay?'

A nurse picked up the baby and carried he or she over to the side where there was loads of medical equipment. What was she doing? Was something wrong? 'Joe.' I gripped his hand. 'Something's wrong.'

'It'll be fine,' he said rubbing his neck.

'No. It's not. Nurse. Please. Is our baby okay? Why isn't it crying?' My stomach churned. This wasn't fair. *Please God don't let our baby die.* 'I'll go and see.' Joe headed over to the nurse, when all of a sudden, our baby let out a high-pitched scream.

'There,' the nurse said. 'Congratulations Mr and Mrs Davies, you have a daughter.' She wrapped our baby in a muslin sheet. 'Come and meet Mummy and Daddy, little one.'

Joe stroked our baby's cheek. 'Oh, she's perfect.'

'She is, isn't she? And look at that mop of dark hair. No wonder I suffered from such bad heartburn.'

'Do you have a name?' the midwife asked.

I glanced at Joe and whispered, 'Melinda.'

He kissed me on the cheek. 'Melinda's perfect if that's what you'd like, babe.'

I smiled at the midwife. 'Her name's Melinda.'

'That's pretty. Would Mummy and Daddy like a cup of tea?'

'Oh, yes, please.' Joe clutched my hand.

'We'll just give your daughter a check over and see what she weighs. Congratulations.'

⋆

Melinda slept in the hospital crib, and Joe leaned back on a plastic chair with his arms folded, while I perched on the bed waiting for the doctor to come and discharge our baby.

'Sorry to keep you waiting, Mr and Mrs Davies, I'm Mr Tanner the paediatrician. I'm sure you're keen to get off with your daughter but if you don't mind, I need to do a quick examination before discharging her.'

'Thanks, Doctor.' Joe leaned over the crib and stroked Melinda's cheek. 'It's rather scary the thought of us taking home this little person.'

'All new parents feel like that.' The doctor smiled. 'Wait until you're home and into a routine, you'll be fine. And if you have any problems, you can contact your midwife or health visitor. Help is always available.'

Joe smiled. 'Thanks.'

The doctor shone a light into each of our baby's eyes, listened to her heart, and checked her hips. 'Right, that's all my tests completed,' Mr Tanner said. 'Have you been discharged yet, Mrs Davies?'

'Yes, I have.'

'In that case, you're good to go. I'll arrange for a nurse to see you off the premises.'

'Thank you, Mr Tanner,' I said.

It wasn't long before a nurse appeared. 'Is your car outside, Mr Davies?'

'No, it's in the car park.'

'Why don't you go on ahead and park up outside the entrance?'

'Okey dokes.' He kissed me on the cheek. 'See you in a minute, babe.'

'If you'd like to get your baby dressed in her outdoor wear and then pass her to me to carry her out.'

'It's okay, I can manage.'

'Hospital rules I'm afraid. I need to see her off the premises.'

'Oh right.' I dressed Melinda in a Babygro and slid her into a quilted sleeping bag before passing her to the nurse.

'Pop your coat on then, Mrs Davies. It's bitter out there today.'

I slipped on my maxi coat and followed the nurse out of the ward, down the corridor and out of the exit to where Joe had parked.

'Bye bye, little one.' The nurse removed the shawl, passing it to me, and laid Melinda inside the carrycot on the back seat.'

'Thank you for everything,' I said before stepping into the passenger seat.

'You're very welcome. Now don't forget you have the telephone numbers for your midwife and health visitor if you have any problems.' The nurse went back through the hospital entrance.

Joe parked in the graveyard car park. I got out, leaned back into the car and took Melinda from the cot and rewrapped the shawl around her.

'Are you sure she'll be okay?' Joe asked. 'The wind's bitter.'

'She'll be fine snuggled in this lot. I won't be long. Do you mind if we have a few minutes on our own?'

'No, course not. I'll come and find you soon.'

Carrying my newborn, I trod across the gravelled footpath until I reached Linda's grave. 'Hi, Linda, I've brought someone to meet you. Her name's Melinda after you. She's lovely, don't you think? Seven pound six ounces and born on thirteenth November just before midday. She was late. I don't think she'd have come out without hospital intervention.'

Melinda gave a little cry.

'I'll never forget you, my friend, and I'll make sure Melinda and Anne-Marie grow up as best friends. Sisters even, like you and me. Anne-Marie's walking now. She's gorgeous and Stu's a great dad. He still misses you so much. You should see the girlie outfits he dresses Anne-Marie in. You'd have approved.'

Joe was at my side with a bunch of flowers. 'It's starting to snow, babe. We need to get back in the car.' He bent down to the grave and laid the burnt-orange chrysanthemums onto the soil.

I passed him Melinda. 'You two go. I shan't be long.'

'Promise? I don't want you catching a chill.'

'Promise. I'll be fine.' I waited for Joe to leave before continuing to chat to Linda. 'Your mam's doing well. It was tricky there for a while but she responded to treatment. Last night she had Anne-Marie to stay overnight for the first time since her breakdown. Stu was reluctant at first but Keith promised he'd make sure he kept an eye on her to ensure nothing went wrong. I think we may have the old Sandra back. I'll invite her over in a few days to meet Melinda.'

I wiped my eyes. Everything had changed. I'd lost my best friend but somehow had managed to come through it. Joe and I would have lots of stories to tell our baby about how hard our journey was to get here. From the first day I met him in Elmo's I was in love and that had never changed. Even when we thought there was no hope, I knew we had to continue a relationship in some form, even if that meant as brother and sister.

Then there was the revelation that Peggy wasn't my birth mother at all and that Joe and I could be together. But because he'd married that mad cow Miranda thinking there was no hope, we had yet another obstacle to climb. And then he'd been critically ill after his irate wife stabbed him out of jealousy. All this had made us stronger. But then Linda had died. That awful accident. Once again, our marriage was postponed until I was ready and it was one of the happiest days of my life when we finally married in March this year with a few friends and our family around us.

It had taken us almost nine years from the first time we were engaged to tie the knot but we got there in the end and our daughter was growing inside me before our wedding night.

'I was lucky, Lind. I got my happy ever after, unlike you. You were cheated out of your life. Fate stole Stu of his wife, and Anne-Marie her mam. But you'll never be forgotten, my friend.' My knees trembled. I'd been standing for too long. Snowflakes fell turning my black coat white. I shivered. 'I should go, Lind, but I'll be back soon. Love you, my best friend.'

I made my way back to the car and climbed into the passenger seat.

'You okay?'

'Think so.' I dabbed my eyes with a handkerchief.

Joe turned on the ignition. He touched my leg. 'Ready?'

I nodded. 'Let's go home.'

We had the rest of our lives to look forward to. Mum and Dad would always be my real parents but Peggy and Adam came a close second. And if things continued with Denise and Gordon as they were going, then I'd soon have another set of parents to call mine too. I was lucky. After all, how many people could say they had three sets of parents? And Melinda, plus any of our other children if we had more, would never be short of a grandparent, nor an aunt with Jen and Kate, and I supposed even Teresa. I hadn't given up on her yet.

Joe pulled up outside the house and passed me the keys. 'Fancy opening up and I'll bring in our precious cargo?'

'Sure.' I closed the car door behind me, put the keys in the front door and turned the lock.

Joe followed with Melinda fast asleep in the carrycot. 'Welcome to your new home, little one.'

Acknowledgements

Special thanks to my friend Maureen Cullen. Not only for her perceptive and thoughtful editing in *The Woodhaerst Women* but for her continuous support, encouragement and faith in me.

A big thank you to my fabulous beta readers for their invaluable feedback, and to Colin Ward(inasmanywords) for the cover design.

Finally, a big thank you to my husband, children, family and friends for their continued support and faith in me.

About the author

Patricia M Osborne was born in Liverpool but now lives in West Sussex. She is married with grown-up children and grandchildren. In 2019 she graduated with an MA in Creative Writing. She is a published novelist, poet and short fiction writer. Her debut poetry pamphlet, *Taxus Baccata,* was nominated for the Michael Marks Pamphlet Award.

Patricia has a successful blog at Whitewingsbooks.com featuring other writers. When Patricia isn't working on her own writing, she enjoys sharing her knowledge, acting as a mentor to fellow writers.

You can find out more about Patricia by visiting her website, whitewingsbooks (.com)

Also by

House of Grace Family Saga Trilogy:

House of Grace (Book 1)
The Coal Miner's Son (Book 2)
The Granville Legacy (Book 3)

The Oath (A Victorian era saga)

The Woodhaerst Family Drama Trilogy:

The Woodhaerst Triangle (Book 1)
The Woodhaerst Reunion (Book 2)

Poetry Published by The Hedgehog Poetry Press

The Montefiore Bride

Taxus Baccata

Sherry & Sparkly

Symbiosis

Spirit Mother: Experience the Myth

Stickleback

Nature's Bookends

www.ingramcontent.com/pod-product-compliance
Lightning Source LLC
Chambersburg PA
CBHW020357080526
44584CB00014B/1063